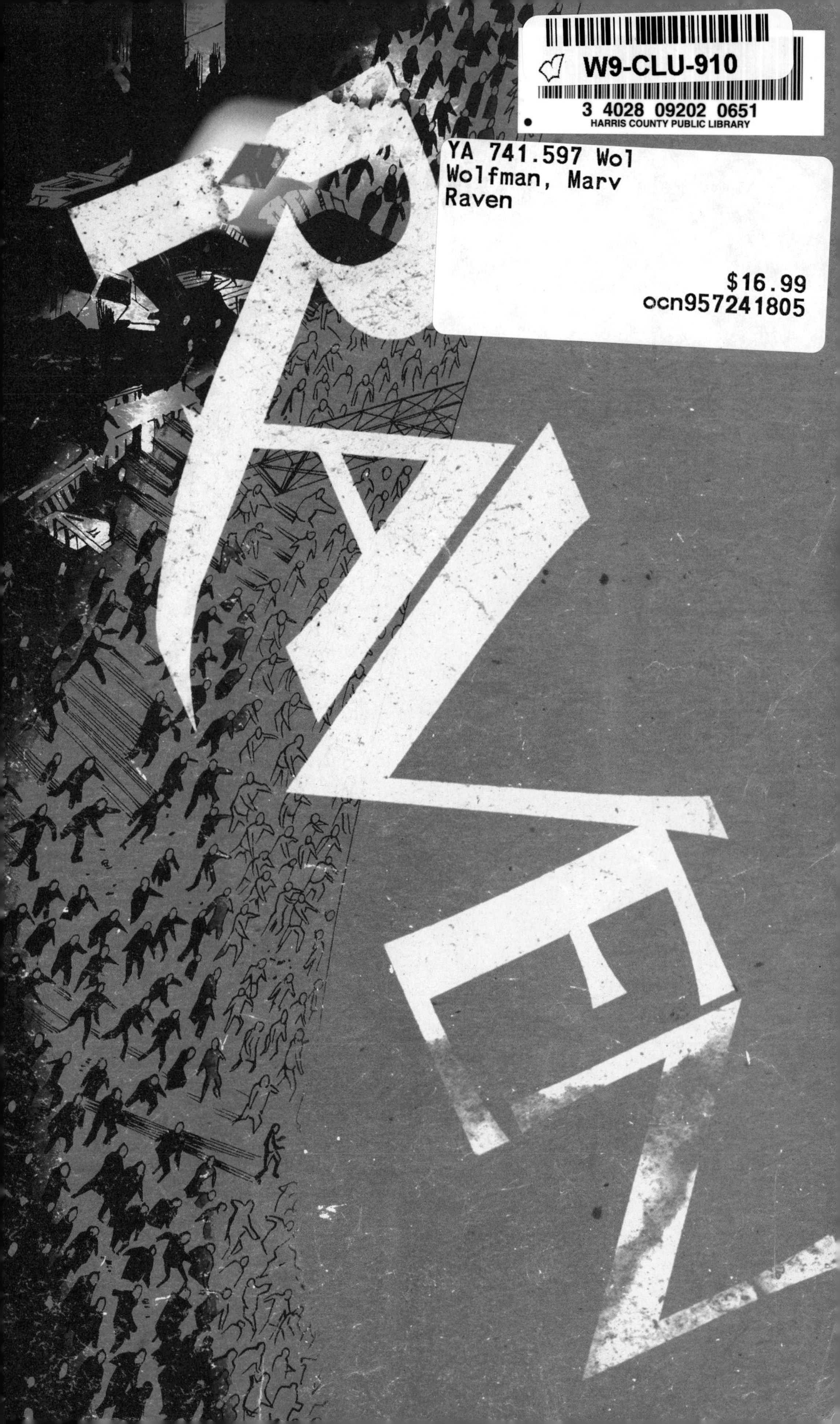
RAVEN

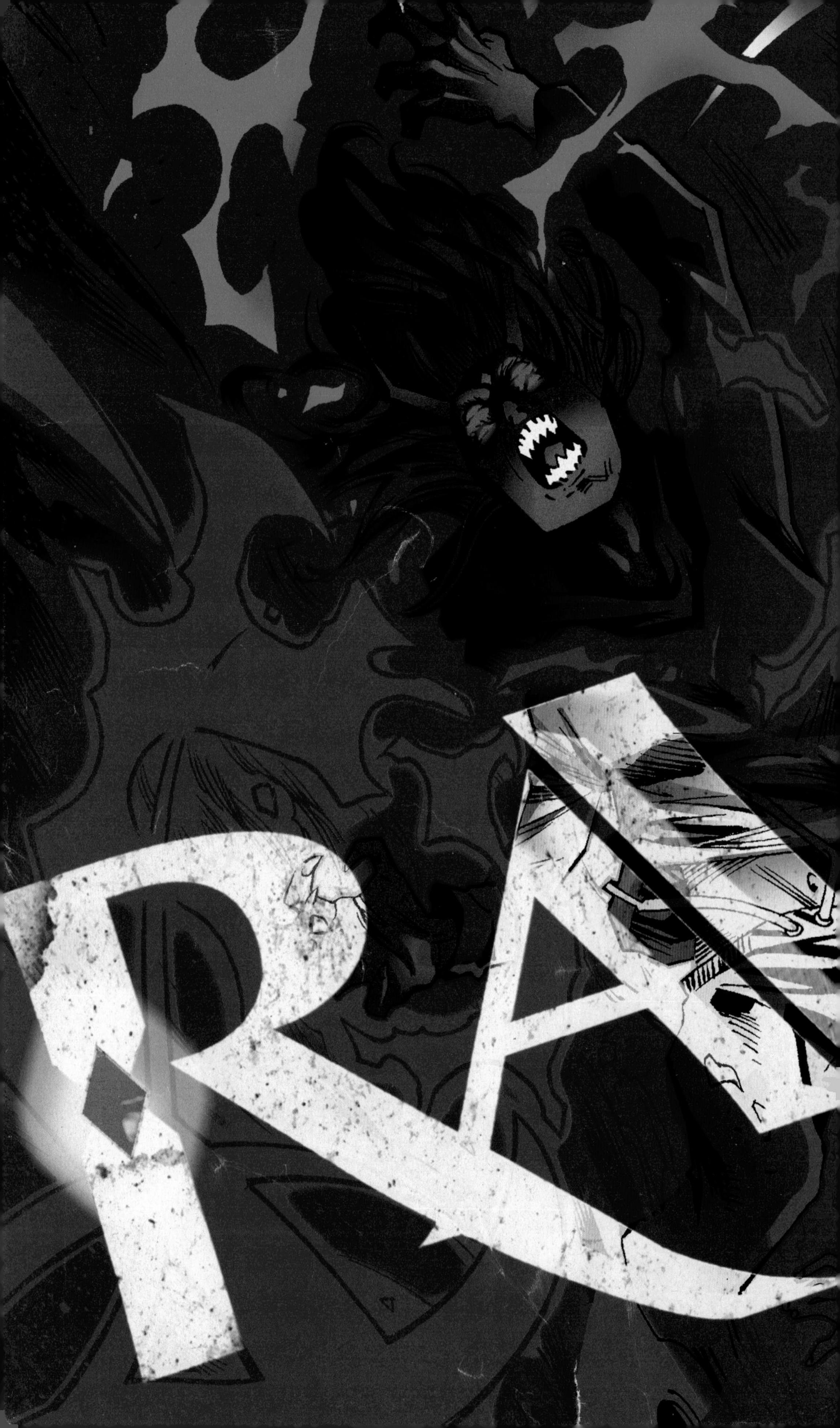
RA

MARV WOLFMAN WRITER

ALISSON BORGES
DIOGENES NEVES
RUY JOSÉ ARTISTS

BLOND COLORIST **A LARGER WORLD** LETTERERS

ALISSON BORGES WITH **BLOND** COLLECTION COVER ARTISTS

MARV WOLFMAN AND **GEORGE PÉREZ**

RAVEN CREATED BY **MARV WOLFMAN** AND **GEORGE PÉREZ**

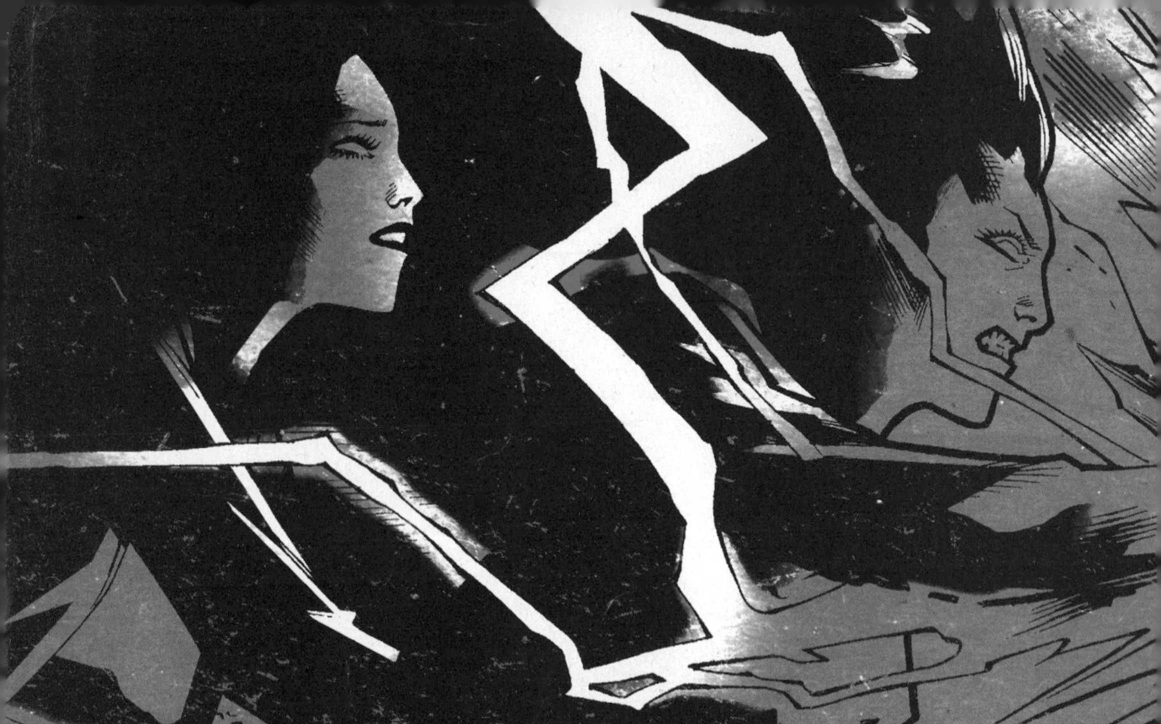

ALEX ANTONE PAUL KAMINSKI Editors – Original Series BRITTANY HOLZHERR Assistant Editor – Original Series
JEB WOODARD Group Editor – Collected Editions LIZ ERICKSON Editor – Collected Edition
STEVE COOK Design Director – Books LOUIS PRANDI Publication Design

BOB HARRAS Senior VP – Editor-in-Chief, DC Comics

DIANE NELSON President DAN DiDIO Publisher JIM LEE Publisher GEOFF JOHNS President & Chief Creative Officer
AMIT DESAI Executive VP – Business & Marketing Strategy, Direct to Consumer & Global Franchise Management
SAM ADES Senior VP – Direct to Consumer BOBBIE CHASE VP – Talent Development
MARK CHIARELLO Senior VP – Art, Design & Collected Editions JOHN CUNNINGHAM Senior VP – Sales & Trade Marketing
ANNE DePIES Senior VP – Business Strategy, Finance & Administration DON FALLETTI VP – Manufacturing Operations
LAWRENCE GANEM VP – Editorial Administration & Talent Relations ALISON GILL Senior VP – Manufacturing & Operations
HANK KANALZ Senior VP – Editorial Strategy & Administration JAY KOGAN VP – Legal Affairs
THOMAS LOFTUS VP – Business Affairs JACK MAHAN VP – Business Affairs
NICK J. NAPOLITANO VP – Manufacturing Administration EDDIE SCANNELL VP – Consumer Marketing
COURTNEY SIMMONS Senior VP – Publicity & Communications JIM (SKI) SOKOLOWSKI VP – Comic Book Specialty Sales & Trade Marketing NANCY SPEARS VP – Mass, Book, Digital Sales & Trade Marketing

DC Comics, 2900 West Alameda Ave., Burbank, CA 91505
Printed by Solisco Printers, Scott, QC, Canada. 4/7/17. First Printing.
ISBN: 978-1-4012-6898-5

Library of Congress Cataloging-in-Publication Data is available.

PEFC Certified
This product is from sustainably managed forests, recycled and controlled sources
PEFC
PEFC/26-31-02
www.pefc.org

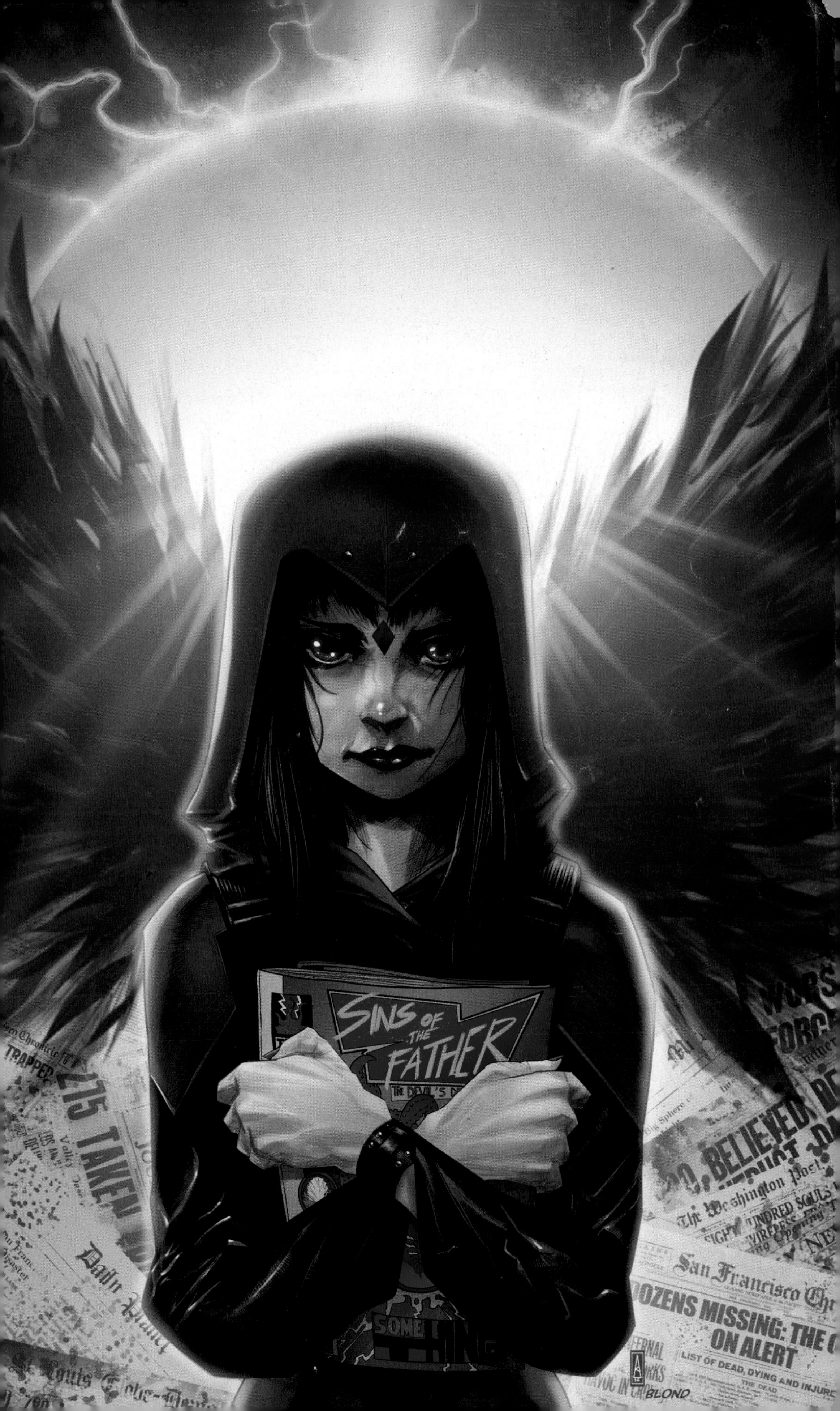
SINS OF THE FATHER
THE DEVIL'S
215 TAKEN
BELIEVED
The Washington Post
San Francisco
DOZENS MISSING: THE
ON ALERT
LIST OF DEAD, DYING AND INJURE
BLOND

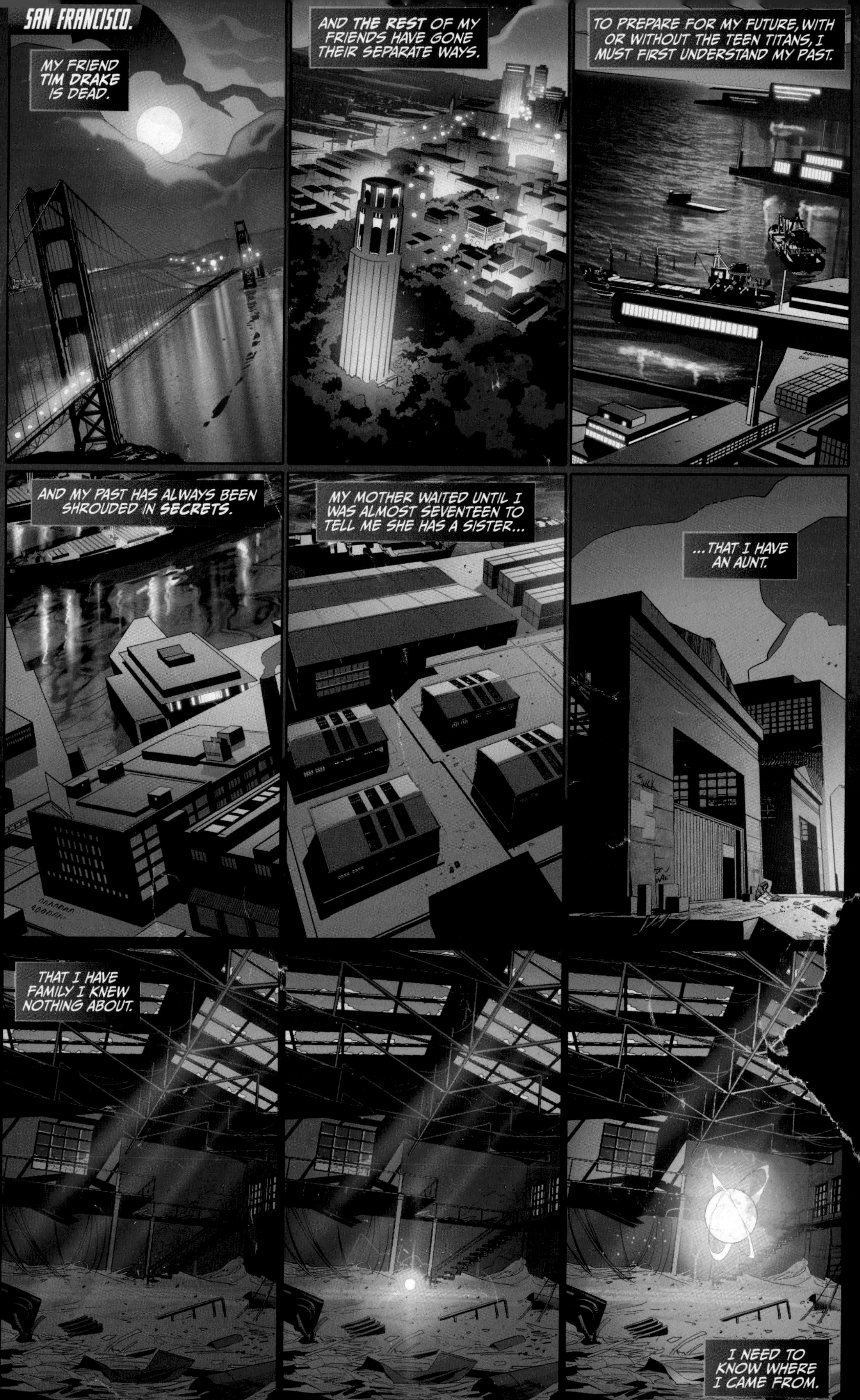

SAN FRANCISCO.
MY FRIEND TIM DRAKE IS DEAD.
AND THE REST OF MY FRIENDS HAVE GONE THEIR SEPARATE WAYS.
TO PREPARE FOR MY FUTURE, WITH OR WITHOUT THE TEEN TITANS, I MUST FIRST UNDERSTAND MY PAST.
AND MY PAST HAS ALWAYS BEEN SHROUDED IN SECRETS.
MY MOTHER WAITED UNTIL I WAS ALMOST SEVENTEEN TO TELL ME SHE HAS A SISTER...
...THAT I HAVE AN AUNT.
THAT I HAVE FAMILY I KNEW NOTHING ABOUT.
I NEED TO KNOW WHERE I CAME FROM.

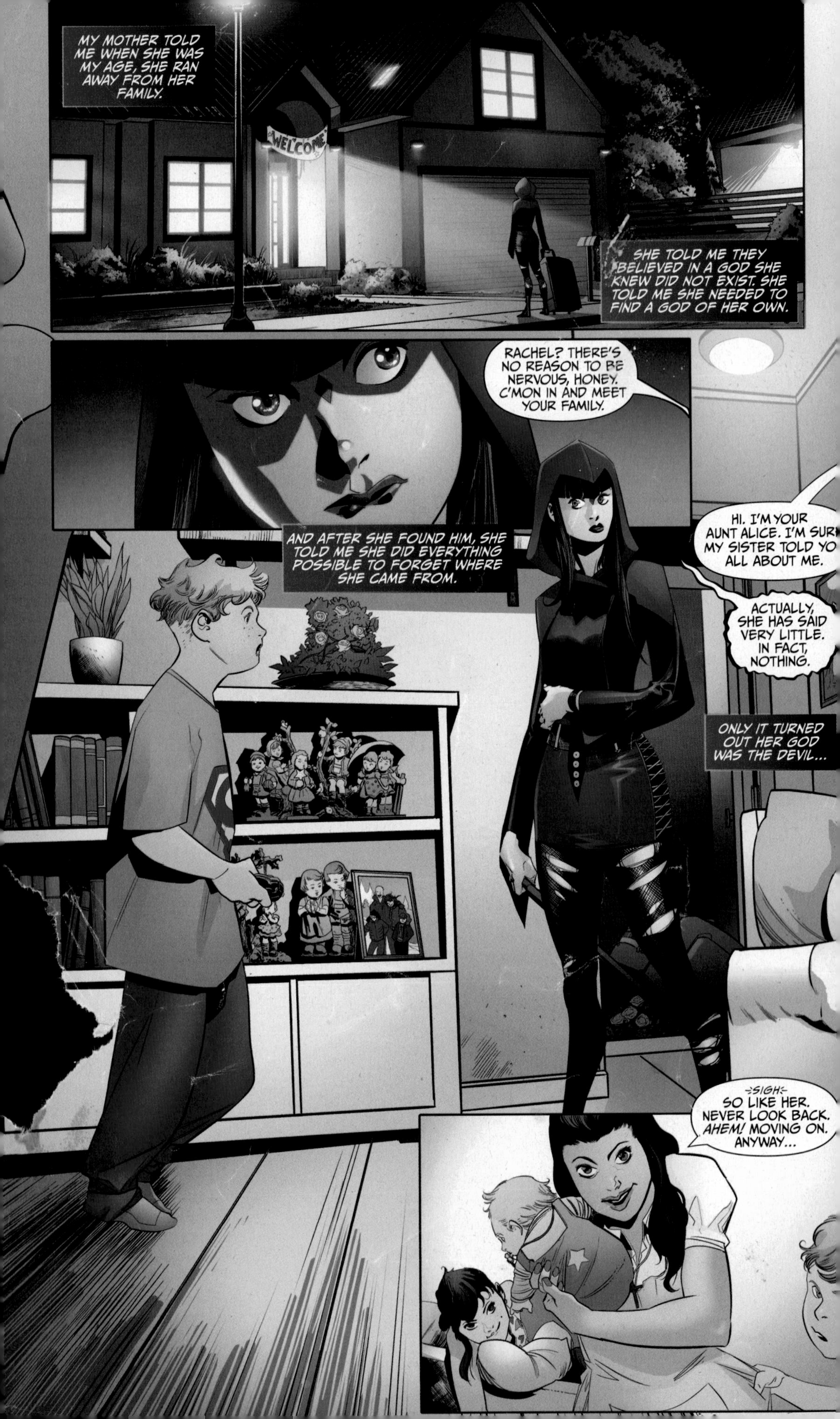

MY MOTHER TOLD ME WHEN SHE WAS MY AGE, SHE RAN AWAY FROM HER FAMILY.
WELCOME
SHE TOLD ME THEY BELIEVED IN A GOD SHE KNEW DID NOT EXIST. SHE TOLD ME SHE NEEDED TO FIND A GOD OF HER OWN.
RACHEL? THERE'S NO REASON TO BE NERVOUS, HONEY. C'MON IN AND MEET YOUR FAMILY.
AND AFTER SHE FOUND HIM, SHE TOLD ME SHE DID EVERYTHING POSSIBLE TO FORGET WHERE SHE CAME FROM.
HI. I'M YOUR AUNT ALICE. I'M SUR MY SISTER TOLD YO ALL ABOUT ME.
ACTUALLY, SHE HAS SAID VERY LITTLE. IN FACT, NOTHING.
ONLY IT TURNED OUT HER GOD WAS THE DEVIL...
SIGH
SO LIKE HER. NEVER LOOK BACK. AHEM! MOVING ON. ANYWAY...

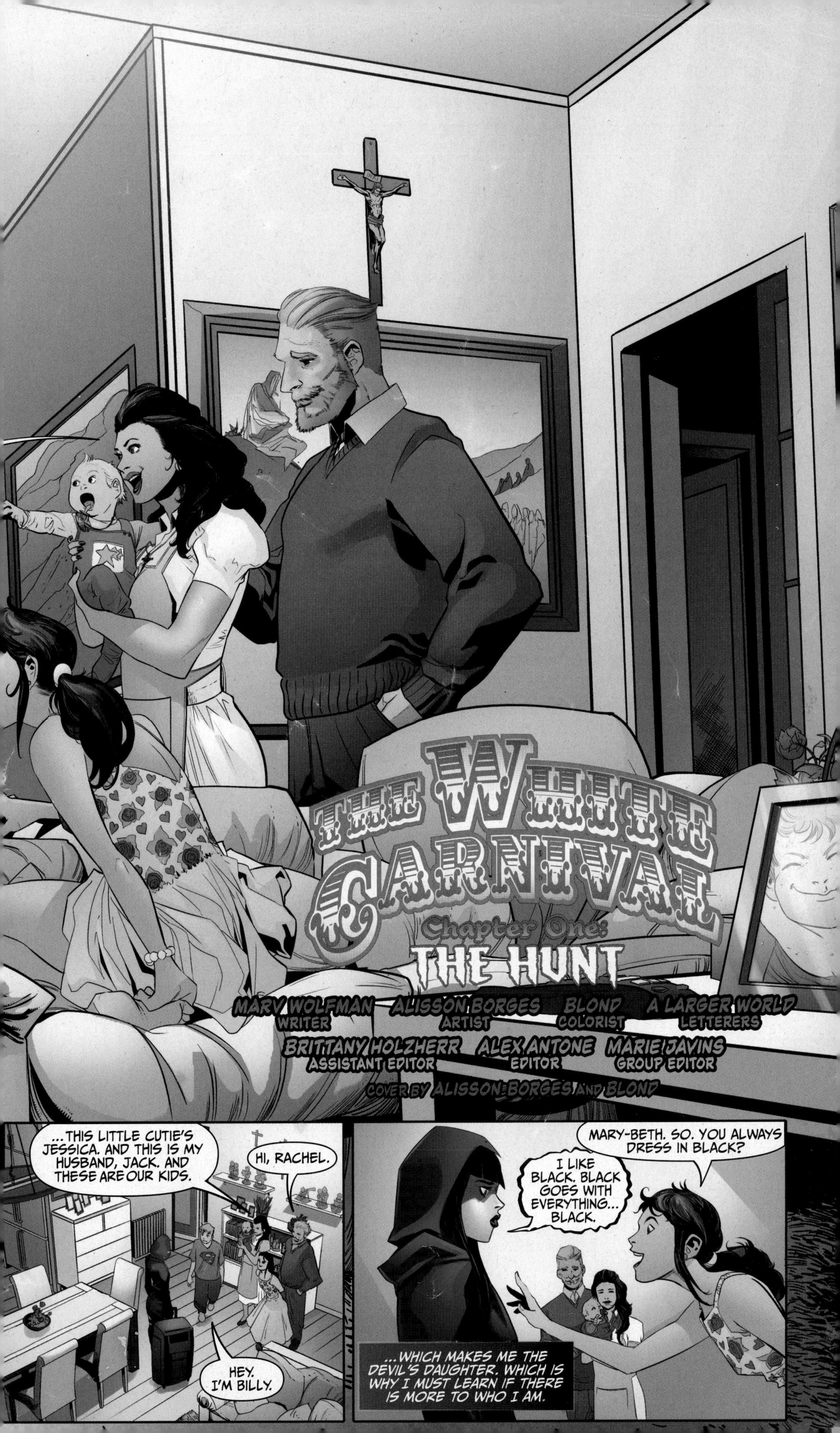
THE WHITE CARNIVAL
Chapter One:
THE HUNT
MARV WOLFMAN WRITER
ALISSON BORGES ARTIST
BLOND COLORIST
A LARGER WORLD LETTERERS
BRITTANY HOLZHERR ASSISTANT EDITOR
ALEX ANTONE EDITOR
MARIE JAVINS GROUP EDITOR
COVER BY ALISSON BORGES AND BLOND
...THIS LITTLE CUTIE'S JESSICA. AND THIS IS MY HUSBAND, JACK. AND THESE ARE OUR KIDS.
HI, RACHEL.
HEY. I'M BILLY.
MARY-BETH. SO. YOU ALWAYS DRESS IN BLACK?
I LIKE BLACK. BLACK GOES WITH EVERYTHING... BLACK.
...WHICH MAKES ME THE DEVIL'S DAUGHTER. WHICH IS WHY I MUST LEARN IF THERE IS MORE TO WHO I AM.

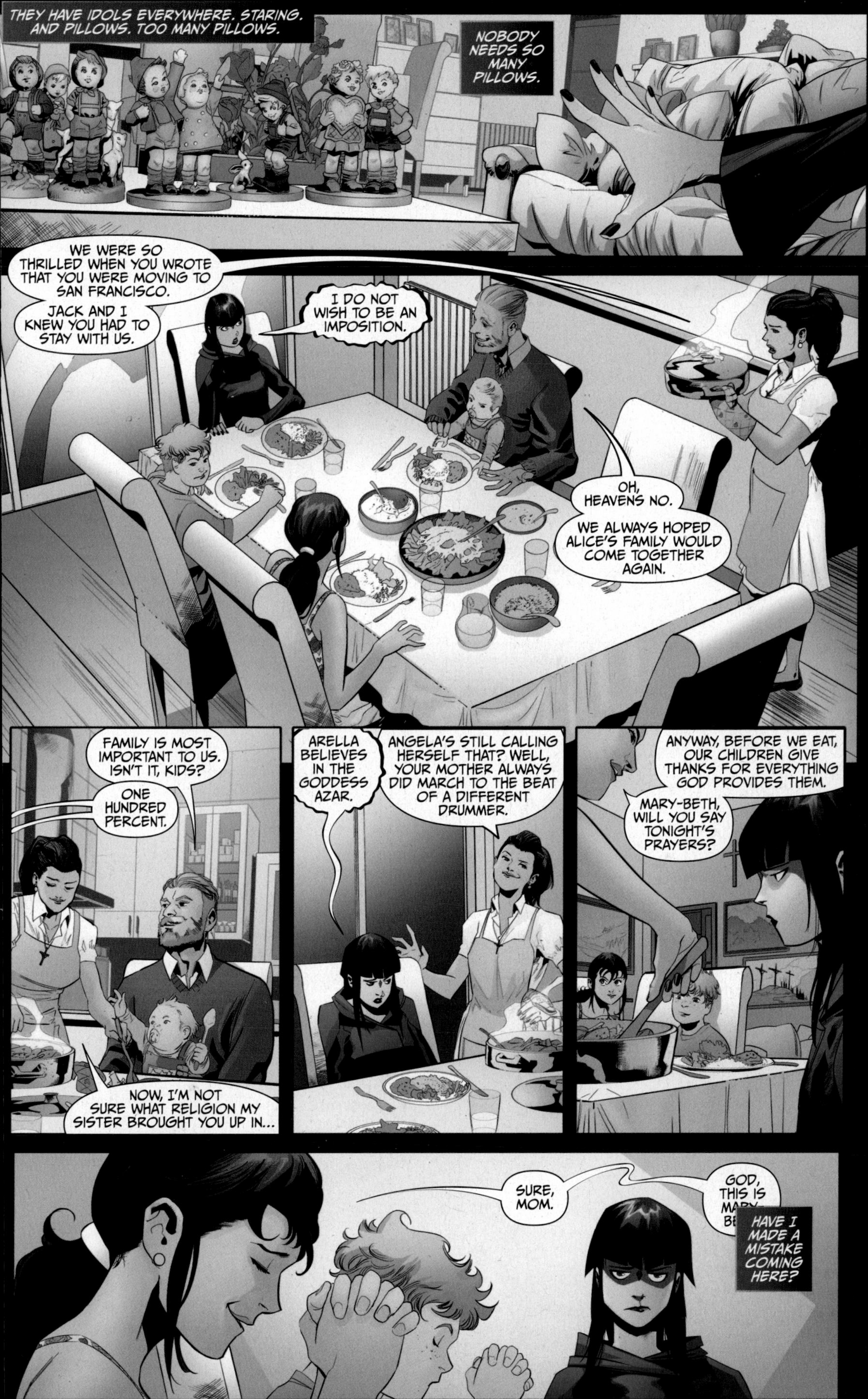
THEY HAVE IDOLS EVERYWHERE. STARING. AND PILLOWS. TOO MANY PILLOWS.
NOBODY NEEDS SO MANY PILLOWS.
WE WERE SO THRILLED WHEN YOU WROTE THAT YOU WERE MOVING TO SAN FRANCISCO.
JACK AND I KNEW YOU HAD TO STAY WITH US.
I DO NOT WISH TO BE AN IMPOSITION.
OH, HEAVENS NO.
WE ALWAYS HOPED ALICE'S FAMILY WOULD COME TOGETHER AGAIN.
FAMILY IS MOST IMPORTANT TO US. ISN'T IT, KIDS?
ONE HUNDRED PERCENT.
NOW, I'M NOT SURE WHAT RELIGION MY SISTER BROUGHT YOU UP IN...
ARELLA BELIEVES IN THE GODDESS AZAR.
ANGELA'S STILL CALLING HERSELF THAT? WELL, YOUR MOTHER ALWAYS DID MARCH TO THE BEAT OF A DIFFERENT DRUMMER.
ANYWAY, BEFORE WE EAT, OUR CHILDREN GIVE THANKS FOR EVERYTHING GOD PROVIDES THEM.
MARY-BETH, WILL YOU SAY TONIGHT'S PRAYERS?
SURE, MOM.
GOD, THIS IS
HAVE I MADE A MISTAKE COMING HERE?

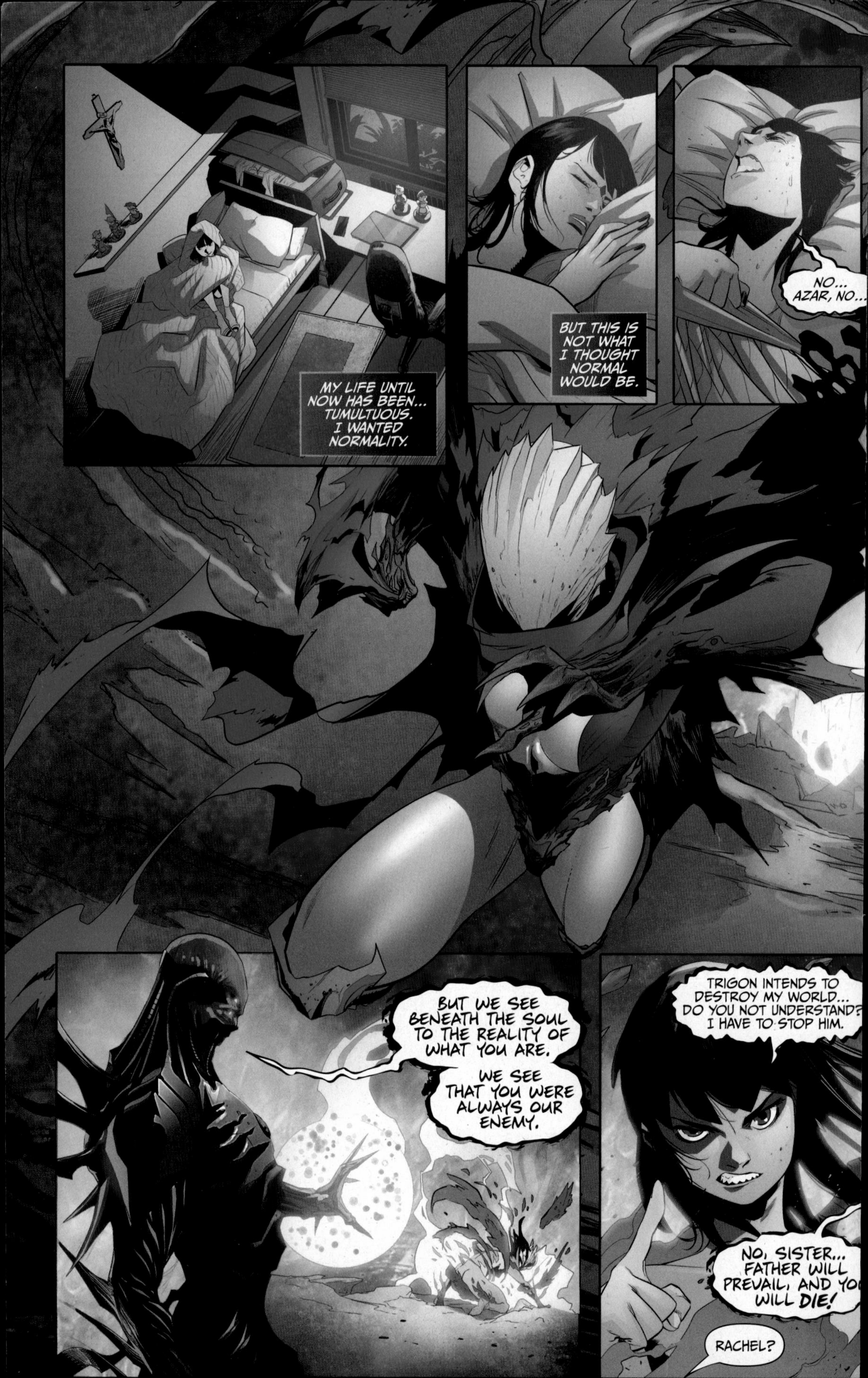
MY LIFE UNTIL NOW HAS BEEN... TUMULTUOUS. I WANTED NORMALITY.
BUT THIS IS NOT WHAT I THOUGHT NORMAL WOULD BE.
NO... AZAR, NO...
BUT WE SEE BENEATH THE SOUL TO THE REALITY OF WHAT YOU ARE.
WE SEE THAT YOU WERE ALWAYS OUR ENEMY.
TRIGON INTENDS TO DESTROY MY WORLD... DO YOU NOT UNDERSTAND? I HAVE TO STOP HIM.
NO, SISTER... FATHER WILL PREVAIL, AND YO WILL DIE!
RACHEL?

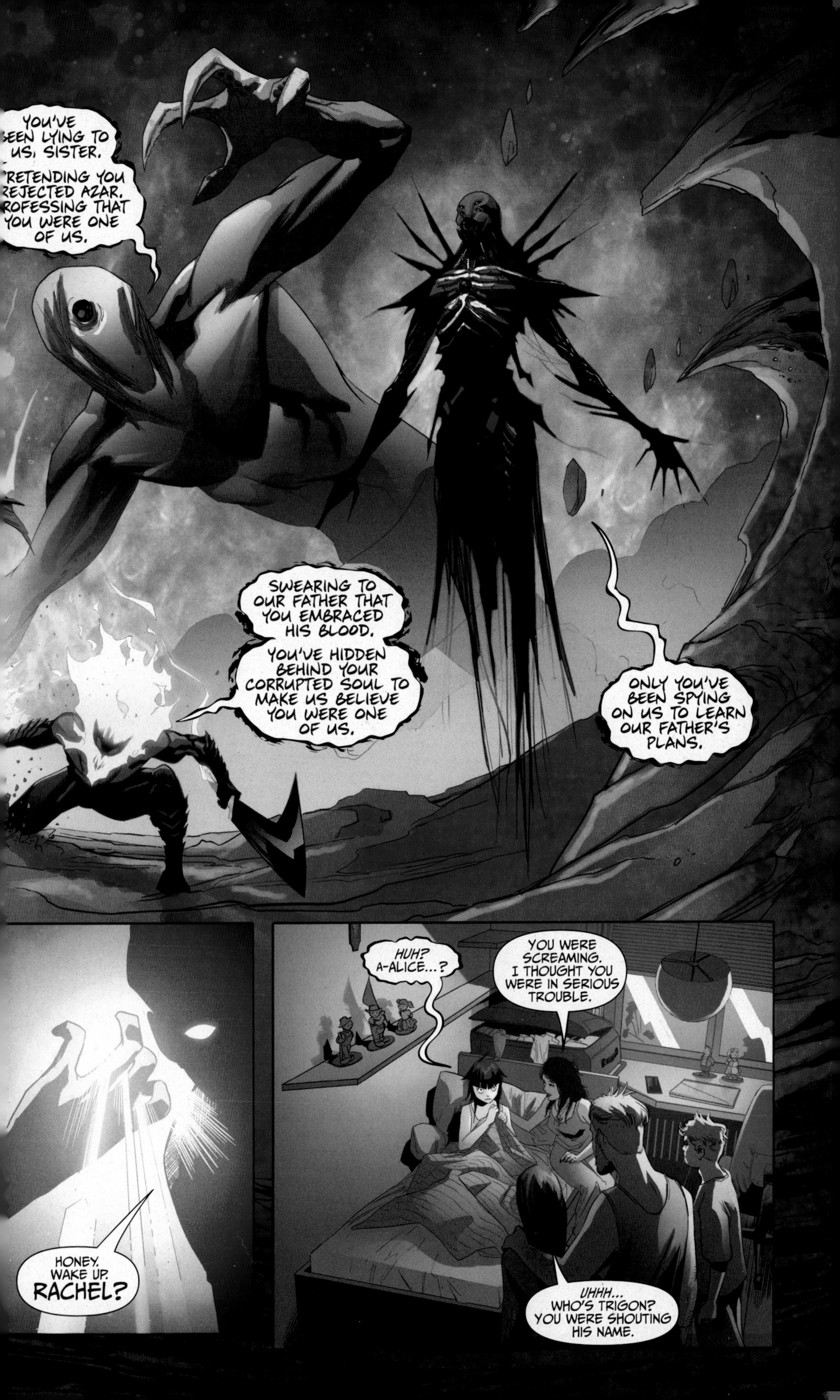
YOU'VE BEEN LYING TO US, SISTER.
PRETENDING YOU REJECTED AZAR. PROFESSING THAT YOU WERE ONE OF US.
SWEARING TO OUR FATHER THAT YOU EMBRACED HIS BLOOD.
YOU'VE HIDDEN BEHIND YOUR CORRUPTED SOUL TO MAKE US BELIEVE YOU WERE ONE OF US.
ONLY YOU'VE BEEN SPYING ON US TO LEARN OUR FATHER'S PLANS.
HONEY. WAKE UP. RACHEL?
HUH? A-ALICE...?
YOU WERE SCREAMING. I THOUGHT YOU WERE IN SERIOUS TROUBLE.
UHHH... WHO'S TRIGON? YOU WERE SHOUTING HIS NAME.

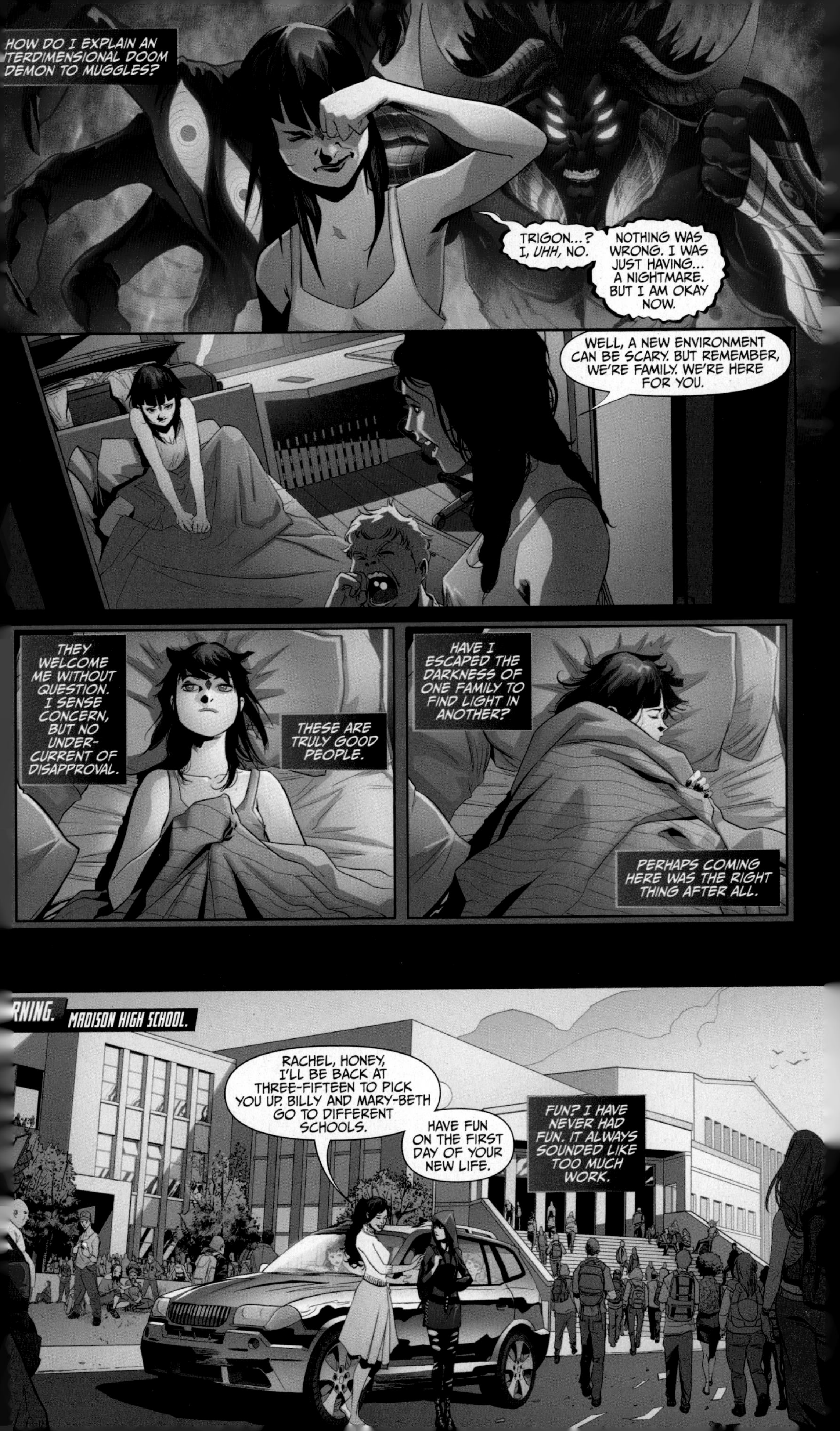

HOW DO I EXPLAIN AN INTERDIMENSIONAL DOOM DEMON TO MUGGLES?
TRIGON...? I, *UHH*, NO.
NOTHING WAS WRONG. I WAS JUST HAVING... A NIGHTMARE. BUT I AM OKAY NOW.
WELL, A NEW ENVIRONMENT CAN BE SCARY. BUT REMEMBER, WE'RE FAMILY. WE'RE HERE FOR YOU.
THEY WELCOME ME WITHOUT QUESTION. I SENSE CONCERN, BUT NO UNDER-CURRENT OF DISAPPROVAL.
THESE ARE TRULY GOOD PEOPLE.
HAVE I ESCAPED THE DARKNESS OF ONE FAMILY TO FIND LIGHT IN ANOTHER?
PERHAPS COMING HERE WAS THE RIGHT THING AFTER ALL.
RNING.
MADISON HIGH SCHOOL.
RACHEL, HONEY, I'LL BE BACK AT THREE-FIFTEEN TO PICK YOU UP. BILLY AND MARY-BETH GO TO DIFFERENT SCHOOLS.
HAVE FUN ON THE FIRST DAY OF YOUR NEW LIFE.
FUN? I HAVE NEVER HAD FUN. IT ALWAYS SOUNDED LIKE TOO MUCH WORK.

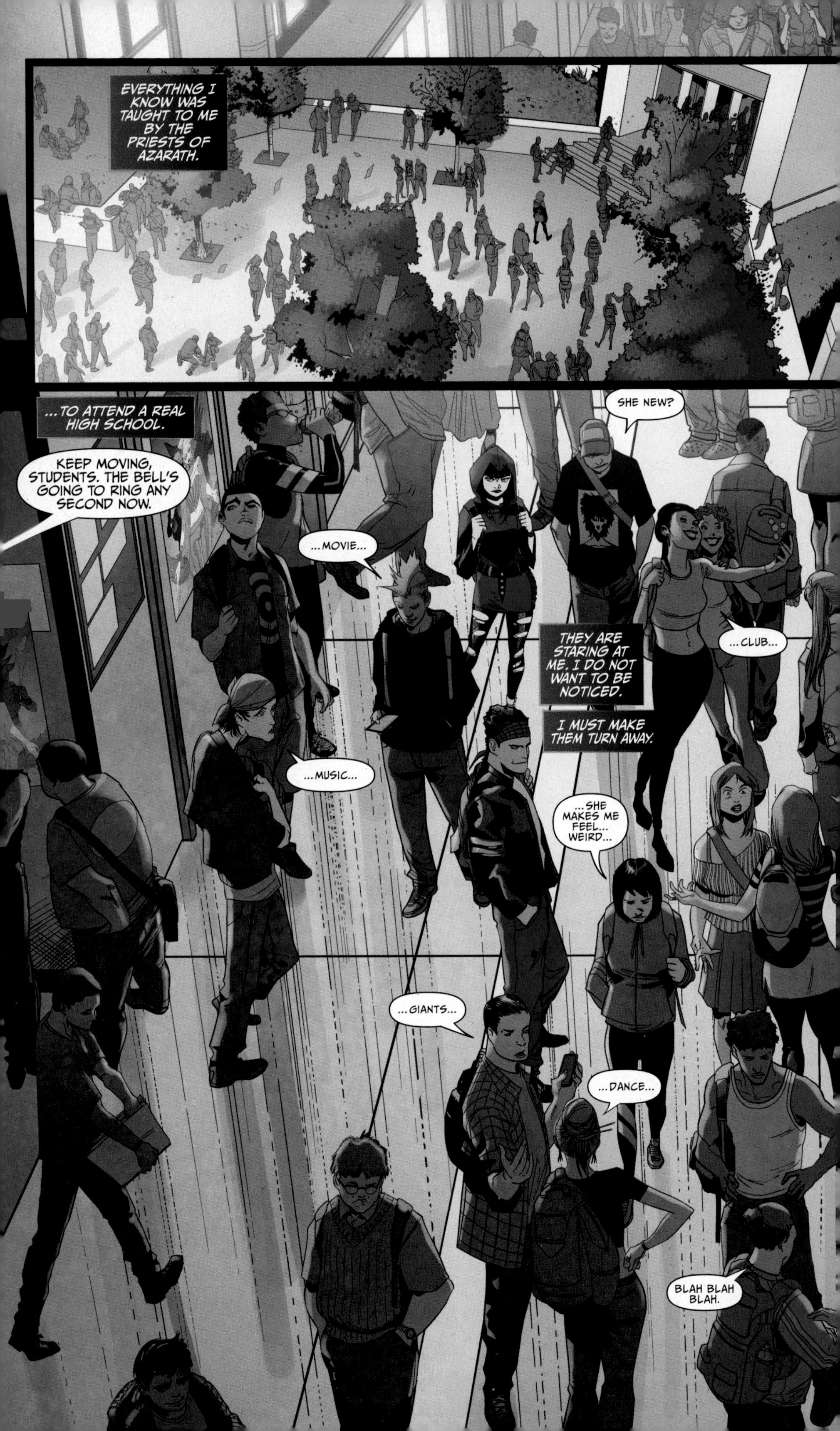
EVERYTHING I KNOW WAS TAUGHT TO ME BY THE PRIESTS OF AZARATH.
...TO ATTEND A REAL HIGH SCHOOL.
KEEP MOVING, STUDENTS. THE BELL'S GOING TO RING ANY SECOND NOW.
SHE NEW?
...MOVIE...
...CLUB...
THEY ARE STARING AT ME. I DO NOT WANT TO BE NOTICED.
I MUST MAKE THEM TURN AWAY.
...MUSIC...
...SHE MAKES ME FEEL... WEIRD...
...GIANTS...
...DANCE...
BLAH BLAH BLAH.

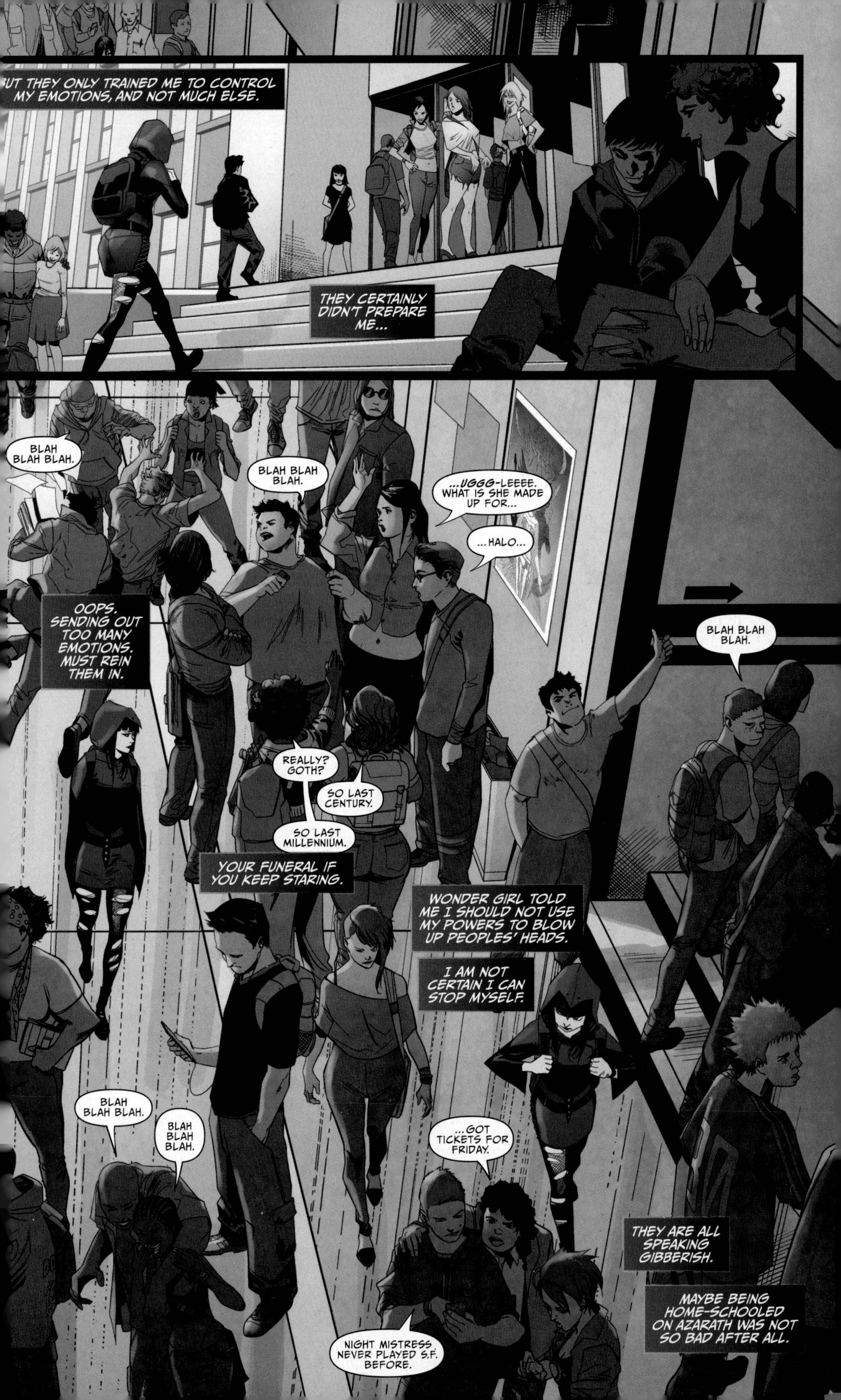
BUT THEY ONLY TRAINED ME TO CONTROL MY EMOTIONS, AND NOT MUCH ELSE.
THEY CERTAINLY DIDN'T PREPARE ME...
BLAH BLAH BLAH.
BLAH BLAH BLAH.
...UGGG-LEEEE. WHAT IS SHE MADE UP FOR...
...HALO...
OOPS. SENDING OUT TOO MANY EMOTIONS. MUST REIN THEM IN.
BLAH BLAH BLAH.
REALLY? GOTH?
SO LAST CENTURY.
SO LAST MILLENNIUM.
YOUR FUNERAL IF YOU KEEP STARING.
WONDER GIRL TOLD ME I SHOULD NOT USE MY POWERS TO BLOW UP PEOPLES' HEADS.
I AM NOT CERTAIN I CAN STOP MYSELF.
BLAH BLAH BLAH.
BLAH BLAH BLAH.
...GOT TICKETS FOR FRIDAY.
THEY ARE ALL SPEAKING GIBBERISH.
MAYBE BEING HOME-SCHOOLED ON AZARATH WAS NOT SO BAD AFTER ALL.
NIGHT MISTRESS NEVER PLAYED S.F. BEFORE.

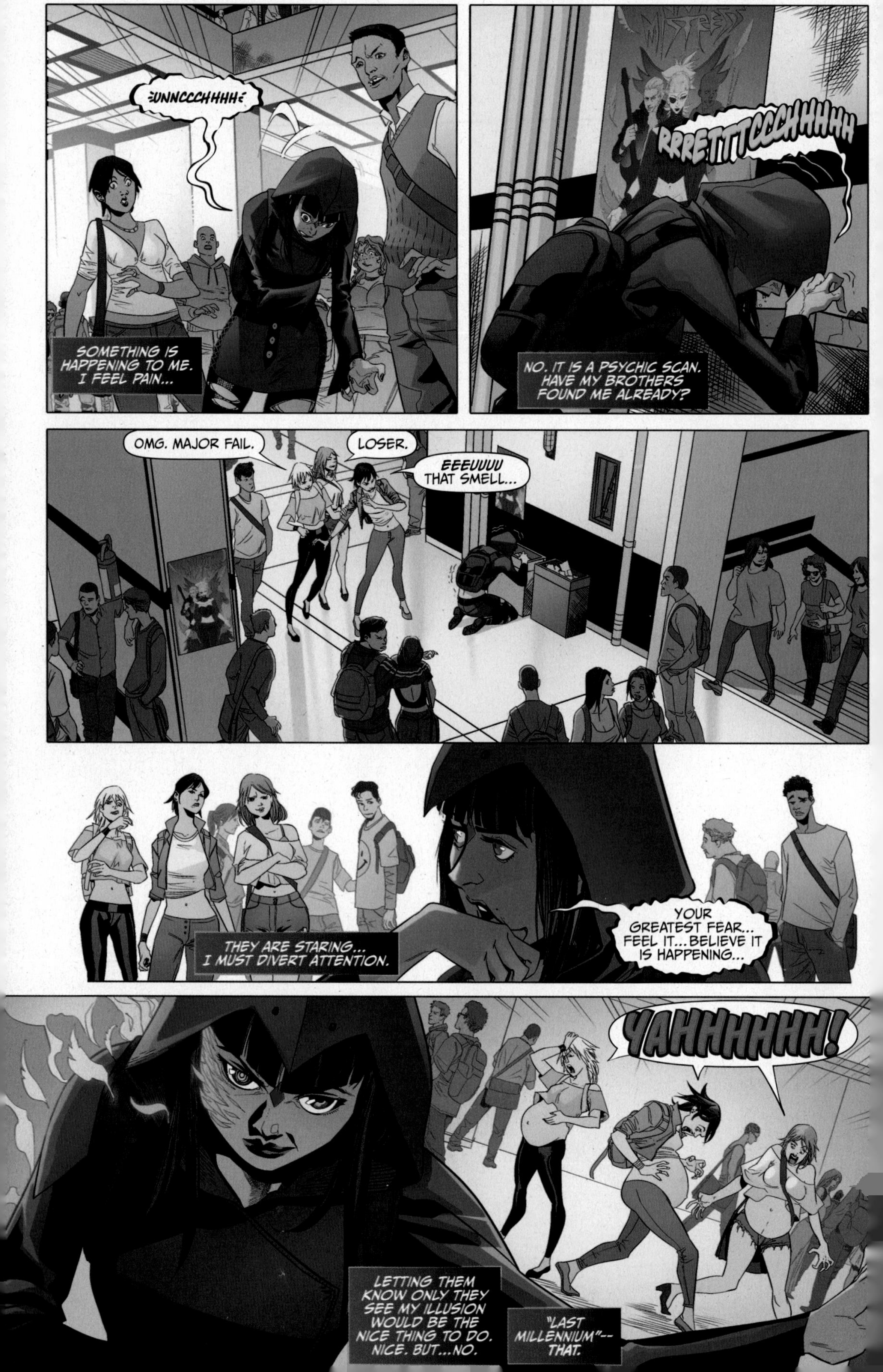
UNNCCCHHHH
SOMETHING IS HAPPENING TO ME. I FEEL PAIN...
RRRETTTCCCHHHHH
NO. IT IS A PSYCHIC SCAN. HAVE MY BROTHERS FOUND ME ALREADY?
OMG. MAJOR FAIL.
LOSER.
EEEUUUU THAT SMELL...
THEY ARE STARING... I MUST DIVERT ATTENTION.
YOUR GREATEST FEAR... FEEL IT...BELIEVE IT IS HAPPENING...
YAHHHHHH!
LETTING THEM KNOW ONLY THEY SEE MY ILLUSION WOULD BE THE NICE THING TO DO. NICE. BUT...NO.
"LAST MILLENNIUM"-- THAT.

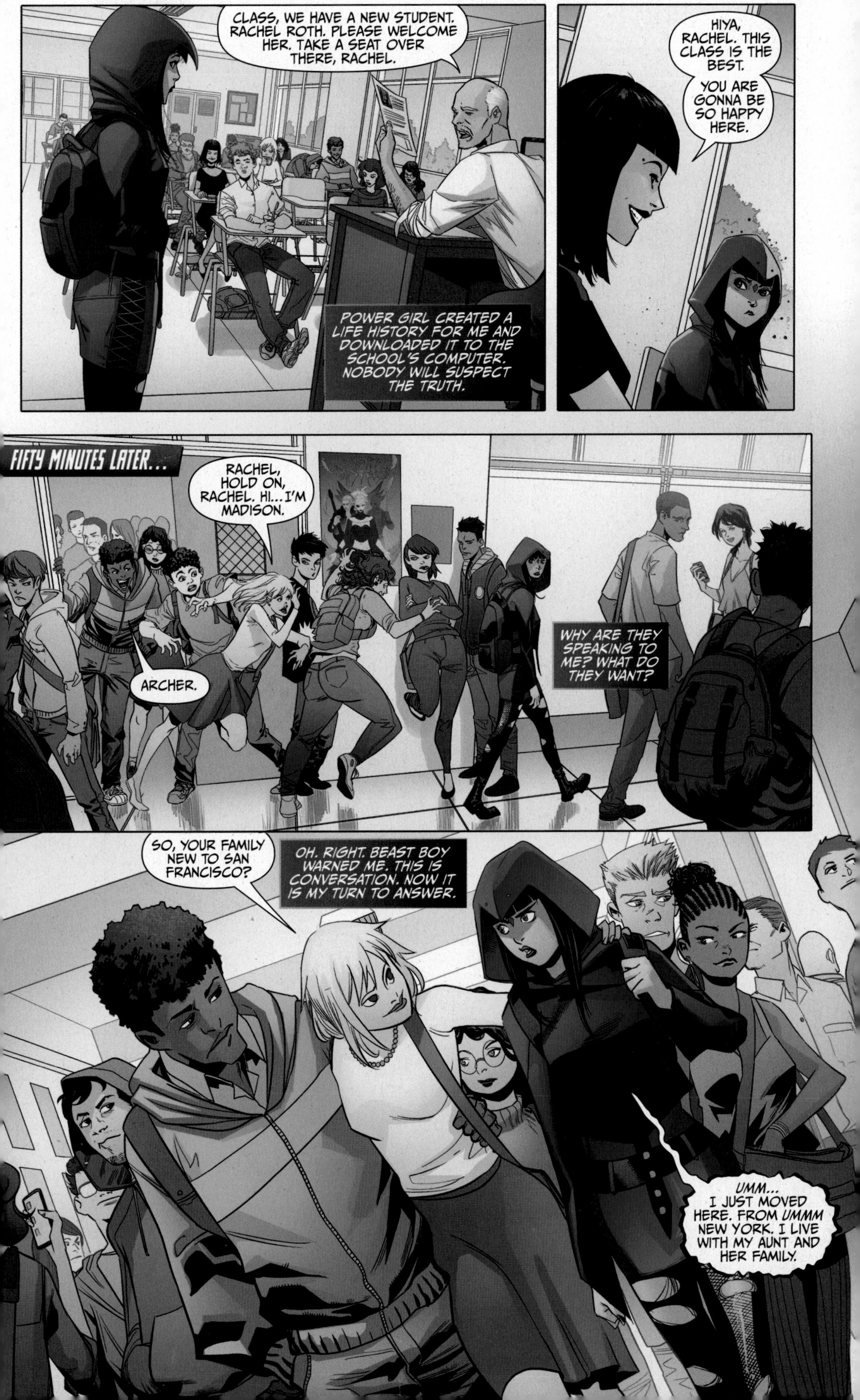
CLASS, WE HAVE A NEW STUDENT. RACHEL ROTH. PLEASE WELCOME HER. TAKE A SEAT OVER THERE, RACHEL.
POWER GIRL CREATED A LIFE HISTORY FOR ME AND DOWNLOADED IT TO THE SCHOOL'S COMPUTER. NOBODY WILL SUSPECT THE TRUTH.
HIYA, RACHEL. THIS CLASS IS THE BEST.
YOU ARE GONNA BE SO HAPPY HERE.
FIFTY MINUTES LATER...
RACHEL, HOLD ON, RACHEL. HI...I'M MADISON.
ARCHER.
WHY ARE THEY SPEAKING TO ME? WHAT DO THEY WANT?
SO, YOUR FAMILY NEW TO SAN FRANCISCO?
OH. RIGHT. BEAST BOY WARNED ME. THIS IS CONVERSATION. NOW IT IS MY TURN TO ANSWER.
UMM... I JUST MOVED HERE. FROM UMMM NEW YORK. I LIVE WITH MY AUNT AND HER FAMILY.

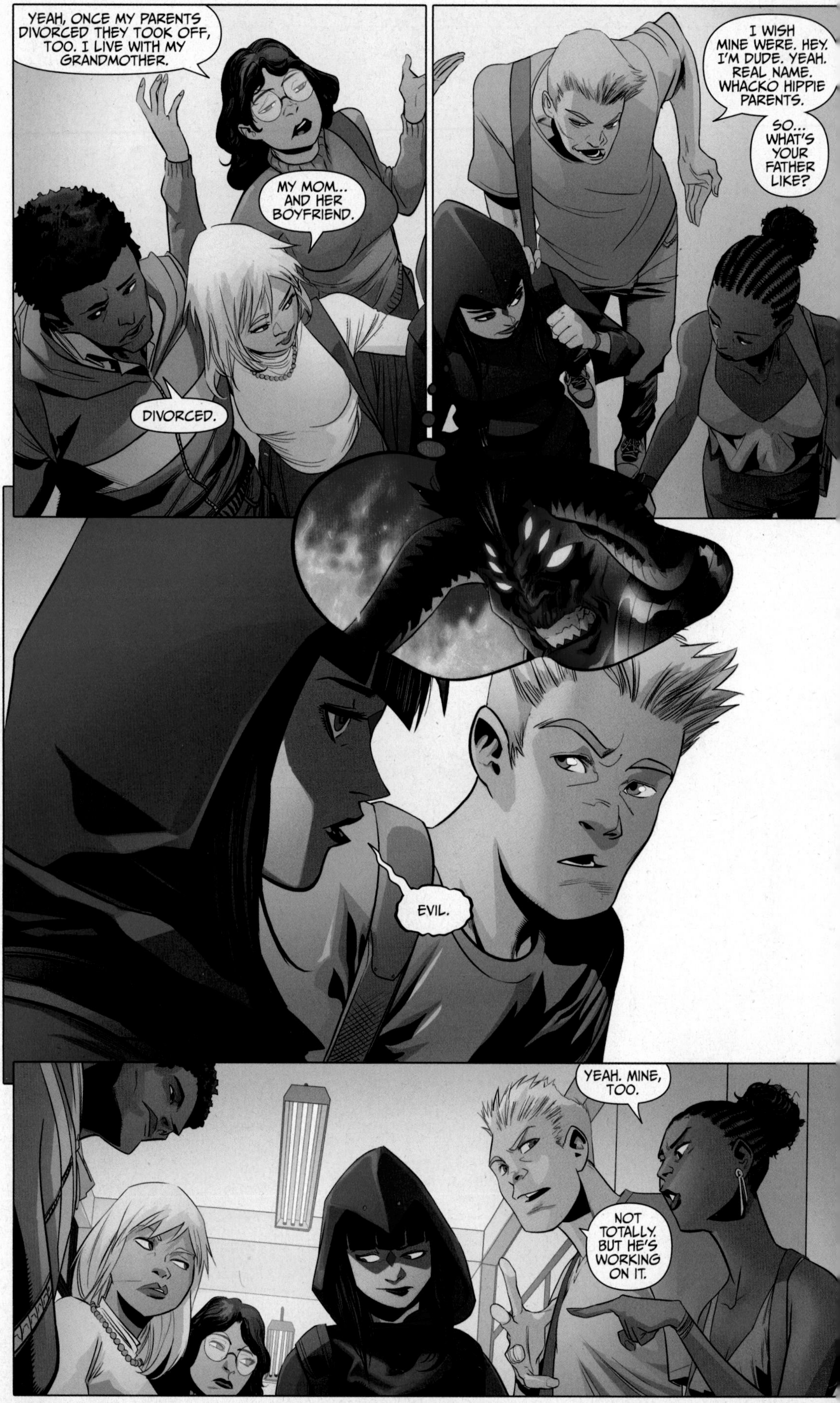
YEAH, ONCE MY PARENTS DIVORCED THEY TOOK OFF, TOO. I LIVE WITH MY GRANDMOTHER.
MY MOM... AND HER BOYFRIEND.
DIVORCED.
I WISH MINE WERE. HEY. I'M DUDE. YEAH. REAL NAME. WHACKO HIPPIE PARENTS.
SO... WHAT'S YOUR FATHER LIKE?
EVIL.
YEAH. MINE, TOO.
NOT TOTALLY. BUT HE'S WORKING ON IT.

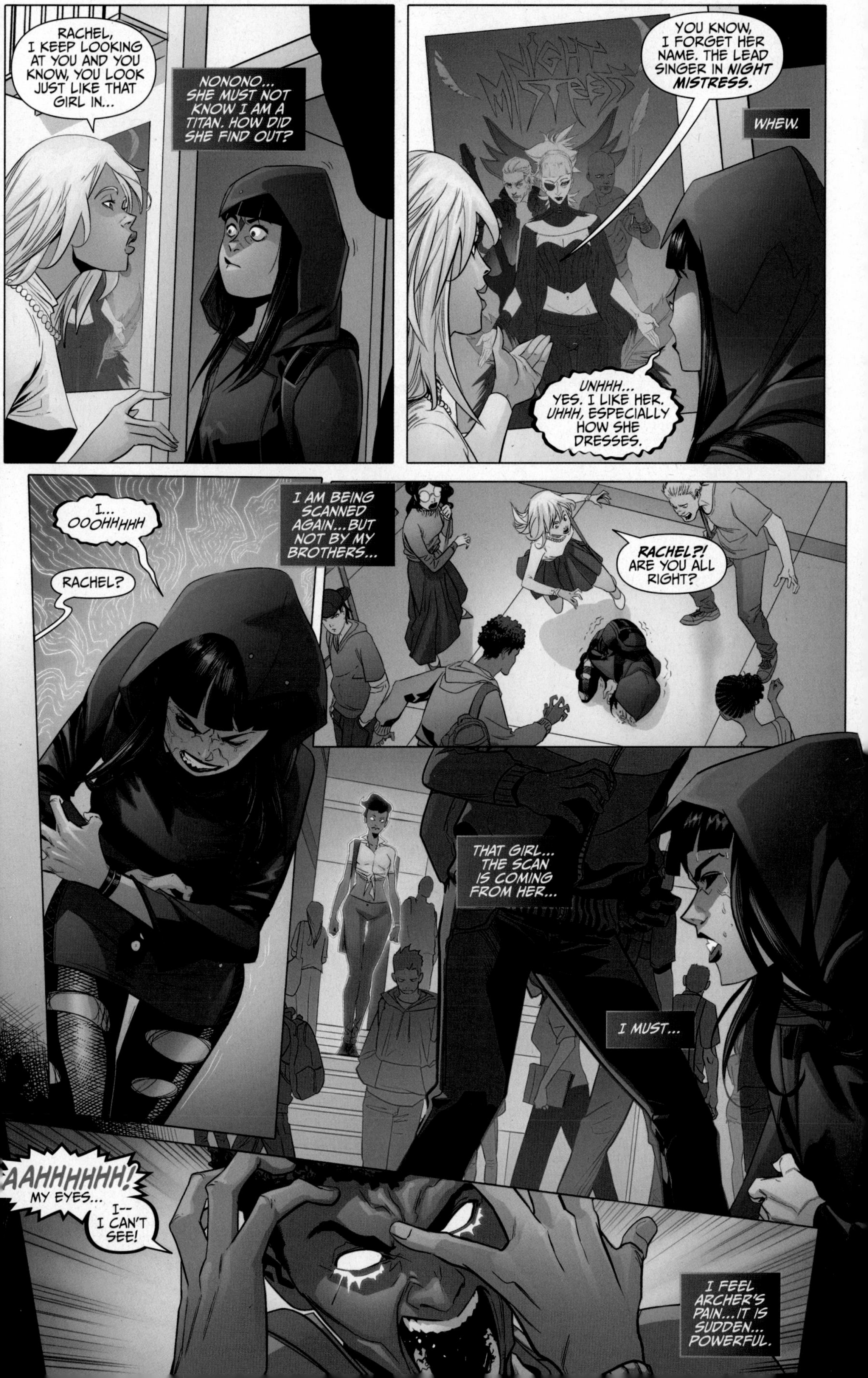
RACHEL, I KEEP LOOKING AT YOU AND YOU KNOW, YOU LOOK JUST LIKE THAT GIRL IN...
NONONO... SHE MUST NOT KNOW I AM A TITAN. HOW DID SHE FIND OUT?
YOU KNOW, I FORGET HER NAME. THE LEAD SINGER IN NIGHT MISTRESS.
NIGHT MISTRESS
WHEW.
UNHHH... YES. I LIKE HER. UHHH, ESPECIALLY HOW SHE DRESSES.
I... OOOHHHHH
RACHEL?
I AM BEING SCANNED AGAIN...BUT NOT BY MY BROTHERS...
RACHEL?! ARE YOU ALL RIGHT?
THAT GIRL... THE SCAN IS COMING FROM HER...
I MUST...
AAHHHHHH! MY EYES...
I-- I CAN'T SEE!
I FEEL ARCHER'S PAIN...IT IS SUDDEN... POWERFUL.

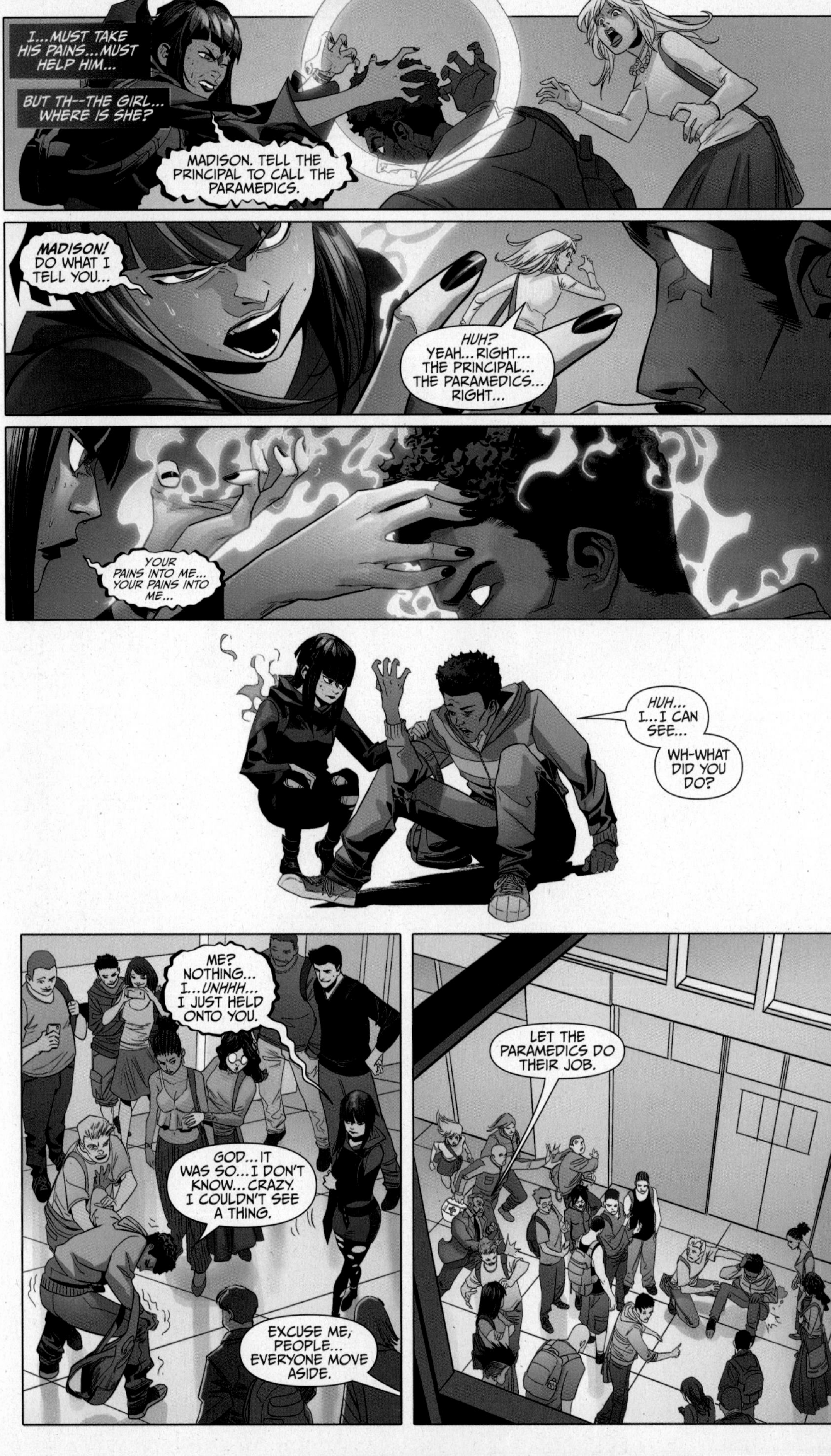
I...MUST TAKE HIS PAINS...MUST HELP HIM...
BUT TH--THE GIRL... WHERE IS SHE?
MADISON. TELL THE PRINCIPAL TO CALL THE PARAMEDICS.
MADISON! DO WHAT I TELL YOU...
HUH? YEAH...RIGHT... THE PRINCIPAL... THE PARAMEDICS... RIGHT...
YOUR PAINS INTO ME... YOUR PAINS INTO ME...
HUH... I...I CAN SEE...
WH-WHAT DID YOU DO?
ME? NOTHING... I...UNHHH... I JUST HELD ONTO YOU.
GOD...IT WAS SO...I DON'T KNOW...CRAZY. I COULDN'T SEE A THING.
EXCUSE ME, PEOPLE... EVERYONE MOVE ASIDE.
LET THE PARAMEDICS DO THEIR JOB.

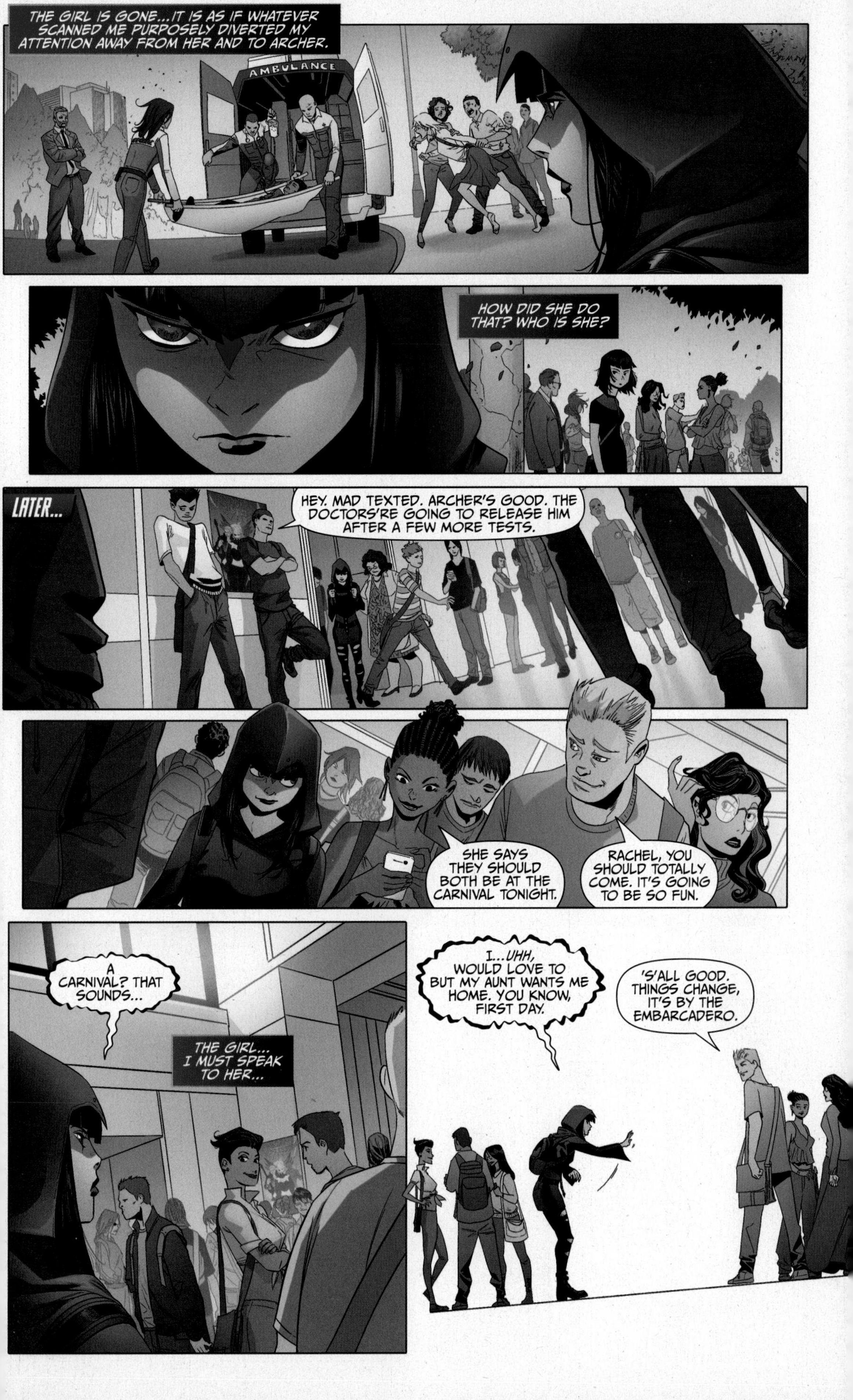
THE GIRL IS GONE...IT IS AS IF WHATEVER SCANNED ME PURPOSELY DIVERTED MY ATTENTION AWAY FROM HER AND TO ARCHER.
AMBULANCE
HOW DID SHE DO THAT? WHO IS SHE?
LATER...
HEY. MAD TEXTED. ARCHER'S GOOD. THE DOCTORS'RE GOING TO RELEASE HIM AFTER A FEW MORE TESTS.
SHE SAYS THEY SHOULD BOTH BE AT THE CARNIVAL TONIGHT.
RACHEL, YOU SHOULD TOTALLY COME. IT'S GOING TO BE SO FUN.
A CARNIVAL? THAT SOUNDS...
THE GIRL... I MUST SPEAK TO HER...
I...UHH, WOULD LOVE TO BUT MY AUNT WANTS ME HOME. YOU KNOW, FIRST DAY.
'S'ALL GOOD. THINGS CHANGE, IT'S BY THE EMBARCADERO.

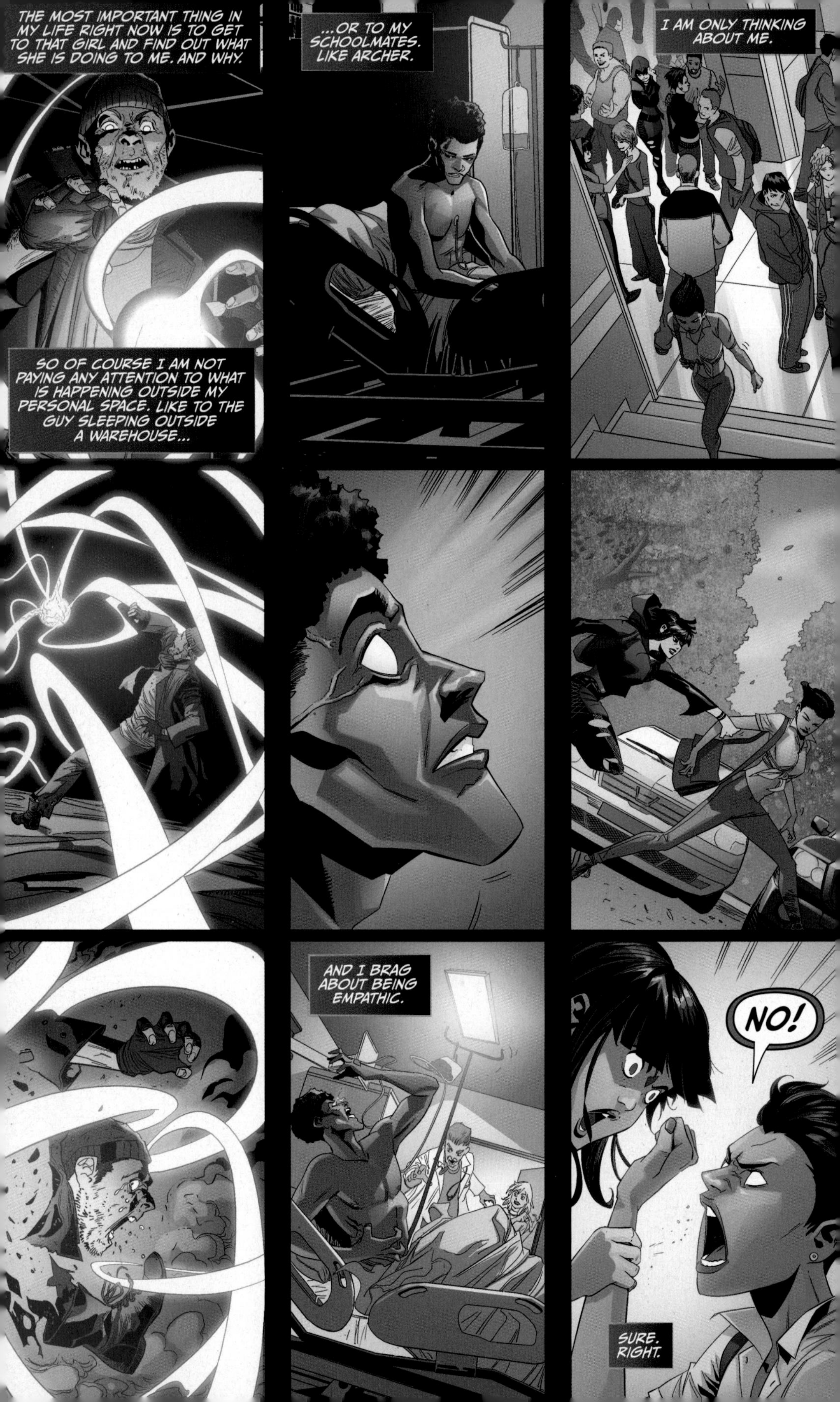
THE MOST IMPORTANT THING IN MY LIFE RIGHT NOW IS TO GET TO THAT GIRL AND FIND OUT WHAT SHE IS DOING TO ME. AND WHY.
SO OF COURSE I AM NOT PAYING ANY ATTENTION TO WHAT IS HAPPENING OUTSIDE MY PERSONAL SPACE. LIKE TO THE GUY SLEEPING OUTSIDE A WAREHOUSE...
...OR TO MY SCHOOLMATES. LIKE ARCHER.
I AM ONLY THINKING ABOUT ME.
AND I BRAG ABOUT BEING EMPATHIC.
NO!
SURE. RIGHT.

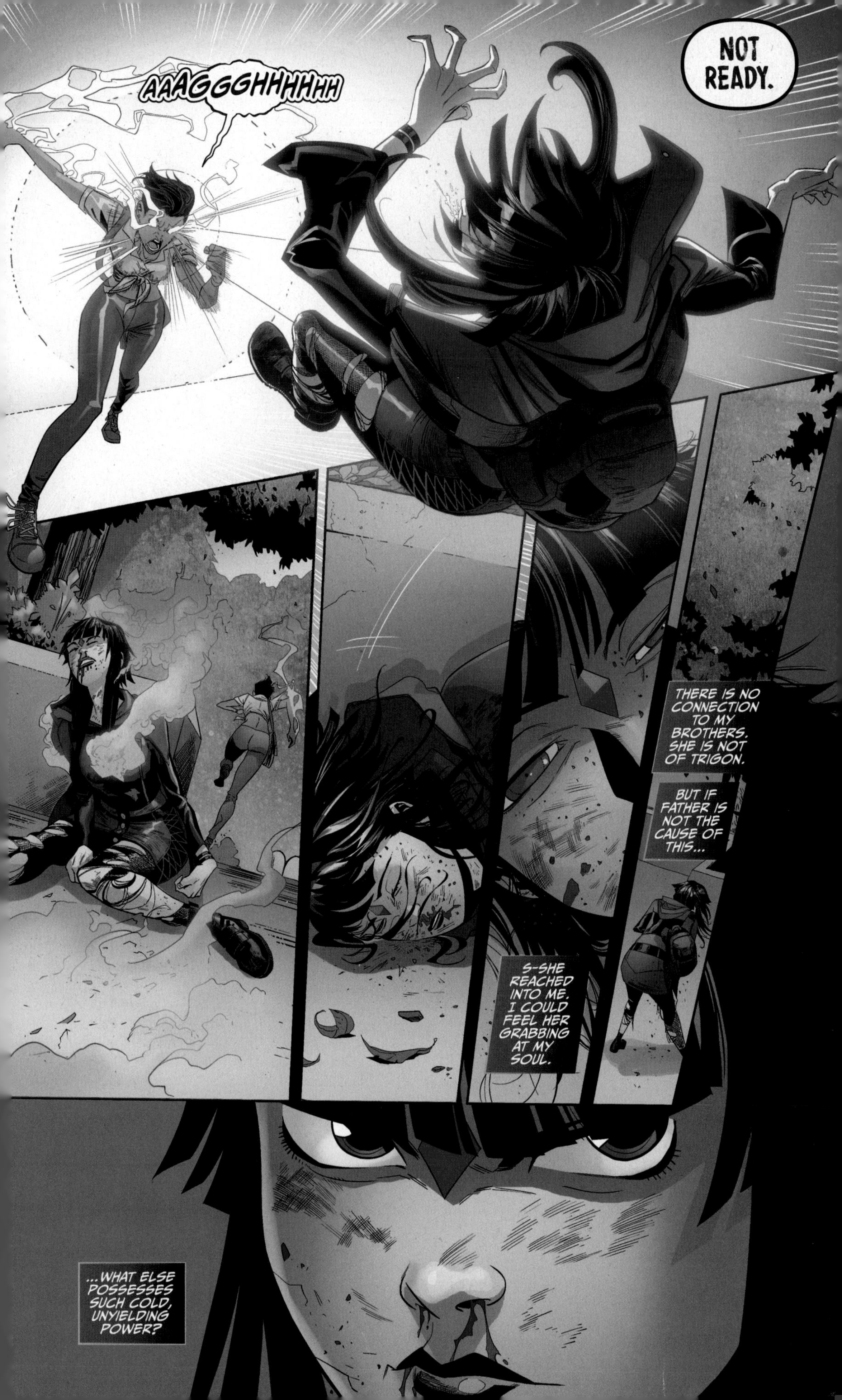
AAAGGGHHHHHH
NOT READY.
S-SHE REACHED INTO ME. I COULD FEEL HER GRABBING AT MY SOUL.
THERE IS NO CONNECTION TO MY BROTHERS. SHE IS NOT OF TRIGON.
BUT IF FATHER IS NOT THE CAUSE OF THIS...
...WHAT ELSE POSSESSES SUCH COLD, UNYIELDING POWER?

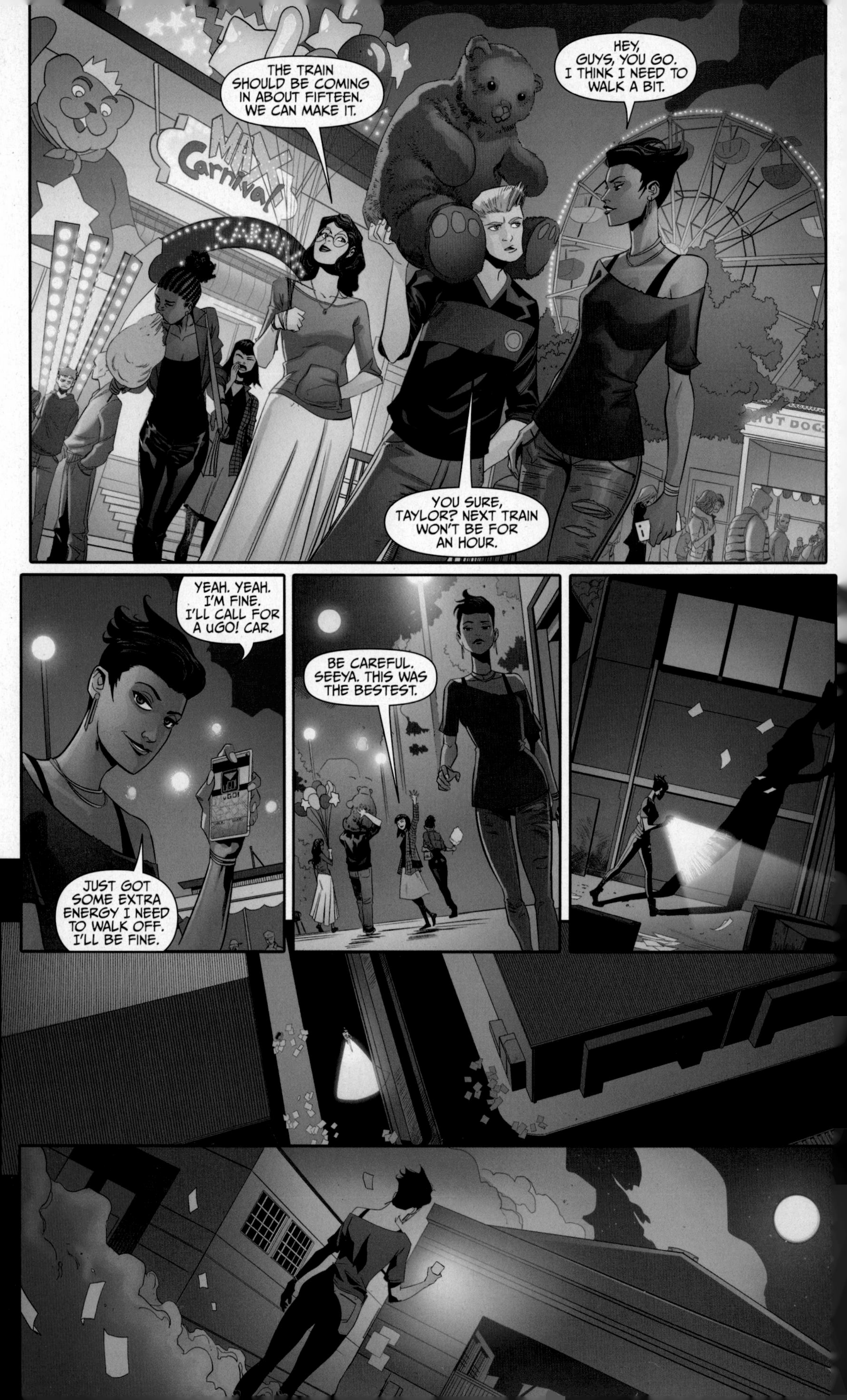
THE TRAIN SHOULD BE COMING IN ABOUT FIFTEEN. WE CAN MAKE IT.
HEY, GUYS, YOU GO. I THINK I NEED TO WALK A BIT.
YOU SURE, TAYLOR? NEXT TRAIN WON'T BE FOR AN HOUR.
YEAH. YEAH. I'M FINE. I'LL CALL FOR A uGO! CAR.
JUST GOT SOME EXTRA ENERGY I NEED TO WALK OFF. I'LL BE FINE.
BE CAREFUL. SEEYA. THIS WAS THE BESTEST.

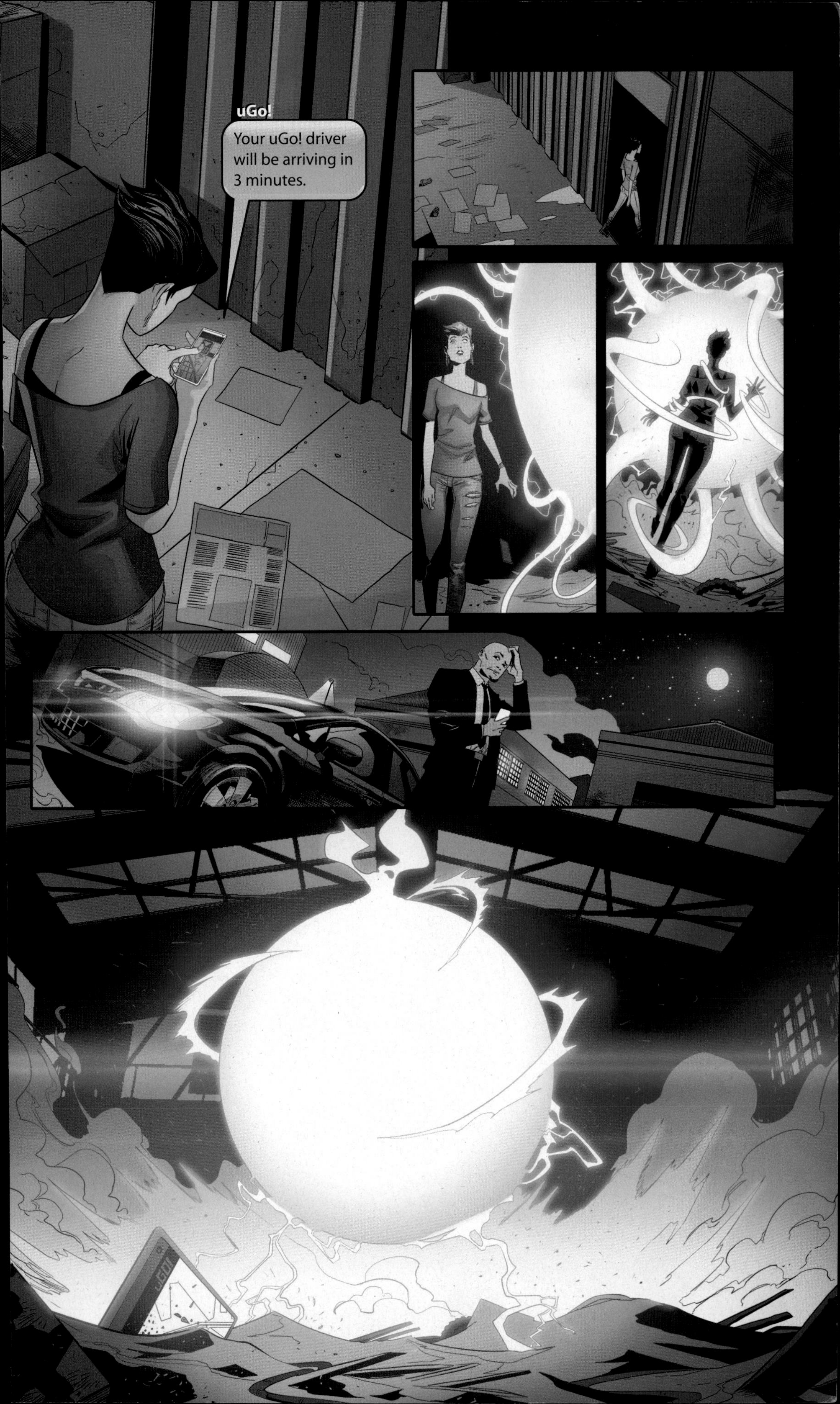
uGo!
Your uGo! driver will be arriving in 3 minutes.
uGo!

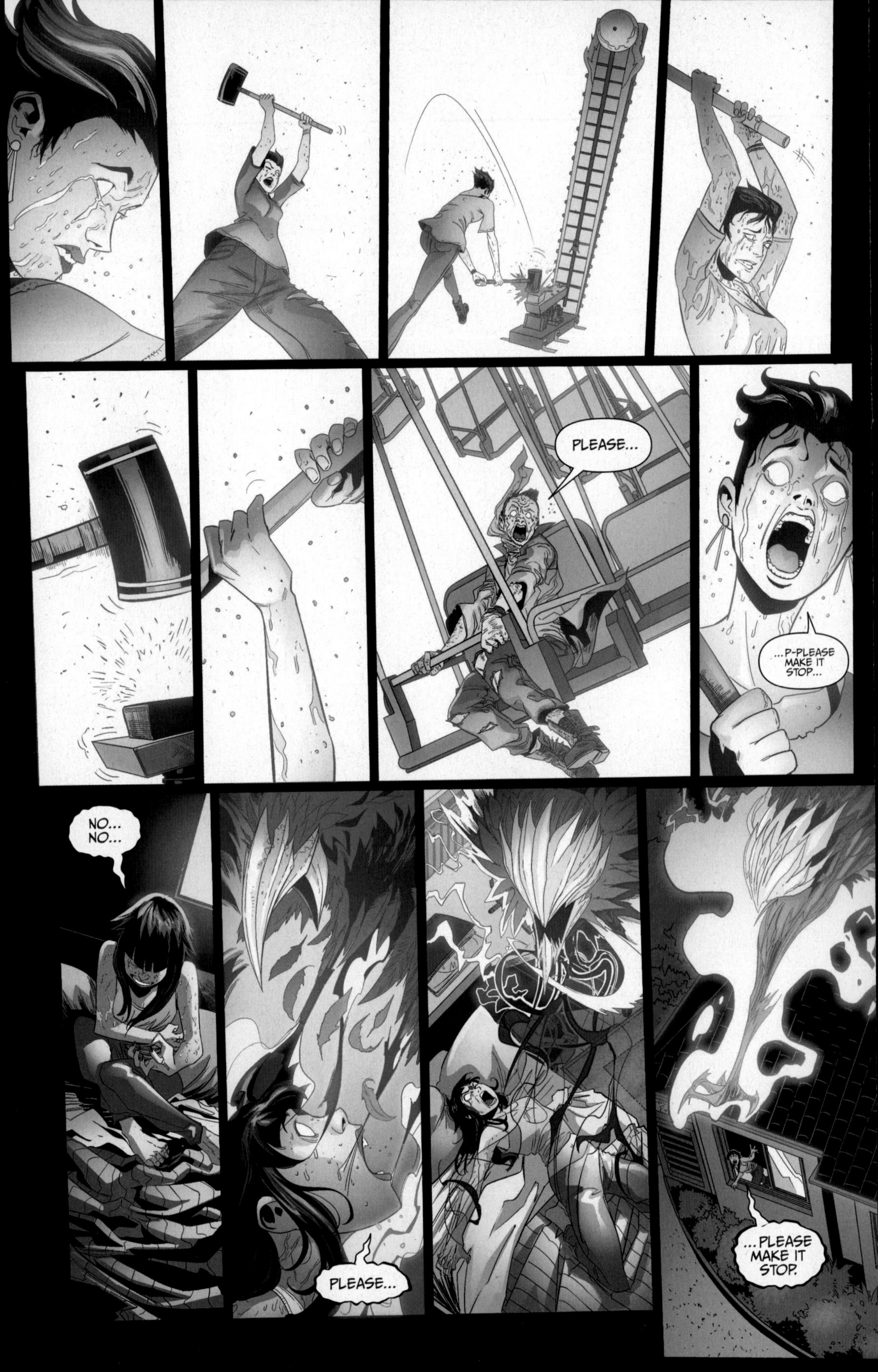
PLEASE...
...P-PLEASE MAKE IT STOP...
NO... NO...
PLEASE...
...PLEASE MAKE IT STOP.

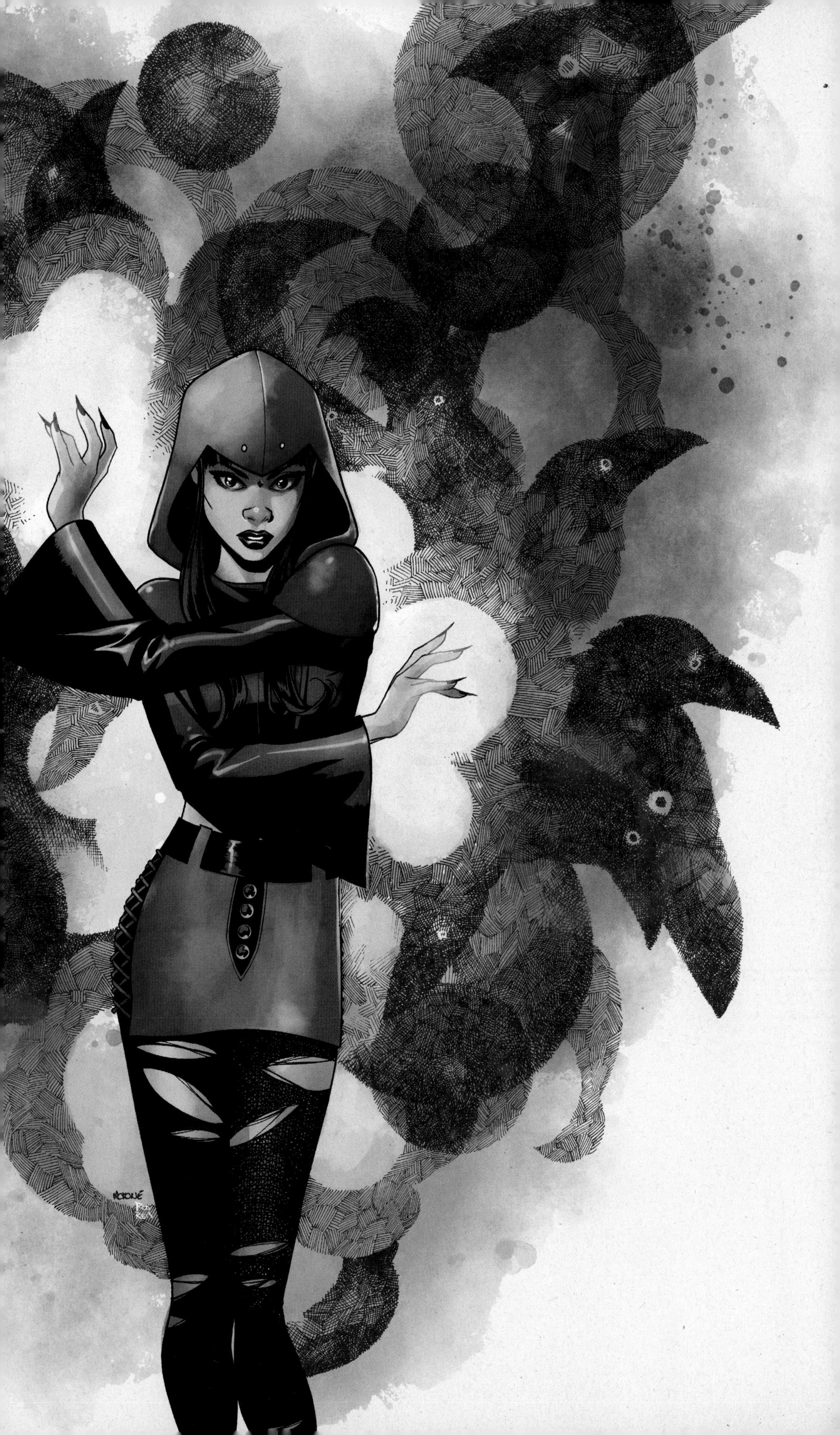

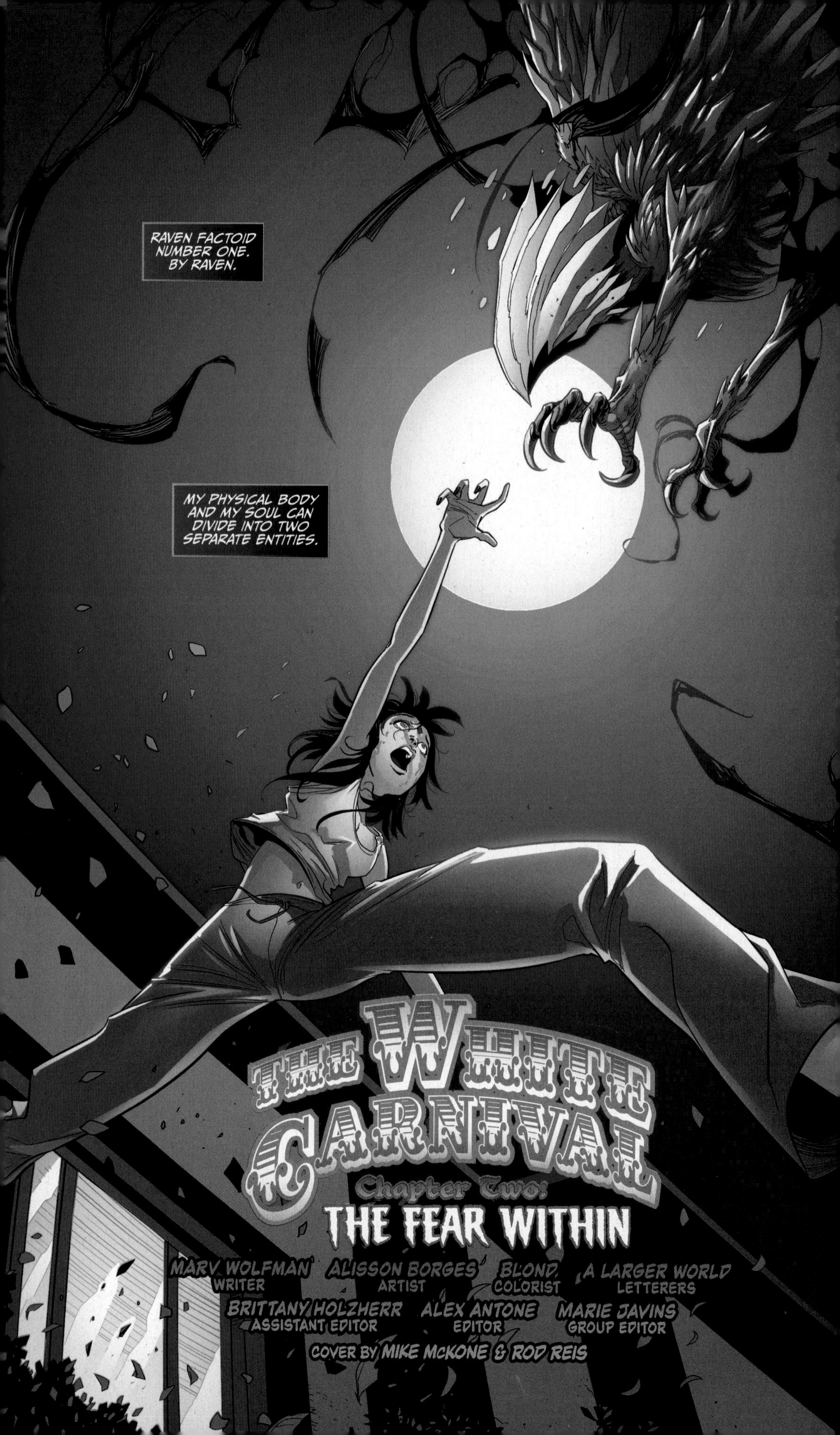

RAVEN FACTOID NUMBER ONE. BY RAVEN.
MY PHYSICAL BODY AND MY SOUL CAN DIVIDE INTO TWO SEPARATE ENTITIES.
THE WHITE CARNIVAL
Chapter Two:
THE FEAR WITHIN
MARV WOLFMAN WRITER
ALISSON BORGES ARTIST
BLOND COLORIST
A LARGER WORLD LETTERERS
BRITTANY HOLZHERR ASSISTANT EDITOR
ALEX ANTONE EDITOR
MARIE JAVINS GROUP EDITOR
COVER BY MIKE McKONE & ROD REIS

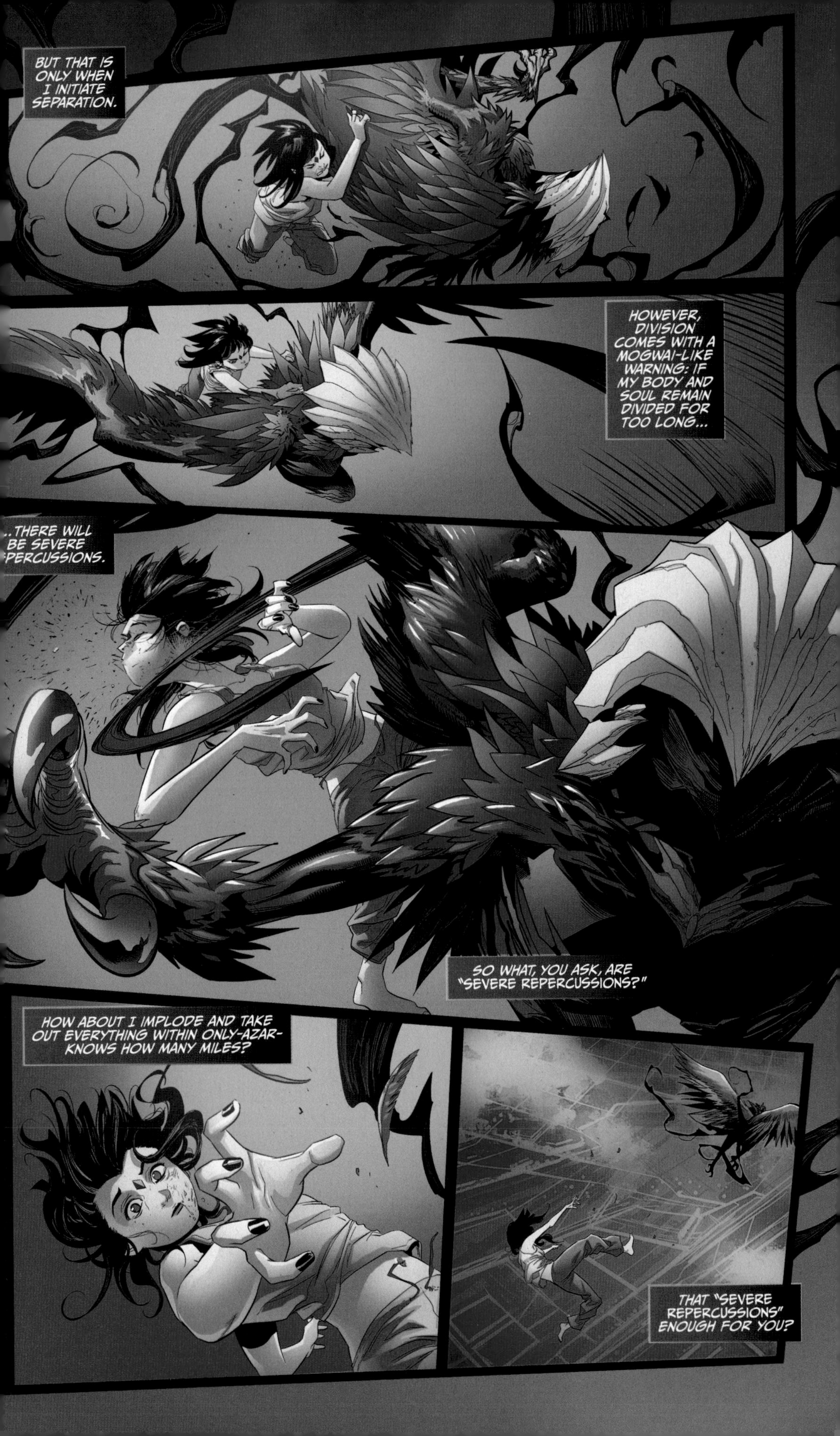
BUT THAT IS ONLY WHEN I INITIATE SEPARATION.
HOWEVER, DIVISION COMES WITH A MOGWAI-LIKE WARNING: IF MY BODY AND SOUL REMAIN DIVIDED FOR TOO LONG...
..THERE WILL BE SEVERE REPERCUSSIONS.
SO WHAT, YOU ASK, ARE "SEVERE REPERCUSSIONS?"
HOW ABOUT I IMPLODE AND TAKE OUT EVERYTHING WITHIN ONLY-AZAR-KNOWS HOW MANY MILES?
THAT "SEVERE REPERCUSSIONS" ENOUGH FOR YOU?

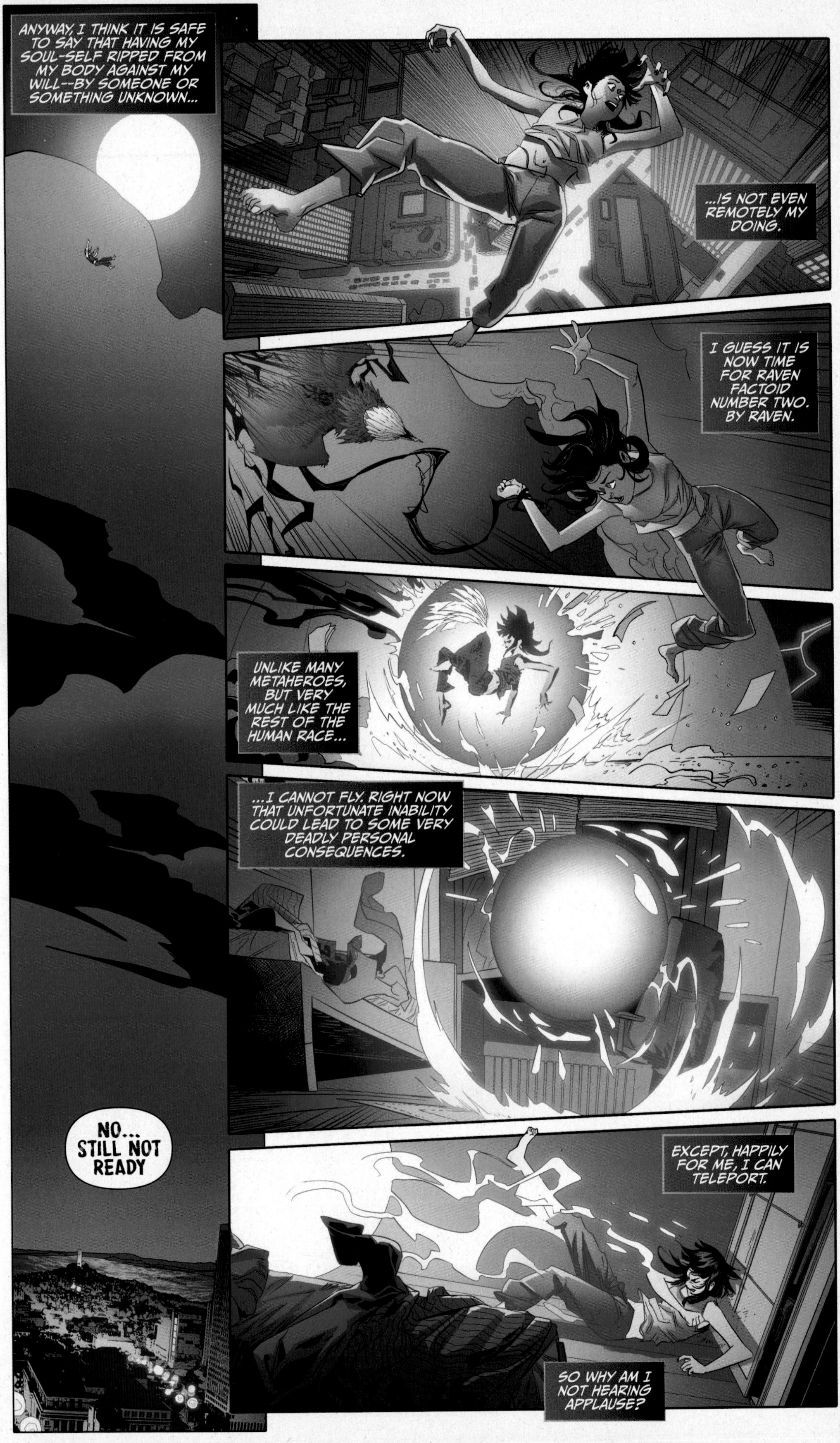
ANYWAY, I THINK IT IS SAFE TO SAY THAT HAVING MY SOUL-SELF RIPPED FROM MY BODY AGAINST MY WILL--BY SOMEONE OR SOMETHING UNKNOWN...
...IS NOT EVEN REMOTELY MY DOING.
I GUESS IT IS NOW TIME FOR RAVEN FACTOID NUMBER TWO. BY RAVEN.
UNLIKE MANY METAHEROES, BUT VERY MUCH LIKE THE REST OF THE HUMAN RACE...
...I CANNOT FLY. RIGHT NOW THAT UNFORTUNATE INABILITY COULD LEAD TO SOME VERY DEADLY PERSONAL CONSEQUENCES.
NO... STILL NOT READY
EXCEPT, HAPPILY FOR ME, I CAN TELEPORT.
SO WHY AM I NOT HEARING APPLAUSE?

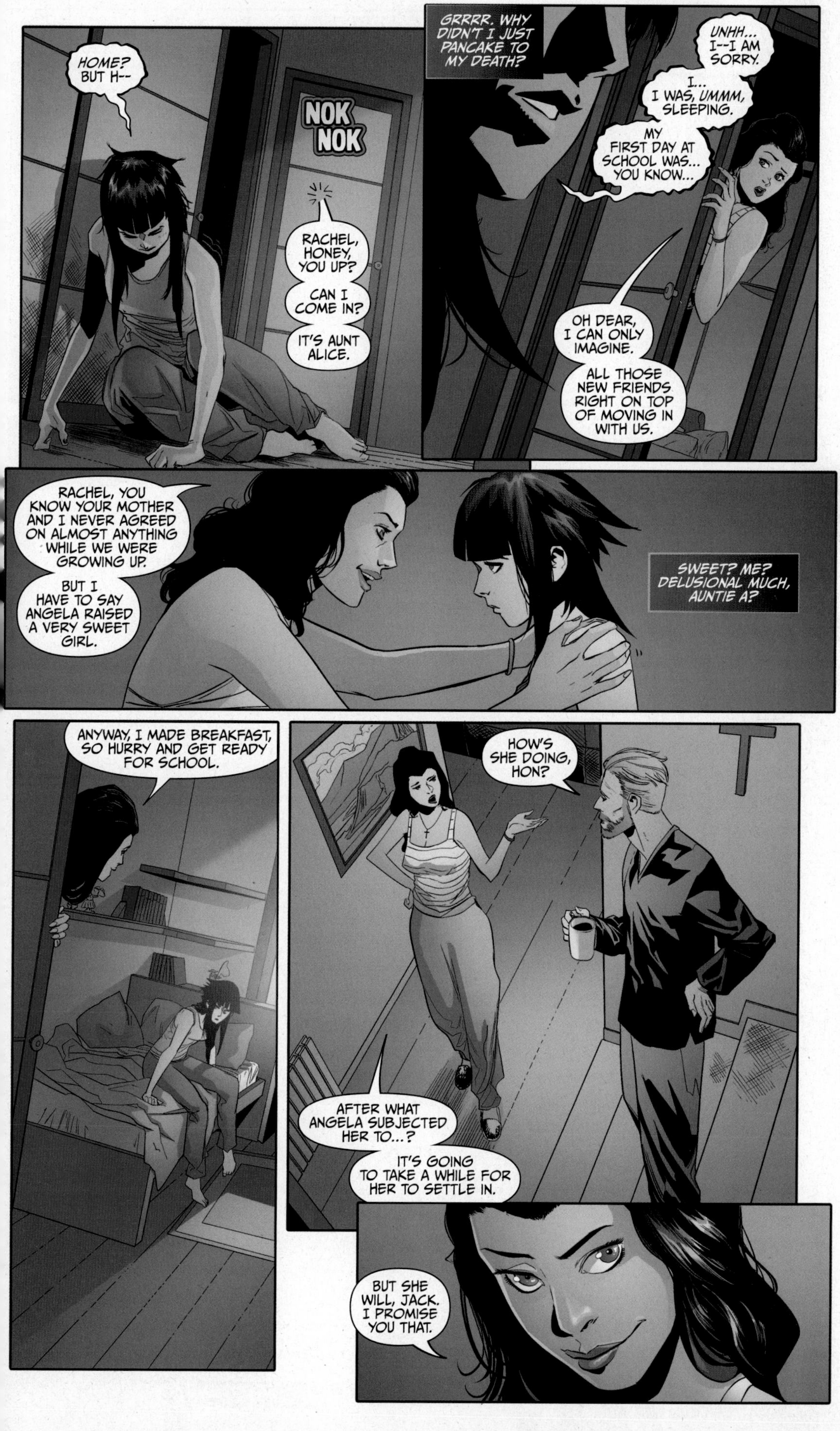
HOME? BUT H--
NOK NOK
RACHEL, HONEY, YOU UP?
CAN I COME IN?
IT'S AUNT ALICE.
GRRRR. WHY DIDN'T I JUST PANCAKE TO MY DEATH?
UNHH... I--I AM SORRY.
I... I WAS, UMMM, SLEEPING.
MY FIRST DAY AT SCHOOL WAS... YOU KNOW...
OH DEAR, I CAN ONLY IMAGINE.
ALL THOSE NEW FRIENDS RIGHT ON TOP OF MOVING IN WITH US.
RACHEL, YOU KNOW YOUR MOTHER AND I NEVER AGREED ON ALMOST ANYTHING WHILE WE WERE GROWING UP.
BUT I HAVE TO SAY ANGELA RAISED A VERY SWEET GIRL.
SWEET? ME? DELUSIONAL MUCH, AUNTIE A?
ANYWAY, I MADE BREAKFAST, SO HURRY AND GET READY FOR SCHOOL.
HOW'S SHE DOING, HON?
AFTER WHAT ANGELA SUBJECTED HER TO...?
IT'S GOING TO TAKE A WHILE FOR HER TO SETTLE IN.
BUT SHE WILL, JACK. I PROMISE YOU THAT.

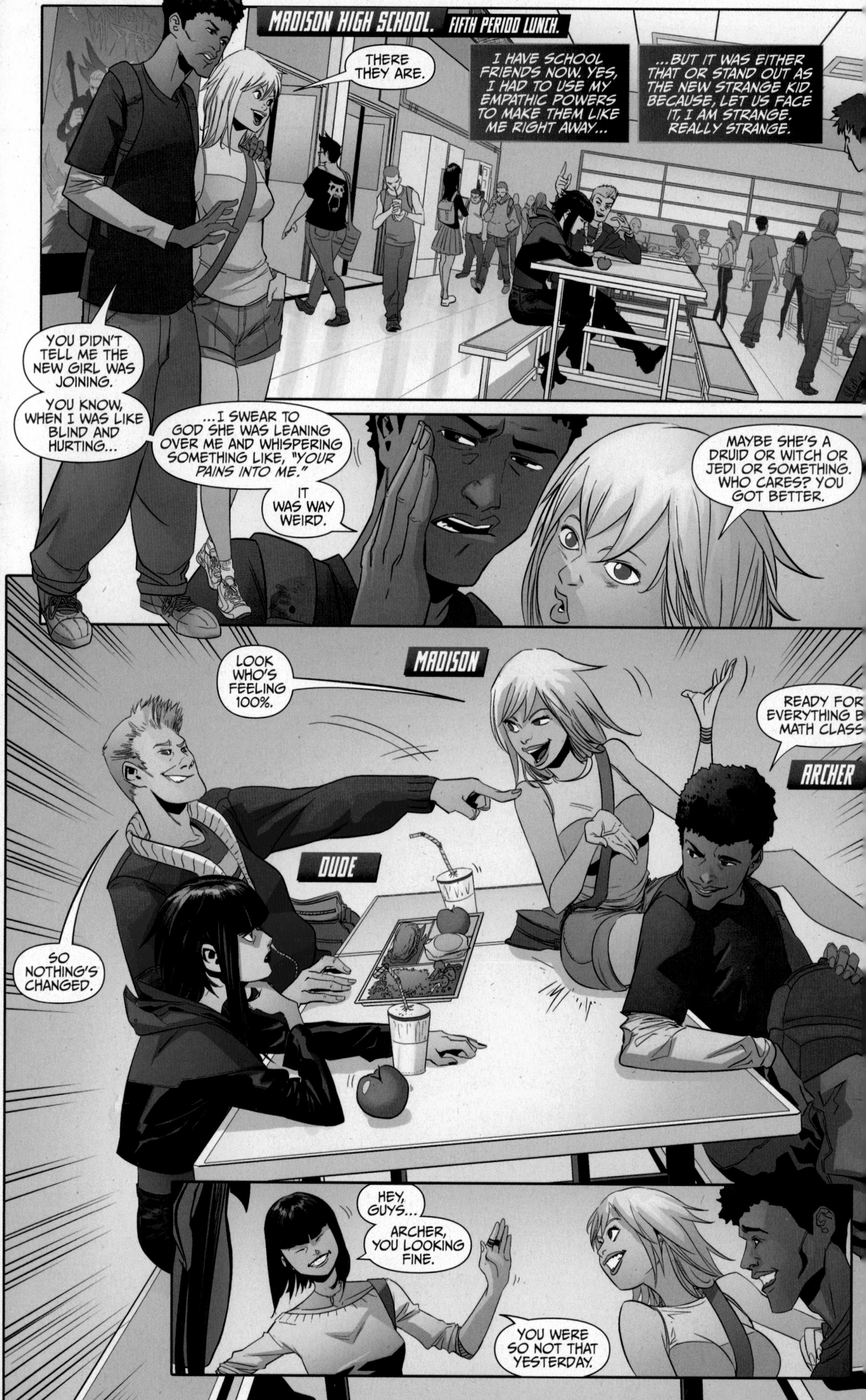
MADISON HIGH SCHOOL. FIFTH PERIOD LUNCH.
THERE THEY ARE.
I HAVE SCHOOL FRIENDS NOW. YES, I HAD TO USE MY EMPATHIC POWERS TO MAKE THEM LIKE ME RIGHT AWAY...
...BUT IT WAS EITHER THAT OR STAND OUT AS THE NEW STRANGE KID. BECAUSE, LET US FACE IT, I AM STRANGE. REALLY STRANGE.
YOU DIDN'T TELL ME THE NEW GIRL WAS JOINING.
YOU KNOW, WHEN I WAS LIKE BLIND AND HURTING...
...I SWEAR TO GOD SHE WAS LEANING OVER ME AND WHISPERING SOMETHING LIKE, "YOUR PAINS INTO ME."
IT WAS WAY WEIRD.
MAYBE SHE'S A DRUID OR WITCH OR JEDI OR SOMETHING. WHO CARES? YOU GOT BETTER.
LOOK WHO'S FEELING 100%.
MADISON
READY FOR EVERYTHING B MATH CLASS
ARCHER
DUDE
SO NOTHING'S CHANGED.
HEY, GUYS...
ARCHER, YOU LOOKING FINE.
YOU WERE SO NOT THAT YESTERDAY.

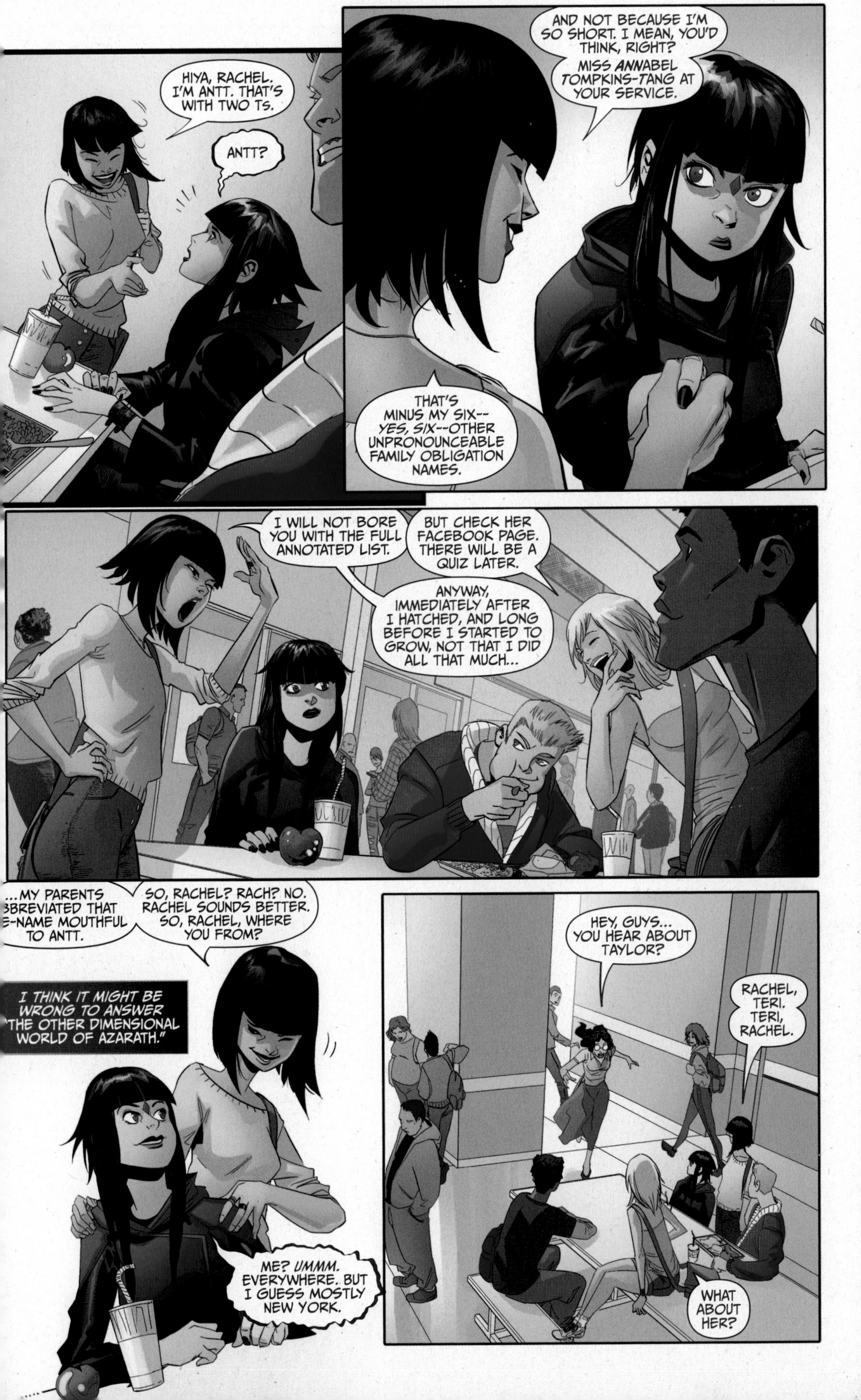
HIYA, RACHEL. I'M ANTT. THAT'S WITH TWO Ts.
ANTT?
AND NOT BECAUSE I'M SO SHORT. I MEAN, YOU'D THINK, RIGHT?
MISS ANNABEL TOMPKINS-TANG AT YOUR SERVICE.
THAT'S MINUS MY SIX-- YES, SIX--OTHER UNPRONOUNCEABLE FAMILY OBLIGATION NAMES.
I WILL NOT BORE YOU WITH THE FULL ANNOTATED LIST.
BUT CHECK HER FACEBOOK PAGE. THERE WILL BE A QUIZ LATER.
ANYWAY, IMMEDIATELY AFTER I HATCHED, AND LONG BEFORE I STARTED TO GROW, NOT THAT I DID ALL THAT MUCH...
...MY PARENTS BBREVIATED THAT E-NAME MOUTHFUL TO ANTT.
SO, RACHEL? RACH? NO. RACHEL SOUNDS BETTER. SO, RACHEL, WHERE YOU FROM?
I THINK IT MIGHT BE WRONG TO ANSWER "THE OTHER DIMENSIONAL WORLD OF AZARATH."
ME? UMMM. EVERYWHERE. BUT I GUESS MOSTLY NEW YORK.
HEY, GUYS... YOU HEAR ABOUT TAYLOR?
RACHEL, TERI. TERI, RACHEL.
WHAT ABOUT HER?

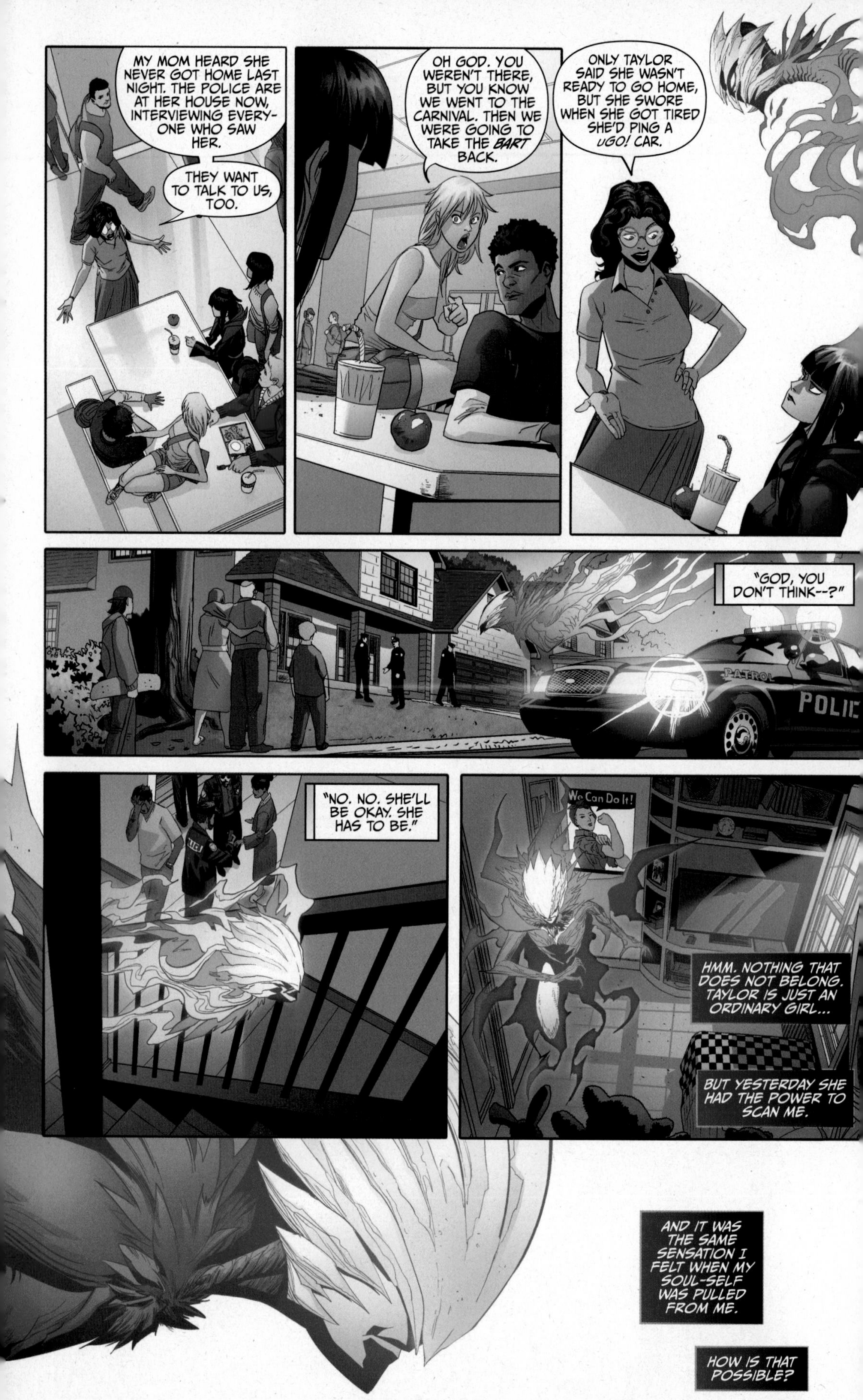
MY MOM HEARD SHE NEVER GOT HOME LAST NIGHT. THE POLICE ARE AT HER HOUSE NOW, INTERVIEWING EVERY-ONE WHO SAW HER.
THEY WANT TO TALK TO US, TOO.
OH GOD. YOU WEREN'T THERE, BUT YOU KNOW WE WENT TO THE CARNIVAL. THEN WE WERE GOING TO TAKE THE BART BACK.
ONLY TAYLOR SAID SHE WASN'T READY TO GO HOME, BUT SHE SWORE WHEN SHE GOT TIRED SHE'D PING A UGO! CAR.
"GOD, YOU DON'T THINK--?"
PATROL
POLIC
"NO. NO. SHE'LL BE OKAY. SHE HAS TO BE."
We Can Do It!
HMM. NOTHING THAT DOES NOT BELONG. TAYLOR IS JUST AN ORDINARY GIRL...
BUT YESTERDAY SHE HAD THE POWER TO SCAN ME.
AND IT WAS THE SAME SENSATION I FELT WHEN MY SOUL-SELF WAS PULLED FROM ME.
HOW IS THAT POSSIBLE?

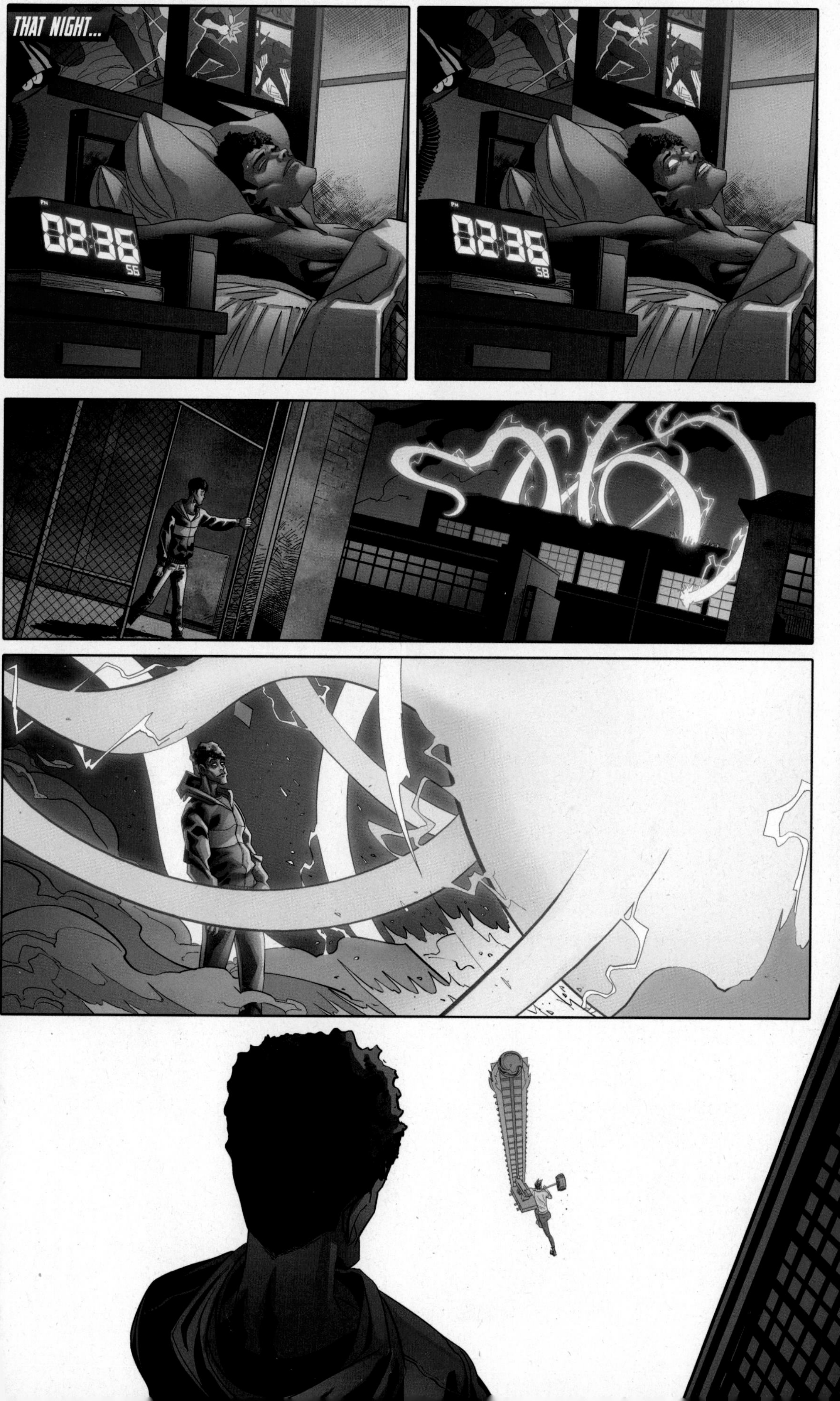
THAT NIGHT...
PM
02:38
56
PM
02:38
58

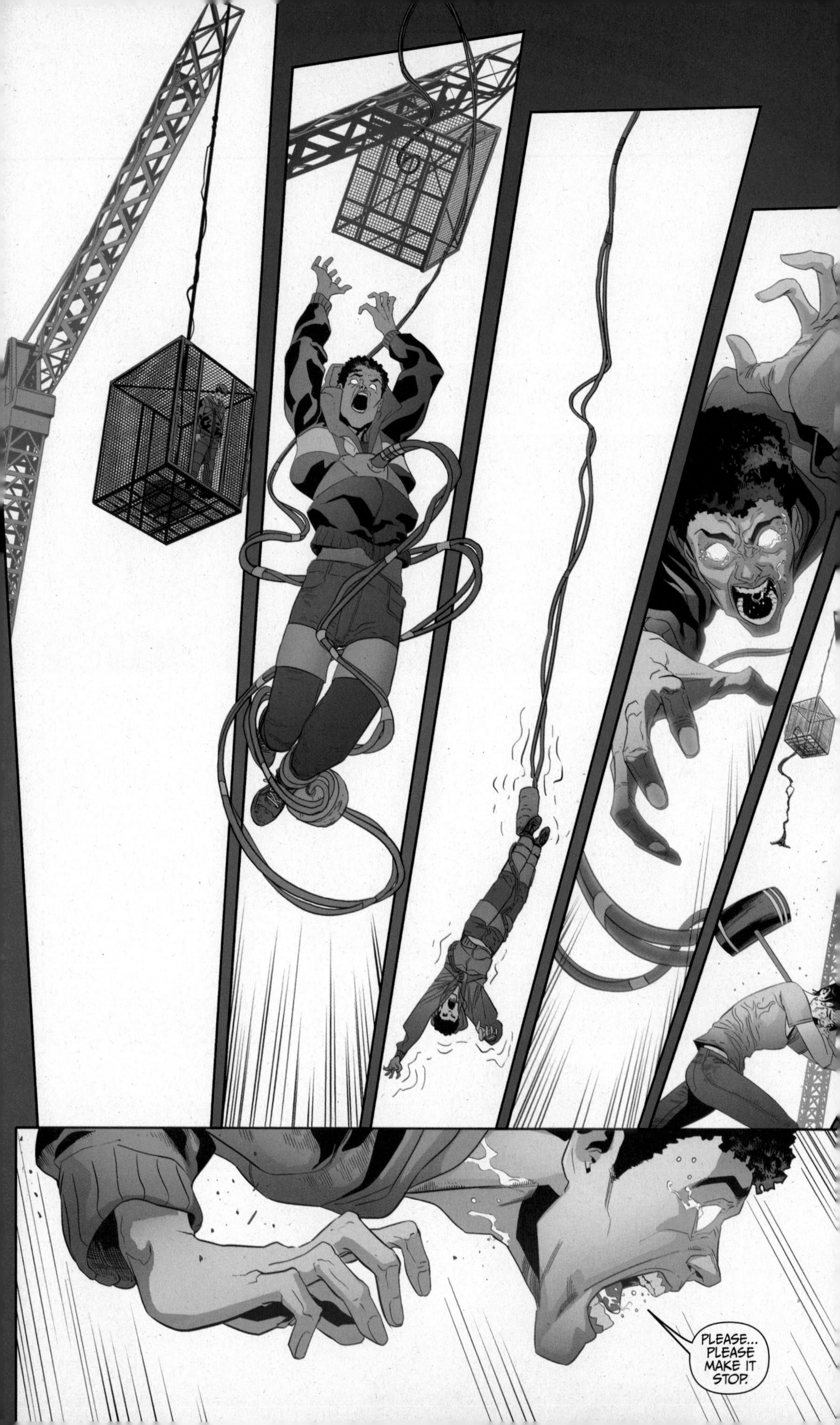
PLEASE... PLEASE MAKE IT STOP.

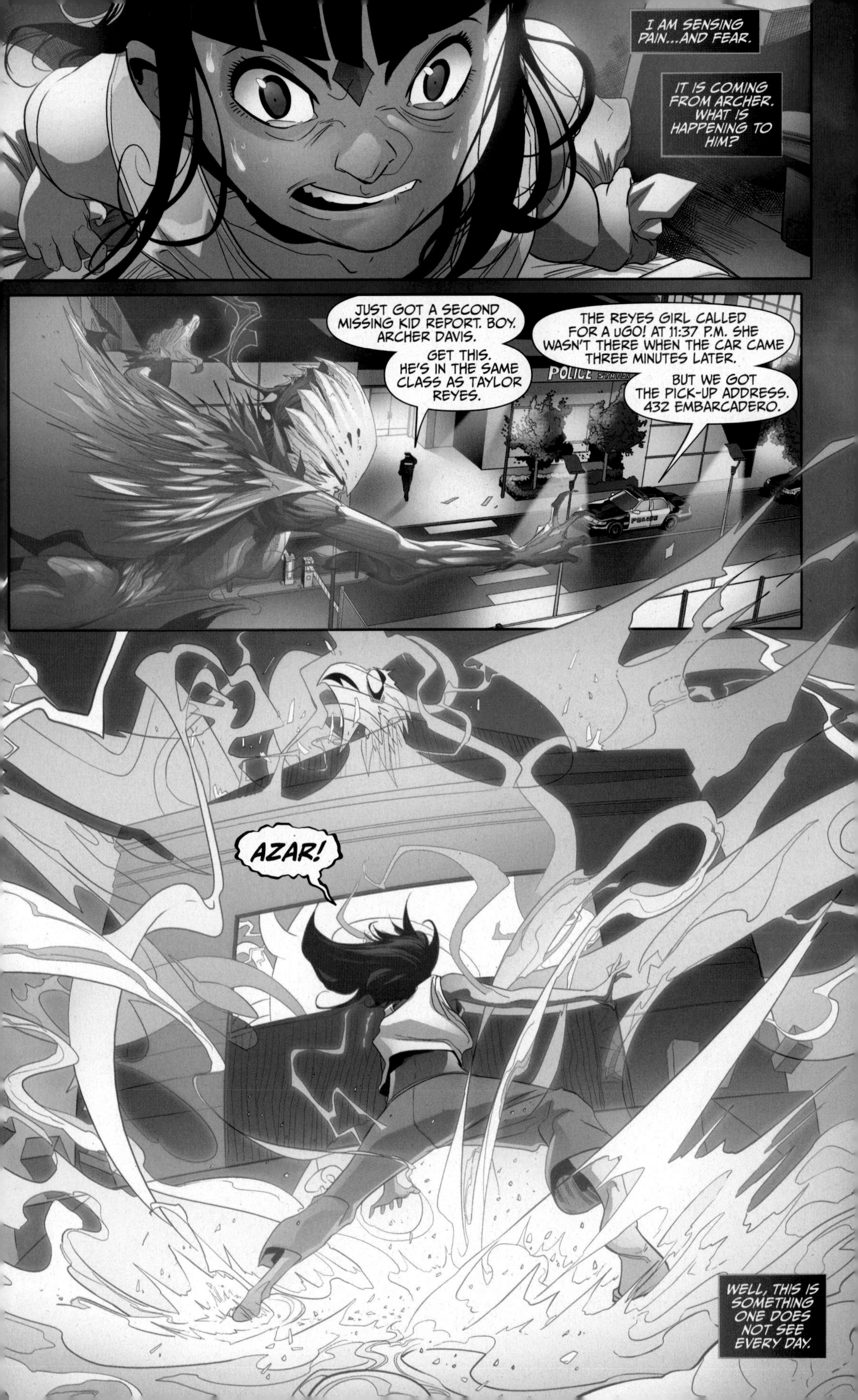
I AM SENSING PAIN...AND FEAR.
IT IS COMING FROM ARCHER. WHAT IS HAPPENING TO HIM?
JUST GOT A SECOND MISSING KID REPORT. BOY. ARCHER DAVIS.
GET THIS. HE'S IN THE SAME CLASS AS TAYLOR REYES.
THE REYES GIRL CALLED FOR A uGO! AT 11:37 P.M. SHE WASN'T THERE WHEN THE CAR CAME THREE MINUTES LATER.
BUT WE GOT THE PICK-UP ADDRESS. 432 EMBARCADERO.
POLICE STATION
AZAR!
WELL, THIS IS SOMETHING ONE DOES NOT SEE EVERY DAY.

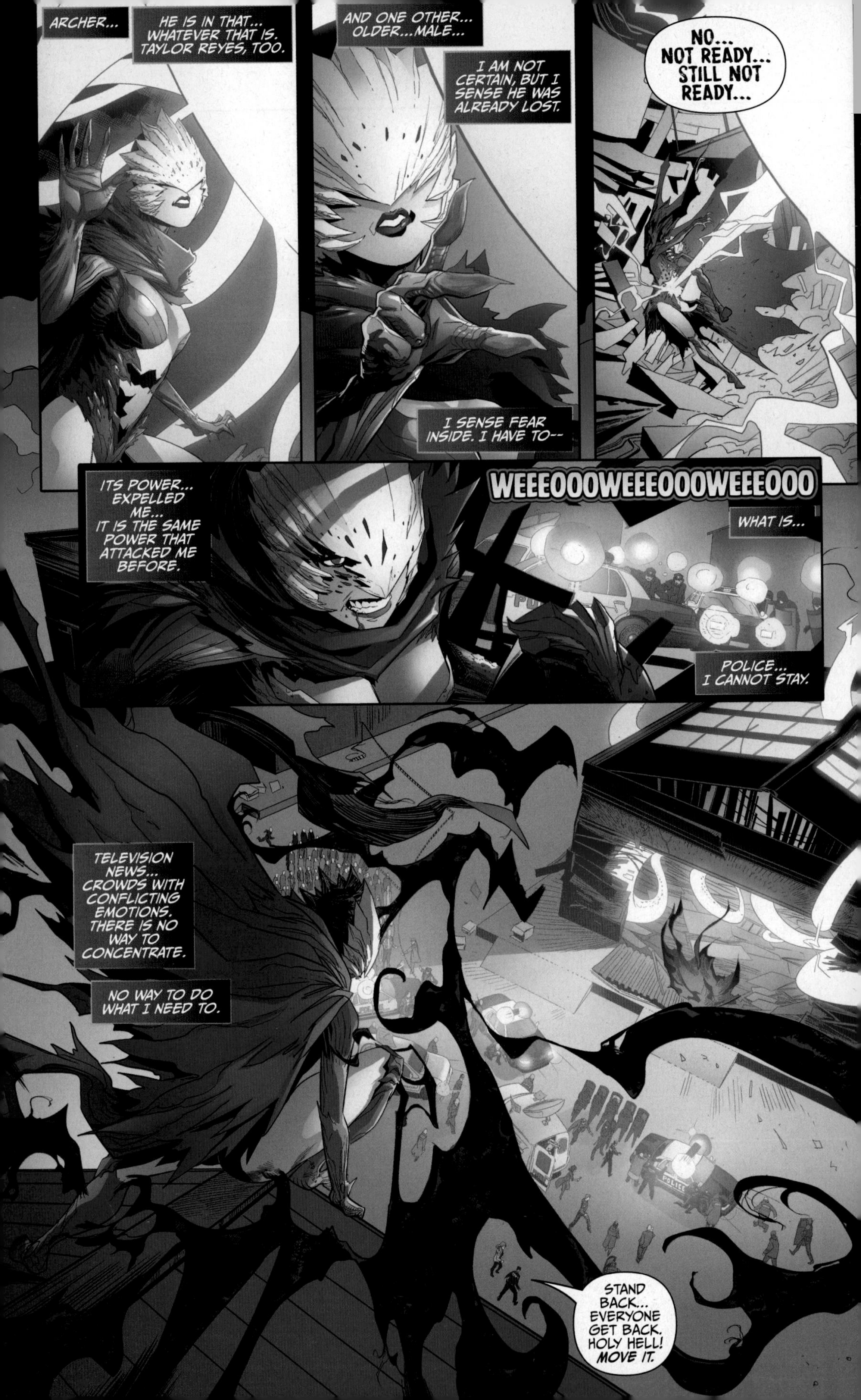
ARCHER...
HE IS IN THAT... WHATEVER THAT IS. TAYLOR REYES, TOO.
AND ONE OTHER... OLDER...MALE...
I AM NOT CERTAIN, BUT I SENSE HE WAS ALREADY LOST.
I SENSE FEAR INSIDE. I HAVE TO--
NO... NOT READY... STILL NOT READY...
ITS POWER... EXPELLED ME... IT IS THE SAME POWER THAT ATTACKED ME BEFORE.
WEEEOOOWEEEOOOWEEEOOO
WHAT IS...
POLICE... I CANNOT STAY.
TELEVISION NEWS... CROWDS WITH CONFLICTING EMOTIONS. THERE IS NO WAY TO CONCENTRATE.
NO WAY TO DO WHAT I NEED TO.
STAND BACK... EVERYONE GET BACK. HOLY HELL! MOVE IT.

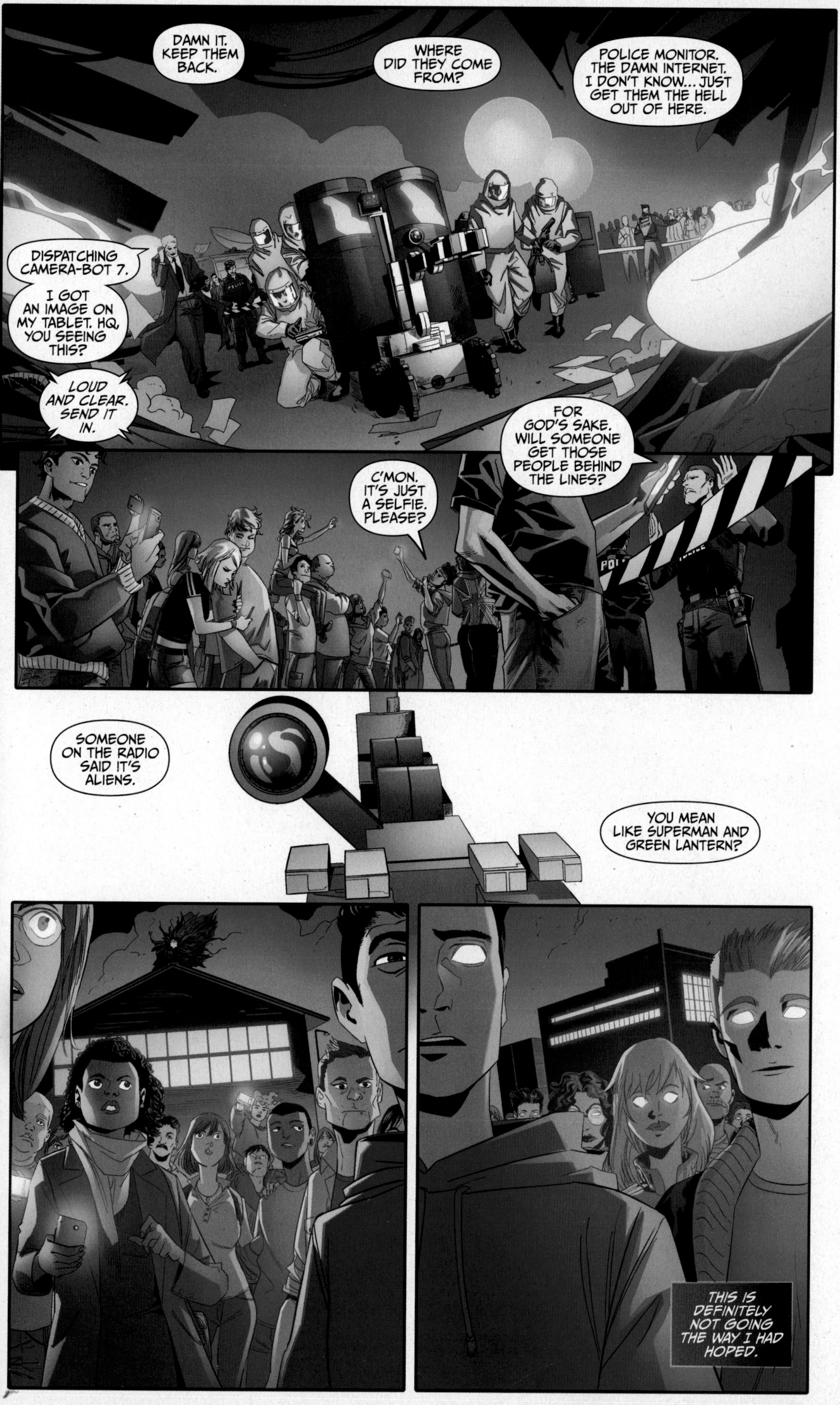
DAMN IT. KEEP THEM BACK.
WHERE DID THEY COME FROM?
POLICE MONITOR. THE DAMN INTERNET. I DON'T KNOW... JUST GET THEM THE HELL OUT OF HERE.
DISPATCHING CAMERA-BOT 7.
I GOT AN IMAGE ON MY TABLET. HQ, YOU SEEING THIS?
LOUD AND CLEAR. SEND IT IN.
C'MON. IT'S JUST A SELFIE. PLEASE?
FOR GOD'S SAKE. WILL SOMEONE GET THOSE PEOPLE BEHIND THE LINES?
SOMEONE ON THE RADIO SAID IT'S ALIENS.
YOU MEAN LIKE SUPERMAN AND GREEN LANTERN?
THIS IS DEFINITELY NOT GOING THE WAY I HAD HOPED.

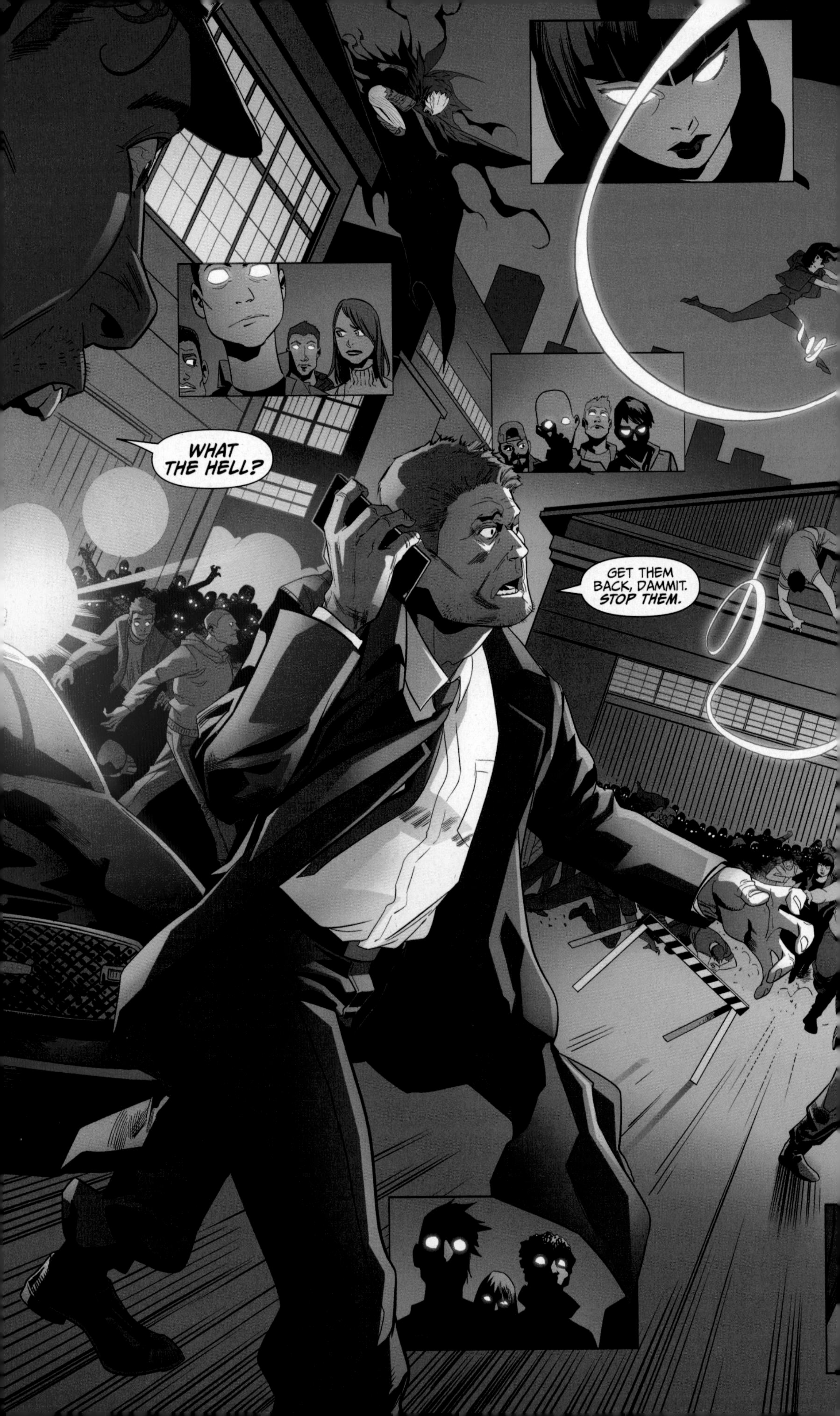
WHAT THE HELL?
GET THEM BACK, DAMMIT. STOP THEM.

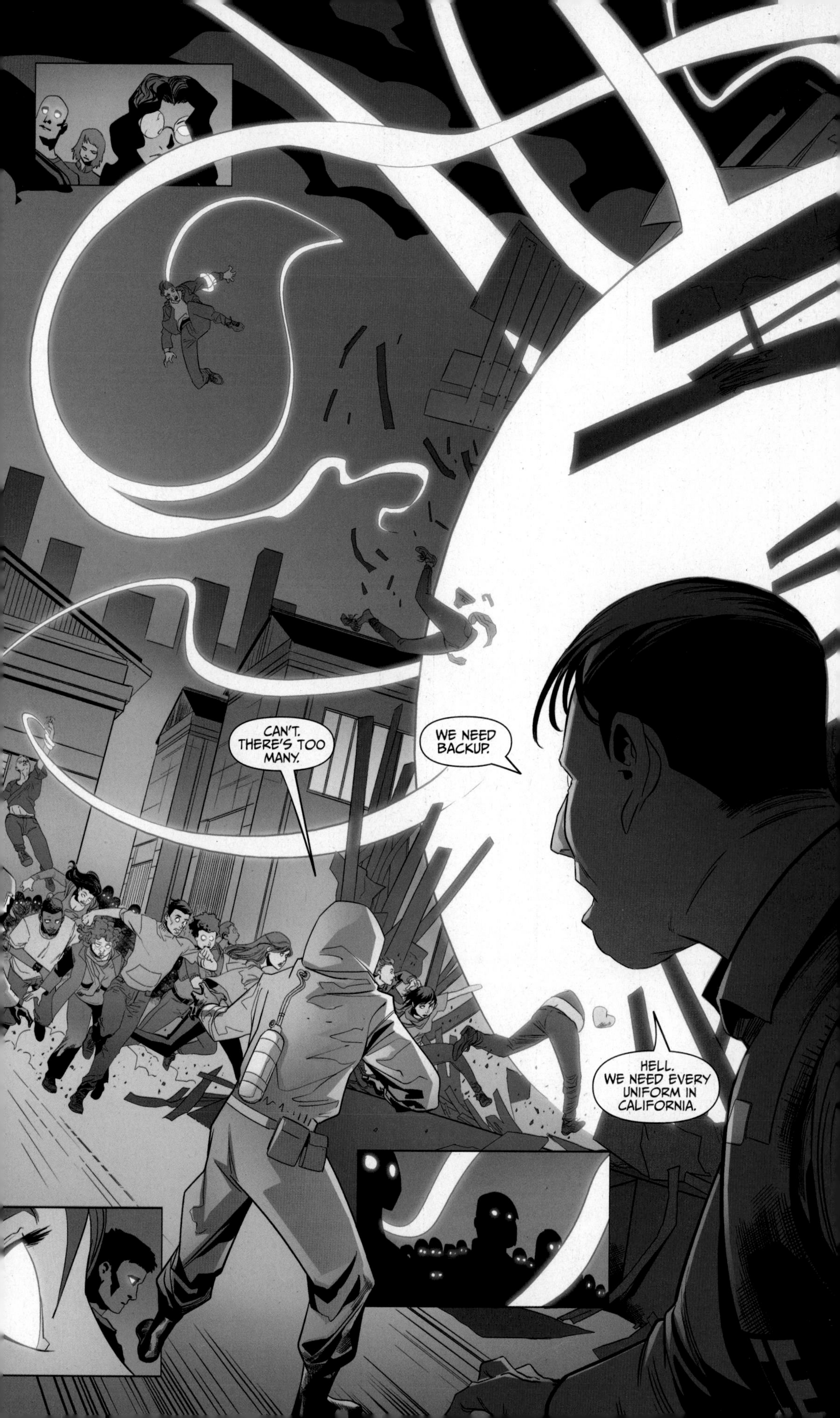
CAN'T. THERE'S TOO MANY.
WE NEED BACKUP.
HELL. WE NEED EVERY UNIFORM IN CALIFORNIA.

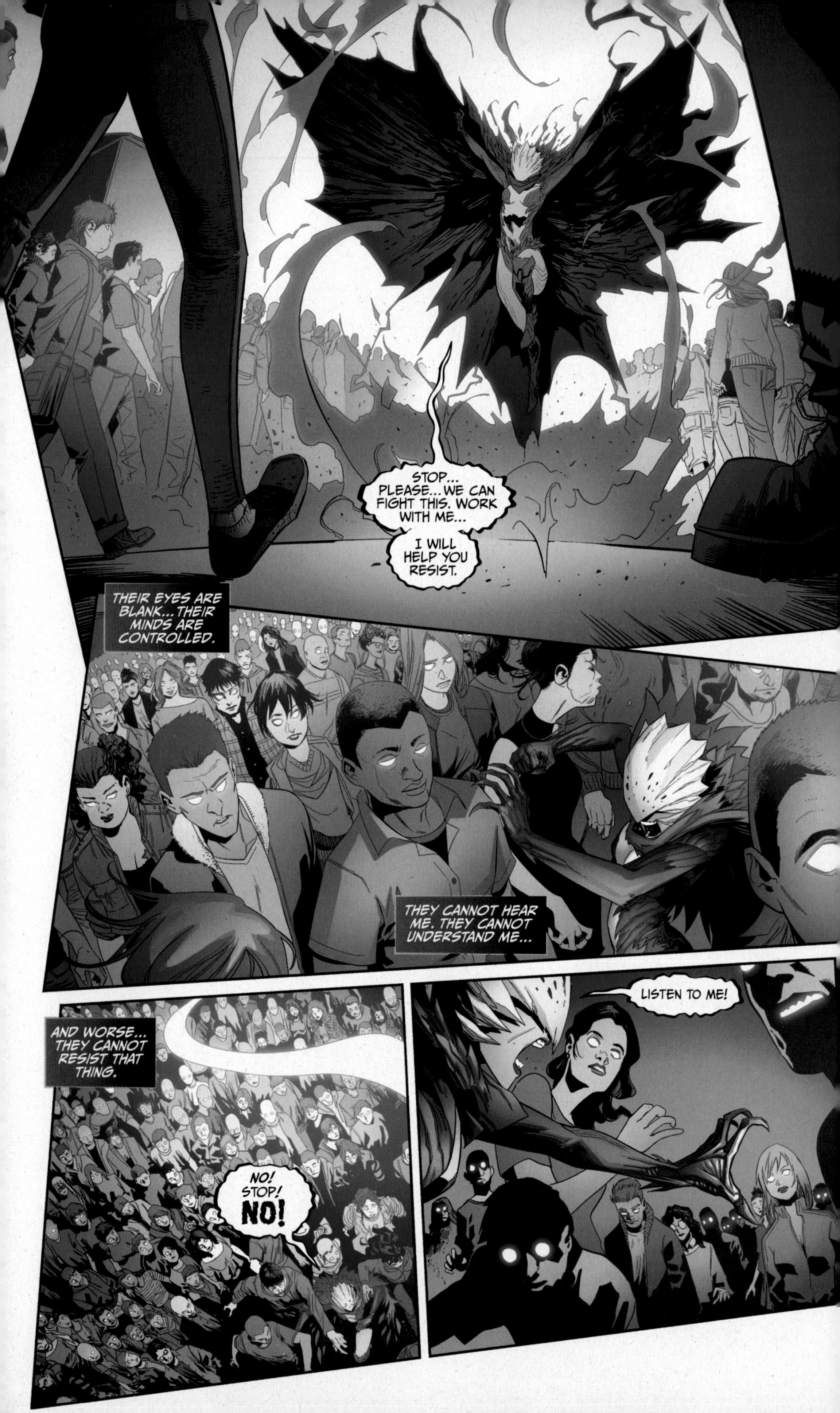
STOP... PLEASE... WE CAN FIGHT THIS. WORK WITH ME...
I WILL HELP YOU RESIST.
THEIR EYES ARE BLANK... THEIR MINDS ARE CONTROLLED.
THEY CANNOT HEAR ME. THEY CANNOT UNDERSTAND ME...
AND WORSE... THEY CANNOT RESIST THAT THING.
NO! STOP! NO!
LISTEN TO ME!

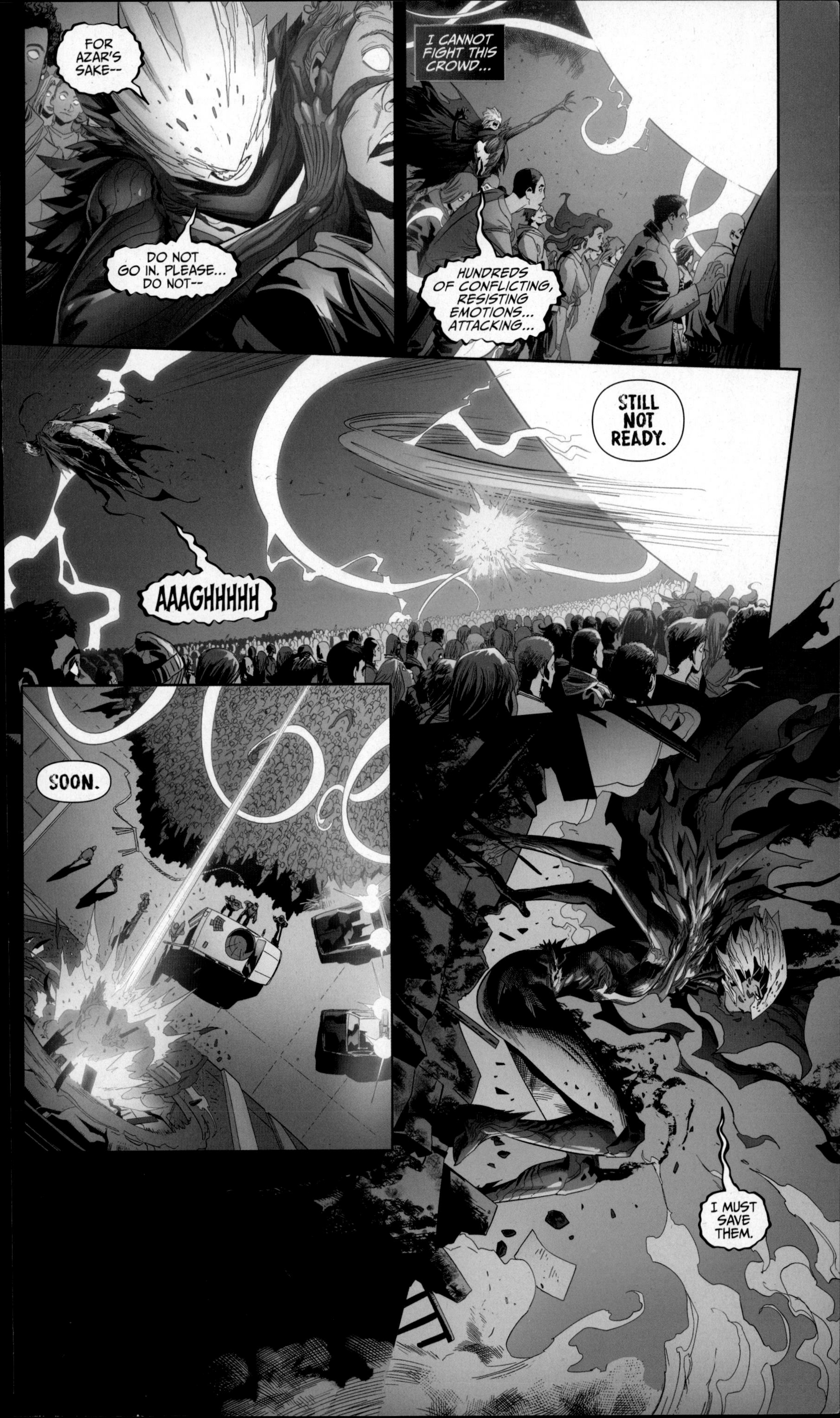
FOR AZAR'S SAKE--
DO NOT GO IN. PLEASE... DO NOT--
I CANNOT FIGHT THIS CROWD...
HUNDREDS OF CONFLICTING, RESISTING EMOTIONS... ATTACKING...
STILL NOT READY.
AAAGHHHHH
SOON.
I MUST SAVE THEM.

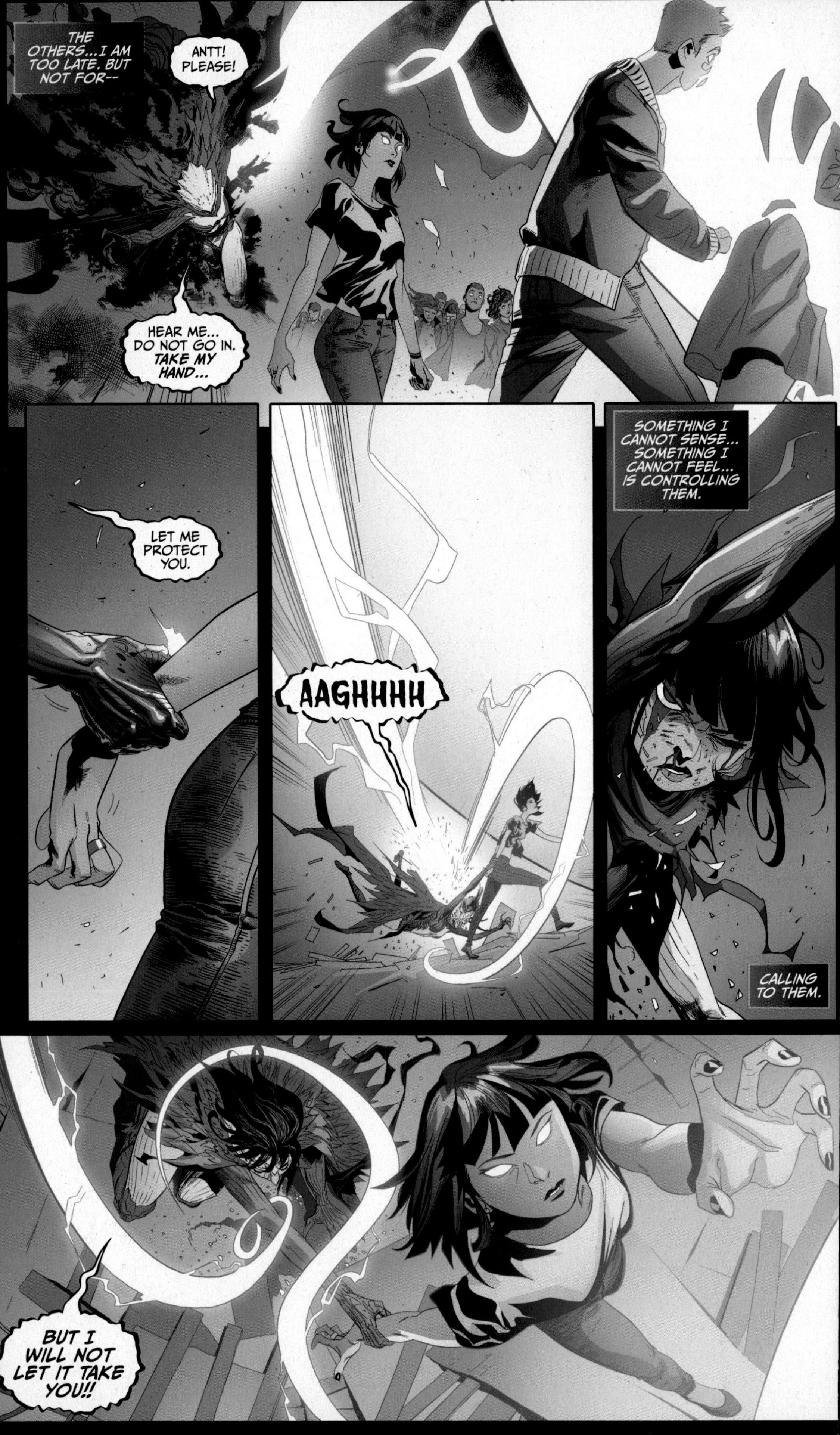
THE OTHERS...I AM TOO LATE. BUT NOT FOR--
ANTT! PLEASE!
HEAR ME... DO NOT GO IN. TAKE MY HAND...
LET ME PROTECT YOU.
AAGHHHH
SOMETHING I CANNOT SENSE... SOMETHING I CANNOT FEEL... IS CONTROLLING THEM.
CALLING TO THEM.
BUT I WILL NOT LET IT TAKE YOU!!

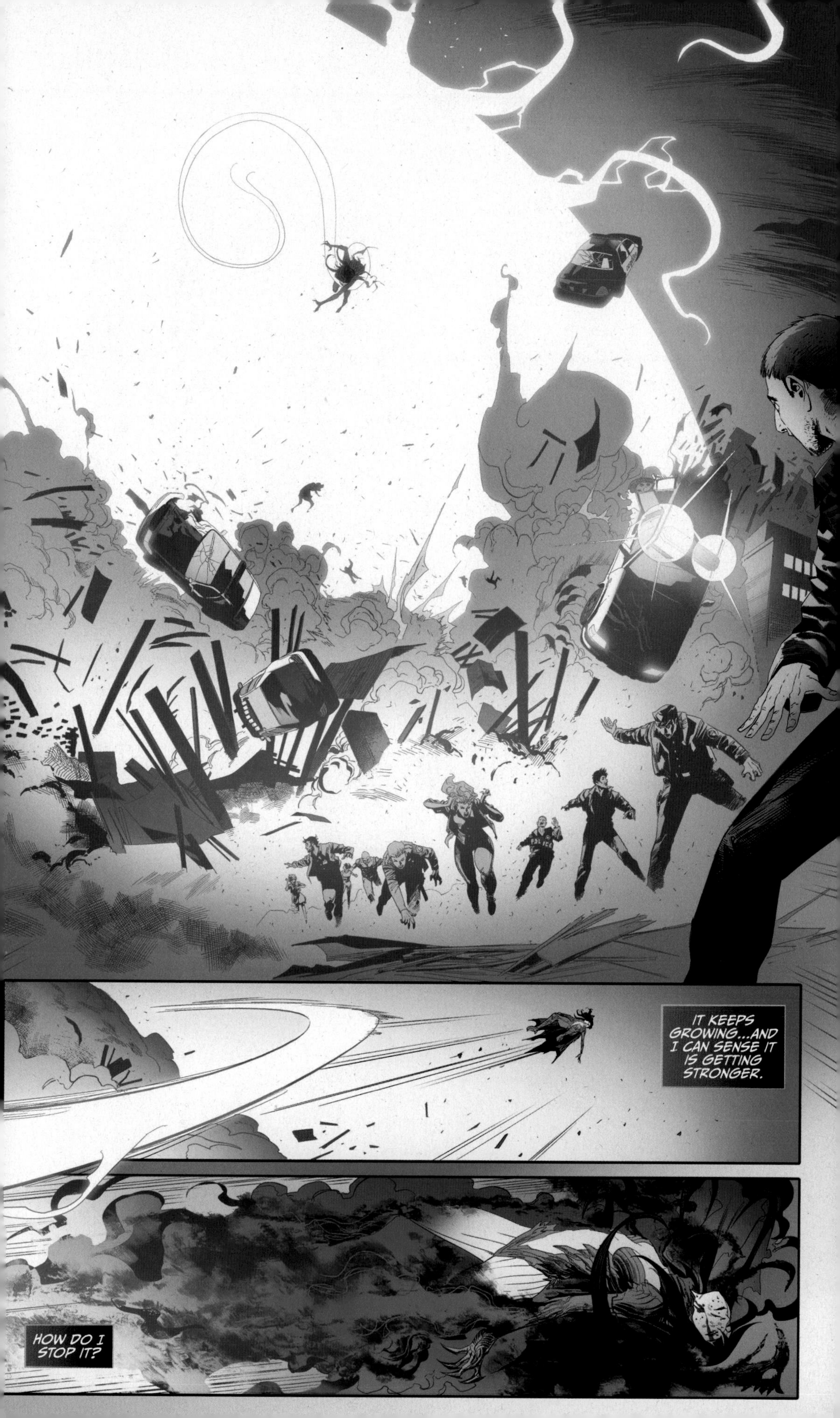
IT KEEPS GROWING...AND I CAN SENSE IT IS GETTING STRONGER.
HOW DO I STOP IT?

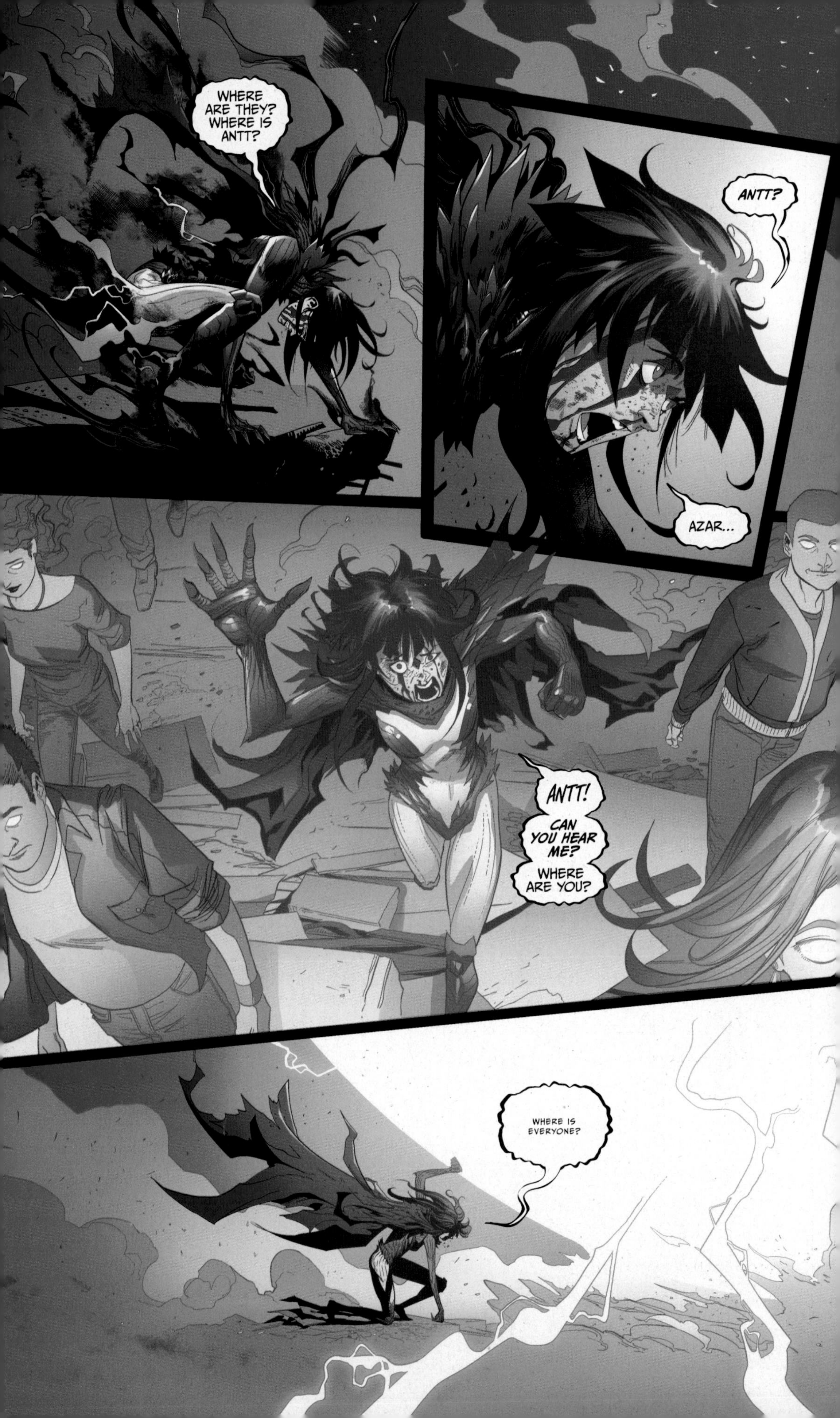
WHERE ARE THEY? WHERE IS ANTT?
ANTT?
AZAR...
ANTT!
CAN YOU HEAR ME?
WHERE ARE YOU?
WHERE IS EVERYONE?

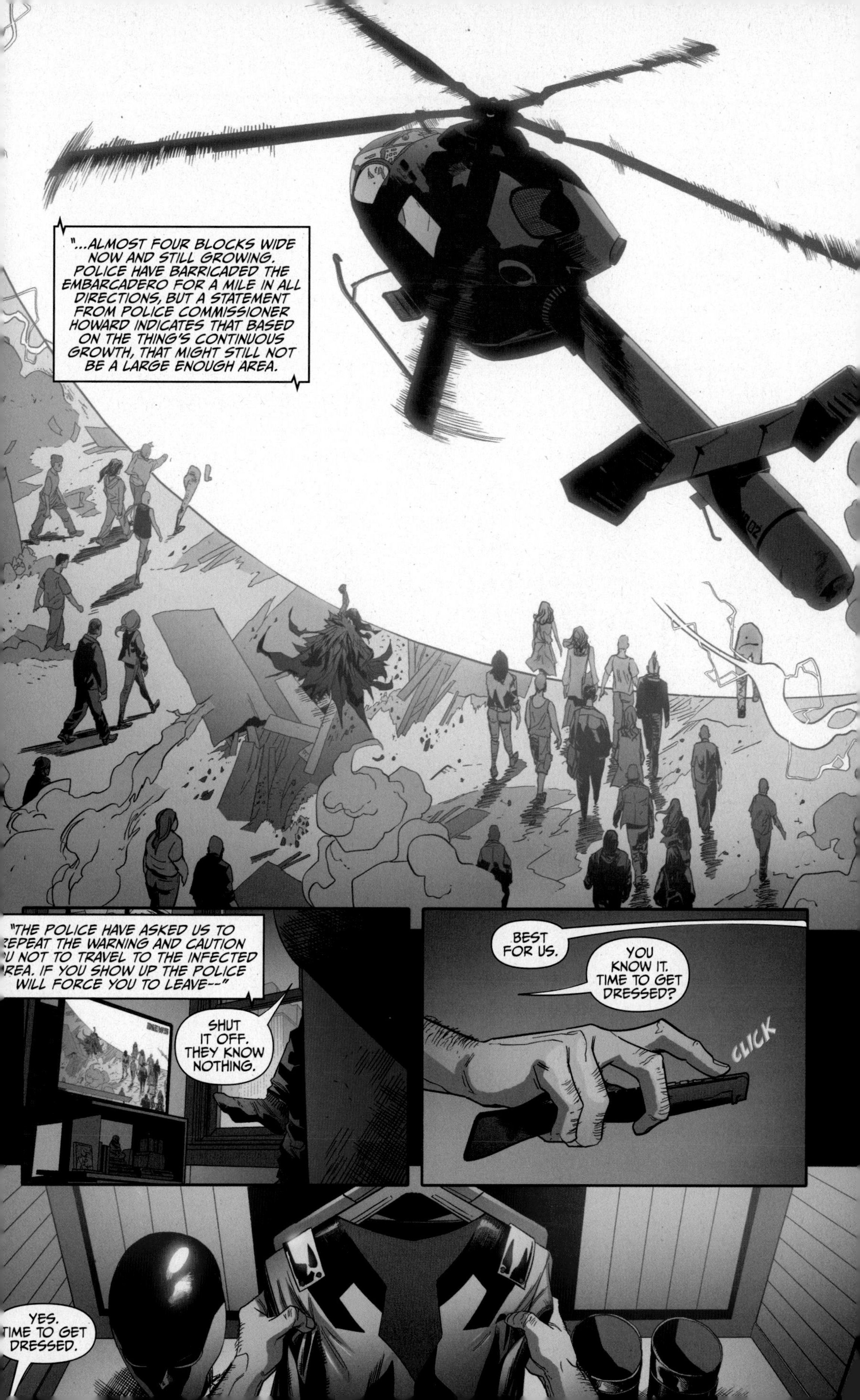
"...ALMOST FOUR BLOCKS WIDE NOW AND STILL GROWING. POLICE HAVE BARRICADED THE EMBARCADERO FOR A MILE IN ALL DIRECTIONS, BUT A STATEMENT FROM POLICE COMMISSIONER HOWARD INDICATES THAT BASED ON THE THING'S CONTINUOUS GROWTH, THAT MIGHT STILL NOT BE A LARGE ENOUGH AREA.
"THE POLICE HAVE ASKED US TO REPEAT THE WARNING AND CAUTION YOU NOT TO TRAVEL TO THE INFECTED AREA. IF YOU SHOW UP THE POLICE WILL FORCE YOU TO LEAVE--"
SHUT IT OFF. THEY KNOW NOTHING.
BEST FOR US.
YOU KNOW IT. TIME TO GET DRESSED?
CLICK
YES. TIME TO GET DRESSED.

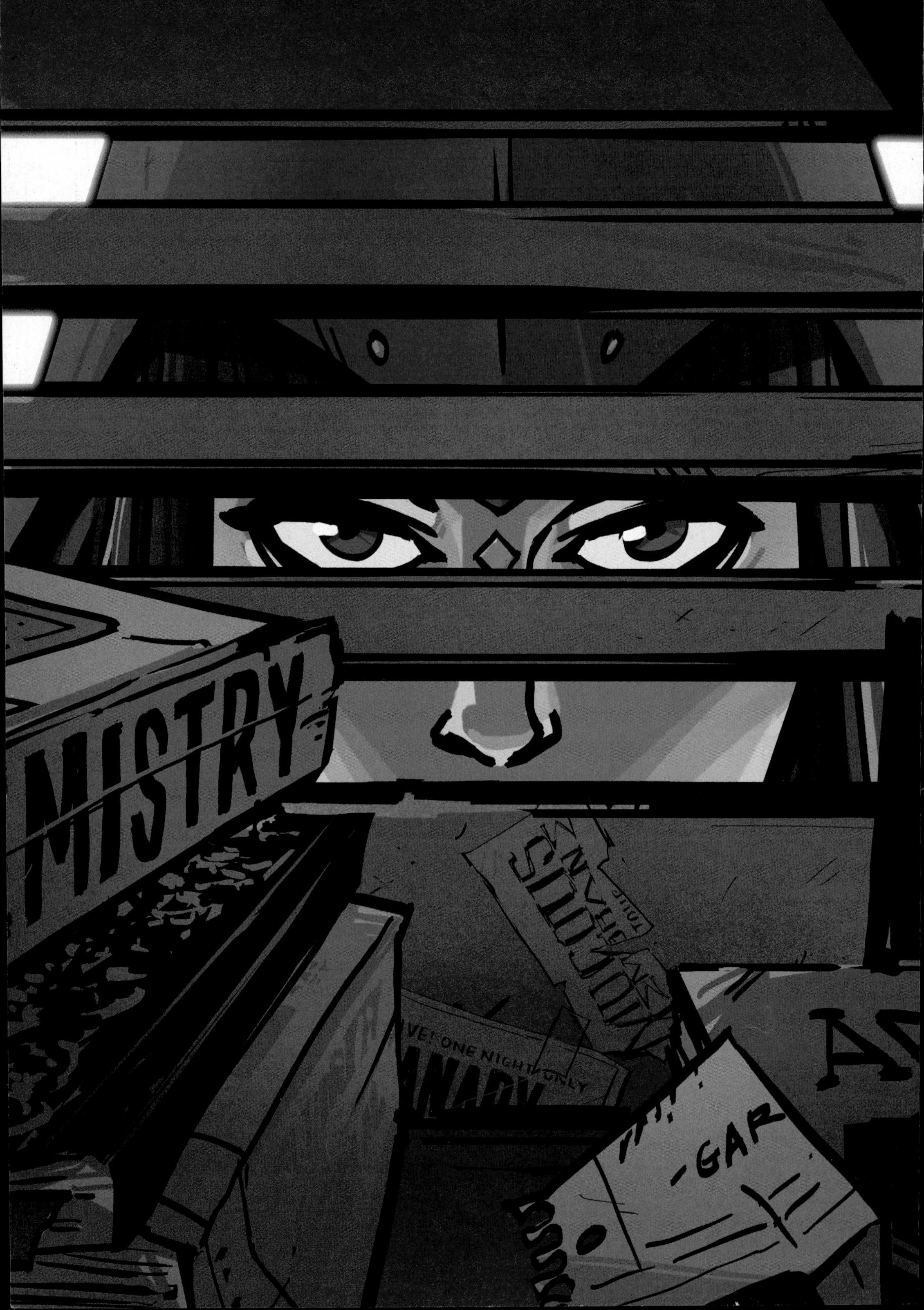
MISTRY
VE! ONE NIGHT ONLY
-GAR

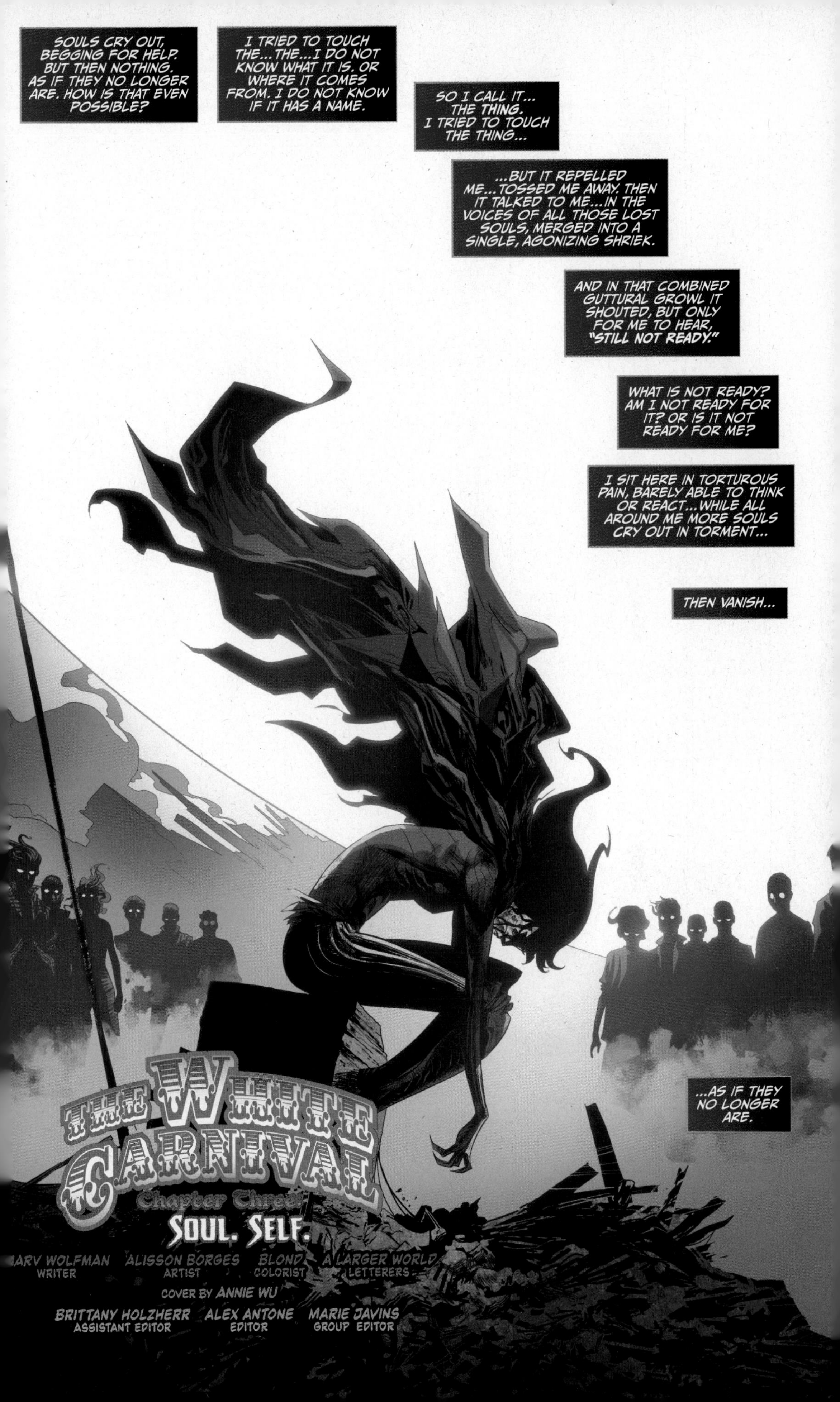
SOULS CRY OUT, BEGGING FOR HELP. BUT THEN NOTHING. AS IF THEY NO LONGER ARE. HOW IS THAT EVEN POSSIBLE?
I TRIED TO TOUCH THE... THE... I DO NOT KNOW WHAT IT IS. OR WHERE IT COMES FROM. I DO NOT KNOW IF IT HAS A NAME.
SO I CALL IT... THE THING. I TRIED TO TOUCH THE THING...
...BUT IT REPELLED ME... TOSSED ME AWAY. THEN IT TALKED TO ME... IN THE VOICES OF ALL THOSE LOST SOULS, MERGED INTO A SINGLE, AGONIZING SHRIEK.
AND IN THAT COMBINED GUTTURAL GROWL IT SHOUTED, BUT ONLY FOR ME TO HEAR, "STILL NOT READY."
WHAT IS NOT READY? AM I NOT READY FOR IT? OR IS IT NOT READY FOR ME?
I SIT HERE IN TORTUROUS PAIN, BARELY ABLE TO THINK OR REACT... WHILE ALL AROUND ME MORE SOULS CRY OUT IN TORMENT...
THEN VANISH...
...AS IF THEY NO LONGER ARE.
THE WHITE CARNIVAL
Chapter Three:
SOUL. SELF.
ARV WOLFMAN WRITER
ALISSON BORGES ARTIST
BLOND COLORIST
A LARGER WORLD LETTERERS
COVER BY ANNIE WU
BRITTANY HOLZHERR ASSISTANT EDITOR
ALEX ANTONE EDITOR
MARIE JAVINS GROUP EDITOR

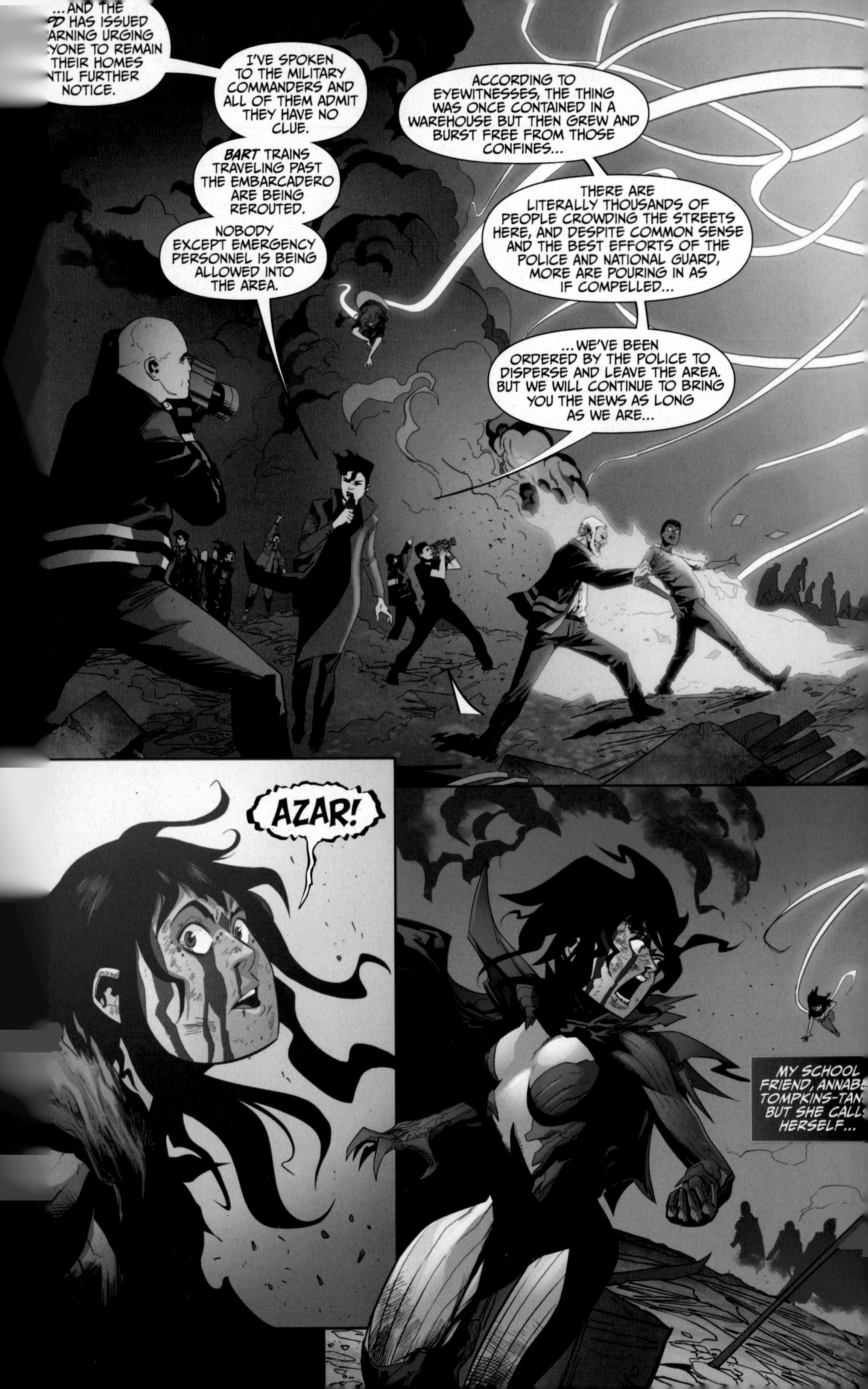
...AND THE PD HAS ISSUED ARNING URGING YONE TO REMAIN THEIR HOMES NTIL FURTHER NOTICE.
I'VE SPOKEN TO THE MILITARY COMMANDERS AND ALL OF THEM ADMIT THEY HAVE NO CLUE.
BART TRAINS TRAVELING PAST THE EMBARCADERO ARE BEING REROUTED.
NOBODY EXCEPT EMERGENCY PERSONNEL IS BEING ALLOWED INTO THE AREA.
ACCORDING TO EYEWITNESSES, THE THING WAS ONCE CONTAINED IN A WAREHOUSE BUT THEN GREW AND BURST FREE FROM THOSE CONFINES...
THERE ARE LITERALLY THOUSANDS OF PEOPLE CROWDING THE STREETS HERE, AND DESPITE COMMON SENSE AND THE BEST EFFORTS OF THE POLICE AND NATIONAL GUARD, MORE ARE POURING IN AS IF COMPELLED...
...WE'VE BEEN ORDERED BY THE POLICE TO DISPERSE AND LEAVE THE AREA. BUT WE WILL CONTINUE TO BRING YOU THE NEWS AS LONG AS WE ARE...
AZAR!
MY SCHOOL FRIEND, ANNAB TOMPKINS-TAN BUT SHE CALL HERSELF...

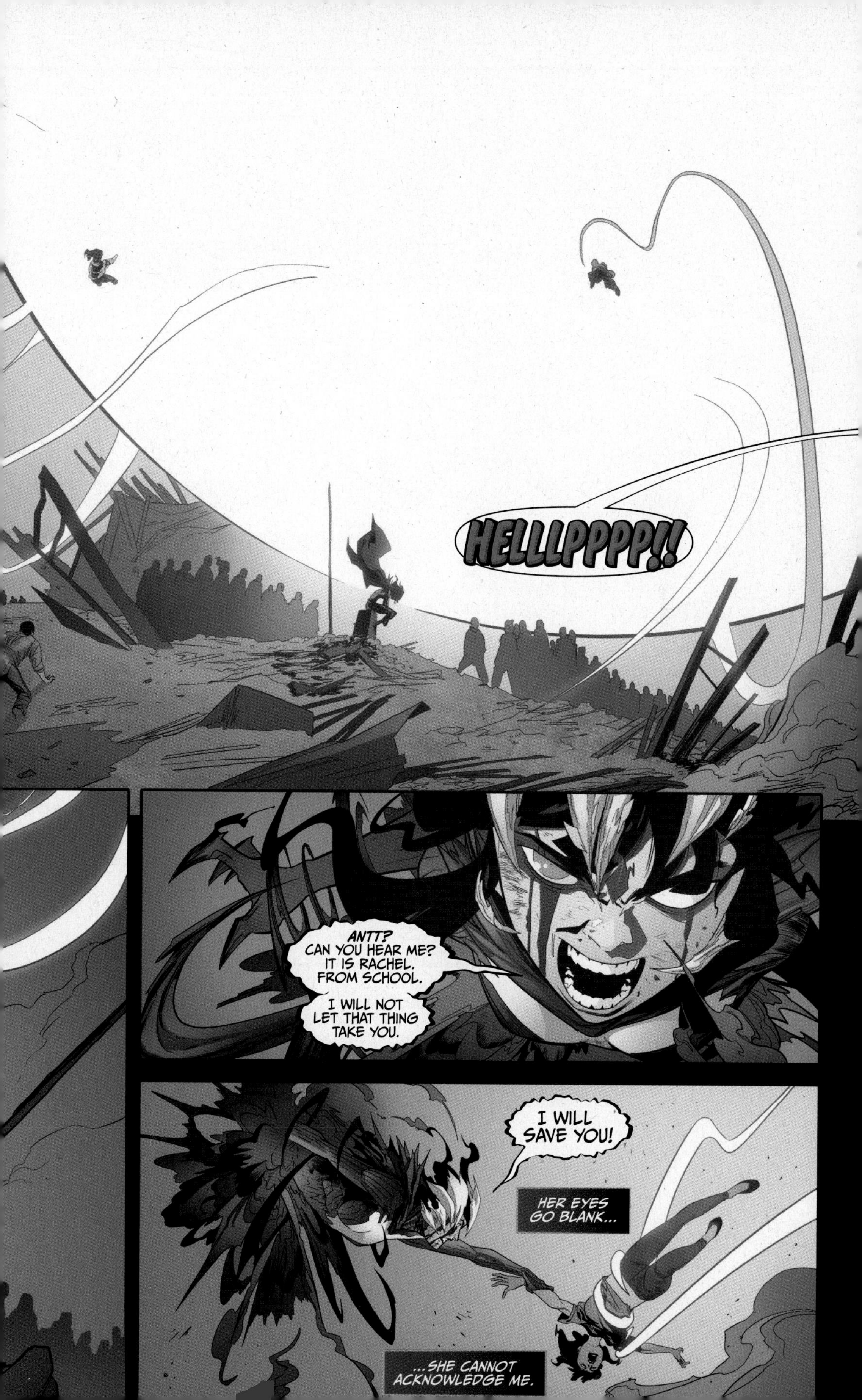
HELLLPPPP!!
ANTT? CAN YOU HEAR ME? IT IS RACHEL. FROM SCHOOL.
I WILL NOT LET THAT THING TAKE YOU.
I WILL SAVE YOU!
HER EYES GO BLANK...
...SHE CANNOT ACKNOWLEDGE ME.

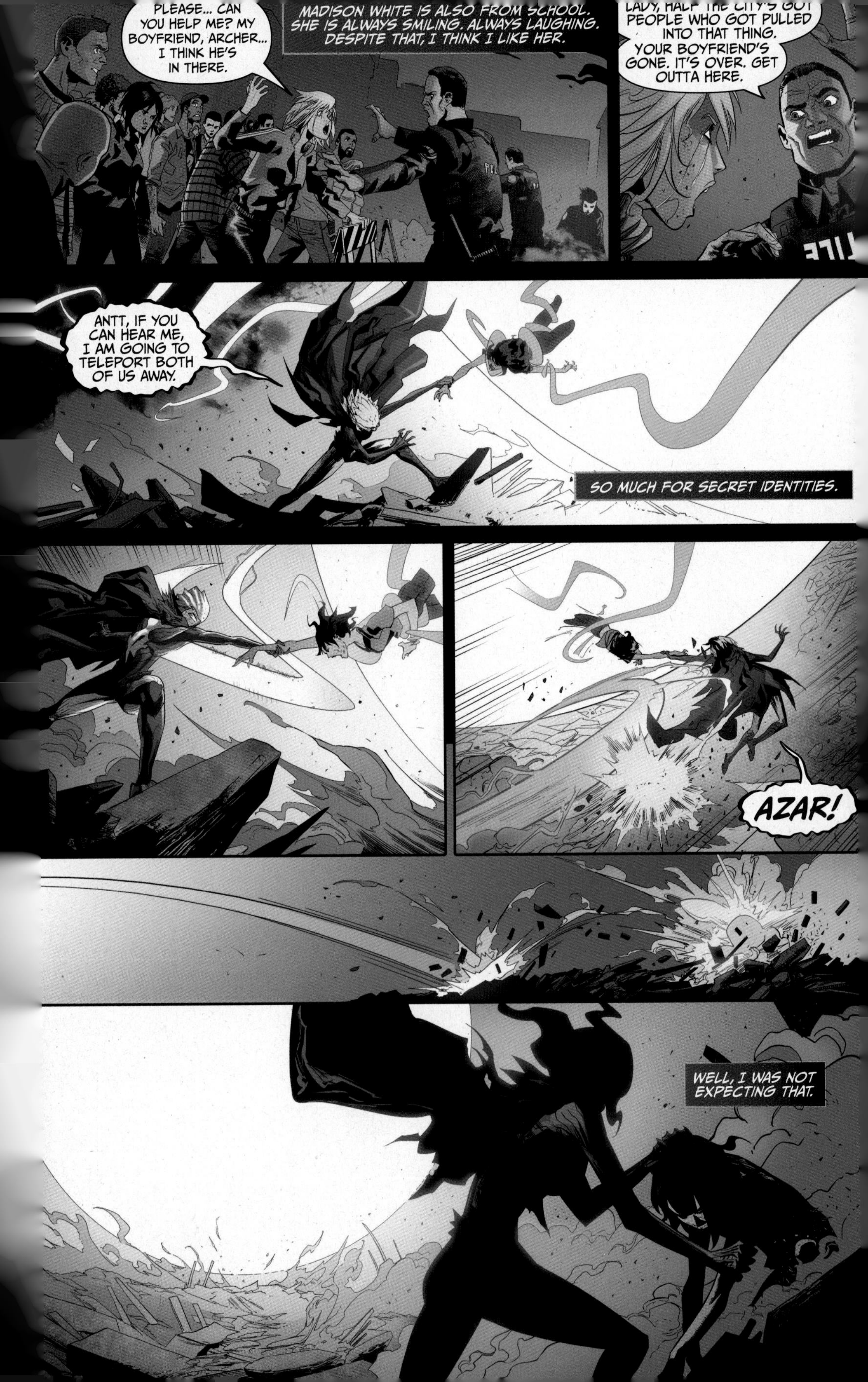

PLEASE... CAN YOU HELP ME? MY BOYFRIEND, ARCHER... I THINK HE'S IN THERE.
MADISON WHITE IS ALSO FROM SCHOOL. SHE IS ALWAYS SMILING. ALWAYS LAUGHING. DESPITE THAT, I THINK I LIKE HER.
LADY, HALF THE CITY'S GOT PEOPLE WHO GOT PULLED INTO THAT THING. YOUR BOYFRIEND'S GONE. IT'S OVER. GET OUTTA HERE.
ANTT, IF YOU CAN HEAR ME, I AM GOING TO TELEPORT BOTH OF US AWAY.
SO MUCH FOR SECRET IDENTITIES.
AZAR!
WELL, I WAS NOT EXPECTING THAT.

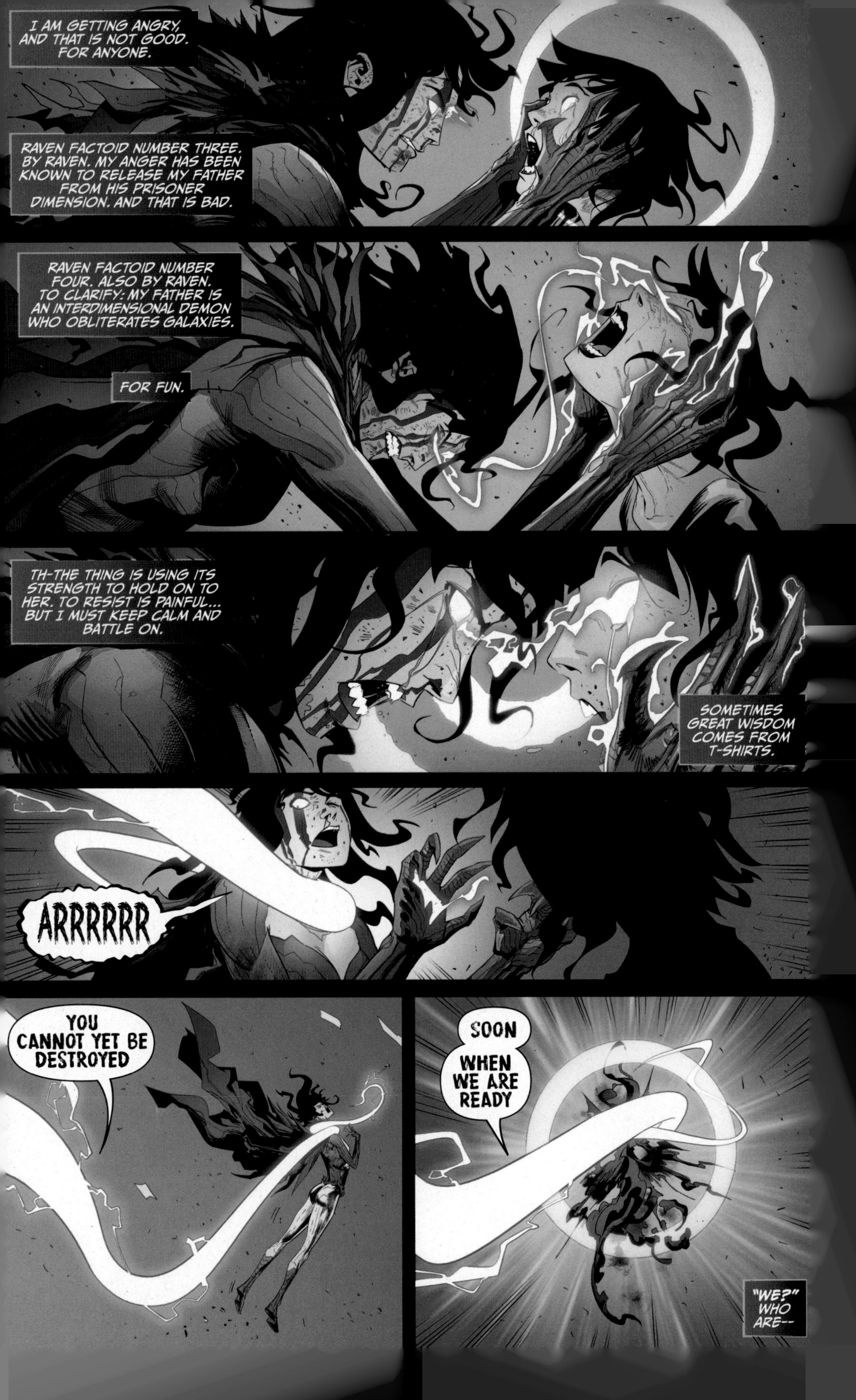
I AM GETTING ANGRY, AND THAT IS NOT GOOD. FOR ANYONE.
RAVEN FACTOID NUMBER THREE. BY RAVEN. MY ANGER HAS BEEN KNOWN TO RELEASE MY FATHER FROM HIS PRISONER DIMENSION. AND THAT IS BAD.
RAVEN FACTOID NUMBER FOUR. ALSO BY RAVEN. TO CLARIFY: MY FATHER IS AN INTERDIMENSIONAL DEMON WHO OBLITERATES GALAXIES.
FOR FUN.
TH-THE THING IS USING ITS STRENGTH TO HOLD ON TO HER. TO RESIST IS PAINFUL... BUT I MUST KEEP CALM AND BATTLE ON.
SOMETIMES GREAT WISDOM COMES FROM T-SHIRTS.
ARRRRRR
YOU CANNOT YET BE DESTROYED
SOON
WHEN WE ARE READY
"WE?" WHO ARE--

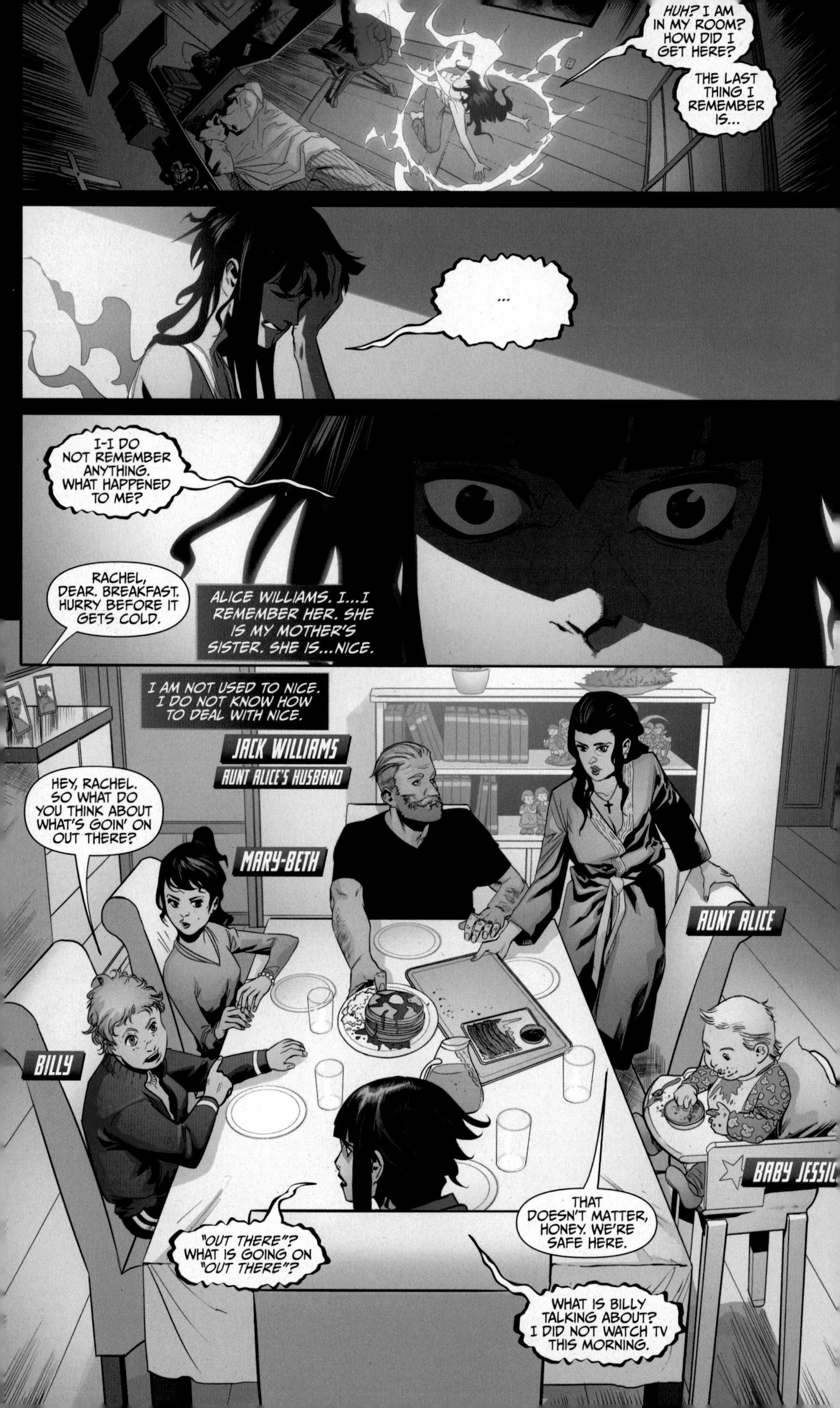
HUH? I AM IN MY ROOM? HOW DID I GET HERE?
THE LAST THING I REMEMBER IS...
...
I-I DO NOT REMEMBER ANYTHING. WHAT HAPPENED TO ME?
RACHEL, DEAR. BREAKFAST. HURRY BEFORE IT GETS COLD.
ALICE WILLIAMS. I...I REMEMBER HER. SHE IS MY MOTHER'S SISTER. SHE IS...NICE.
I AM NOT USED TO NICE. I DO NOT KNOW HOW TO DEAL WITH NICE.
JACK WILLIAMS
AUNT ALICE'S HUSBAND
HEY, RACHEL. SO WHAT DO YOU THINK ABOUT WHAT'S GOIN' ON OUT THERE?
MARY-BETH
AUNT ALICE
BILLY
"OUT THERE"? WHAT IS GOING ON "OUT THERE"?
THAT DOESN'T MATTER, HONEY. WE'RE SAFE HERE.
WHAT IS BILLY TALKING ABOUT? I DID NOT WATCH TV THIS MORNING.

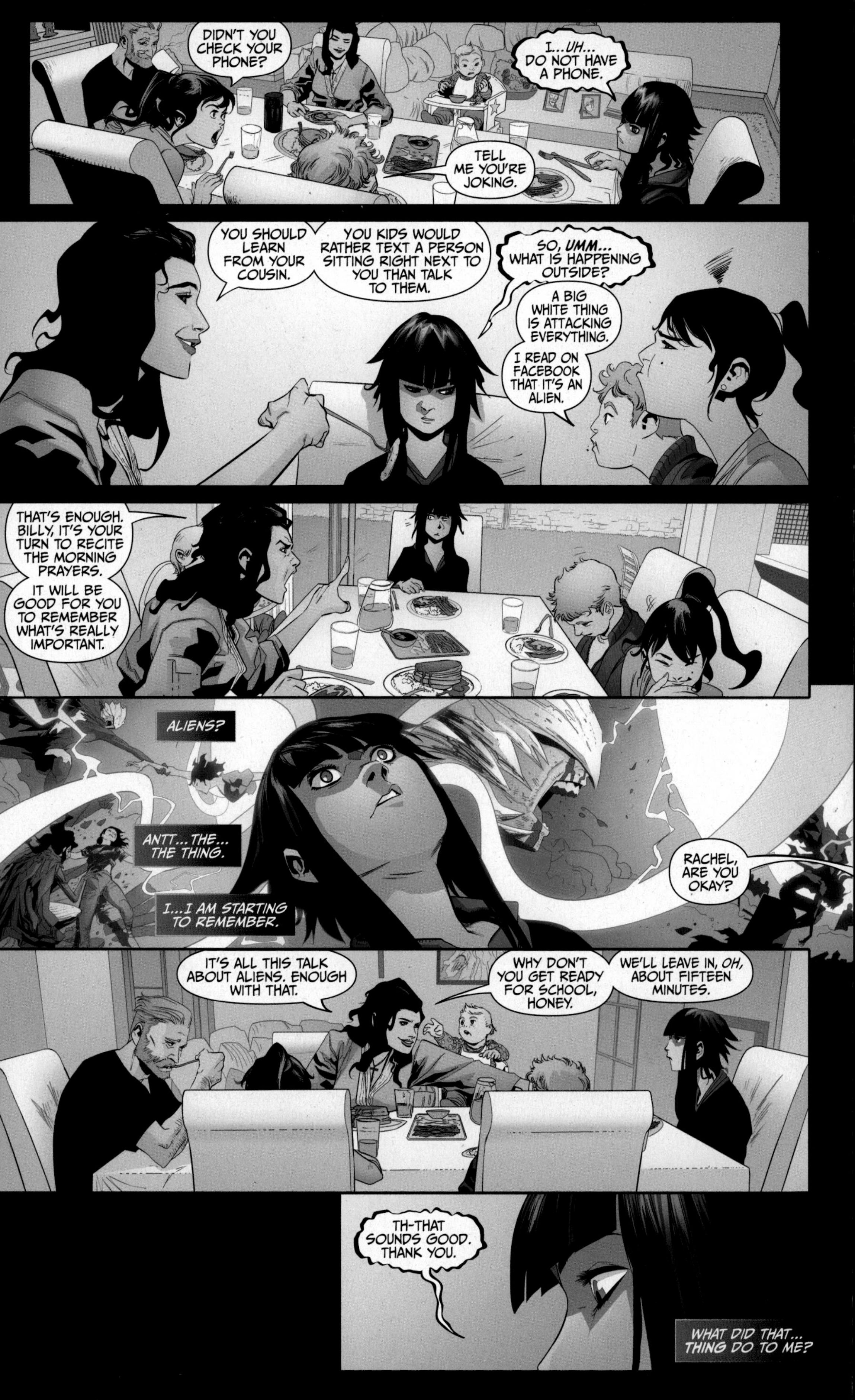
DIDN'T YOU CHECK YOUR PHONE?
I...UH... DO NOT HAVE A PHONE.
TELL ME YOU'RE JOKING.
YOU SHOULD LEARN FROM YOUR COUSIN.
YOU KIDS WOULD RATHER TEXT A PERSON SITTING RIGHT NEXT TO YOU THAN TALK TO THEM.
SO, UMM... WHAT IS HAPPENING OUTSIDE?
A BIG WHITE THING IS ATTACKING EVERYTHING.
I READ ON FACEBOOK THAT IT'S AN ALIEN.
THAT'S ENOUGH. BILLY, IT'S YOUR TURN TO RECITE THE MORNING PRAYERS.
IT WILL BE GOOD FOR YOU TO REMEMBER WHAT'S REALLY IMPORTANT.
ALIENS?
ANTT...THE... THE THING.
I...I AM STARTING TO REMEMBER.
RACHEL, ARE YOU OKAY?
IT'S ALL THIS TALK ABOUT ALIENS. ENOUGH WITH THAT.
WHY DON'T YOU GET READY FOR SCHOOL, HONEY.
WE'LL LEAVE IN, OH, ABOUT FIFTEEN MINUTES.
TH-THAT SOUNDS GOOD. THANK YOU.
WHAT DID THAT... THING DO TO ME?

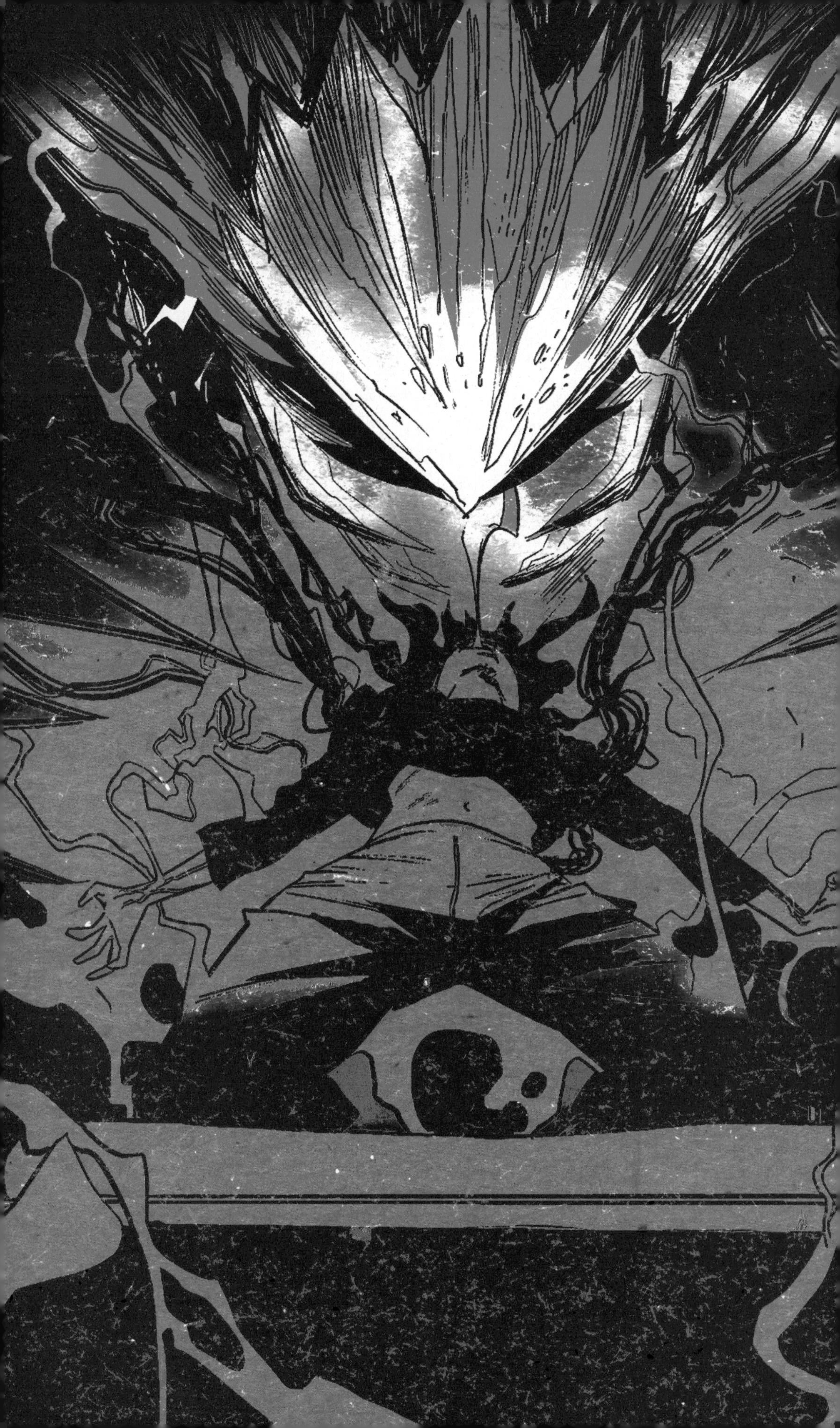

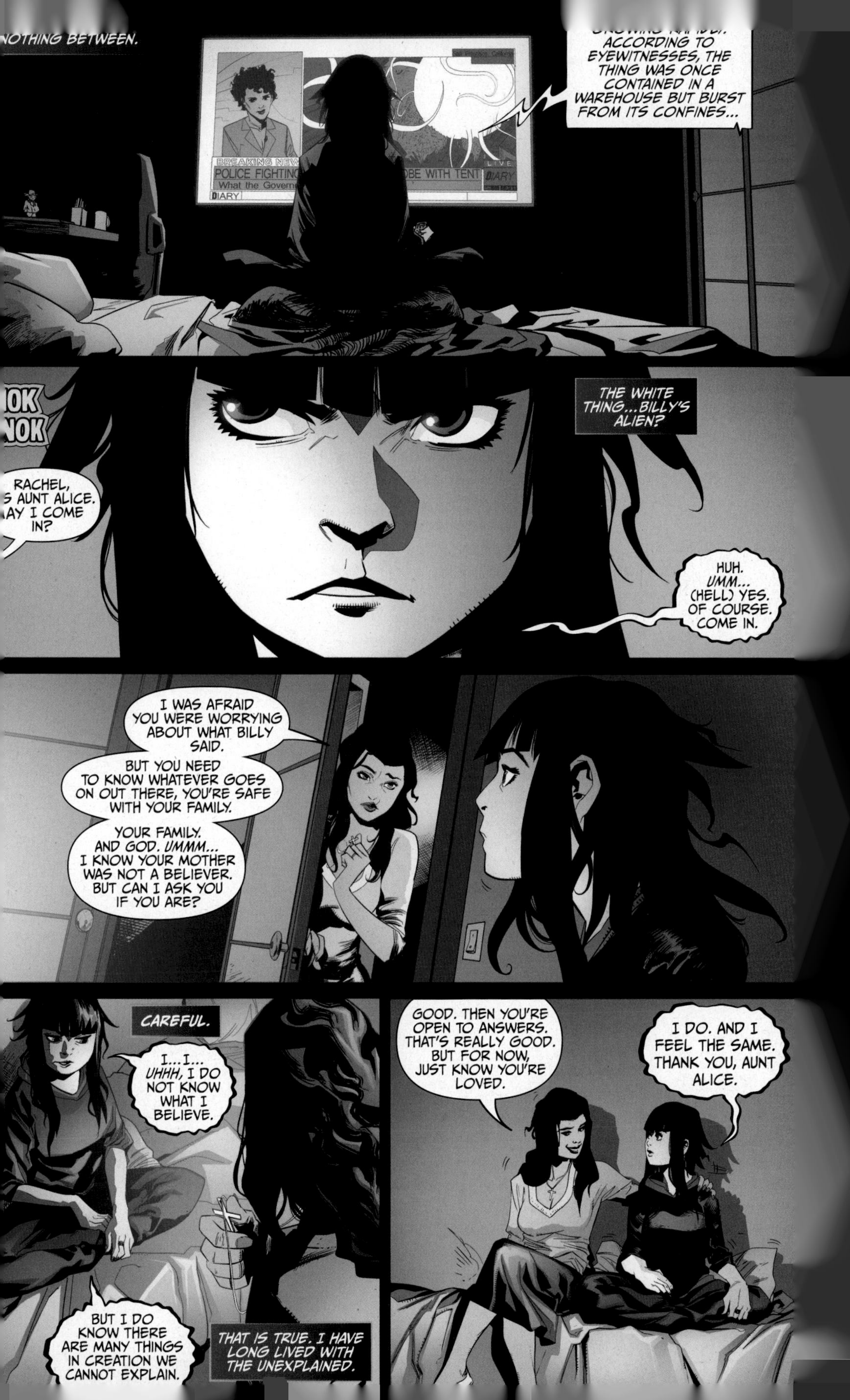

NOTHING BETWEEN.
ACCORDING TO EYEWITNESSES, THE THING WAS ONCE CONTAINED IN A WAREHOUSE BUT BURST FROM ITS CONFINES...
THE WHITE THING...BILLY'S ALIEN?
RACHEL, S AUNT ALICE. AY I COME IN?
HUH. UMM... (HELL) YES. OF COURSE. COME IN.
I WAS AFRAID YOU WERE WORRYING ABOUT WHAT BILLY SAID.
BUT YOU NEED TO KNOW WHATEVER GOES ON OUT THERE, YOU'RE SAFE WITH YOUR FAMILY.
YOUR FAMILY. AND GOD. UMMM... I KNOW YOUR MOTHER WAS NOT A BELIEVER. BUT CAN I ASK YOU IF YOU ARE?
CAREFUL.
I...I... UHHH, I DO NOT KNOW WHAT I BELIEVE.
BUT I DO KNOW THERE ARE MANY THINGS IN CREATION WE CANNOT EXPLAIN.
THAT IS TRUE. I HAVE LONG LIVED WITH THE UNEXPLAINED.
GOOD. THEN YOU'RE OPEN TO ANSWERS. THAT'S REALLY GOOD. BUT FOR NOW, JUST KNOW YOU'RE LOVED.
I DO. AND I FEEL THE SAME. THANK YOU, AUNT ALICE.

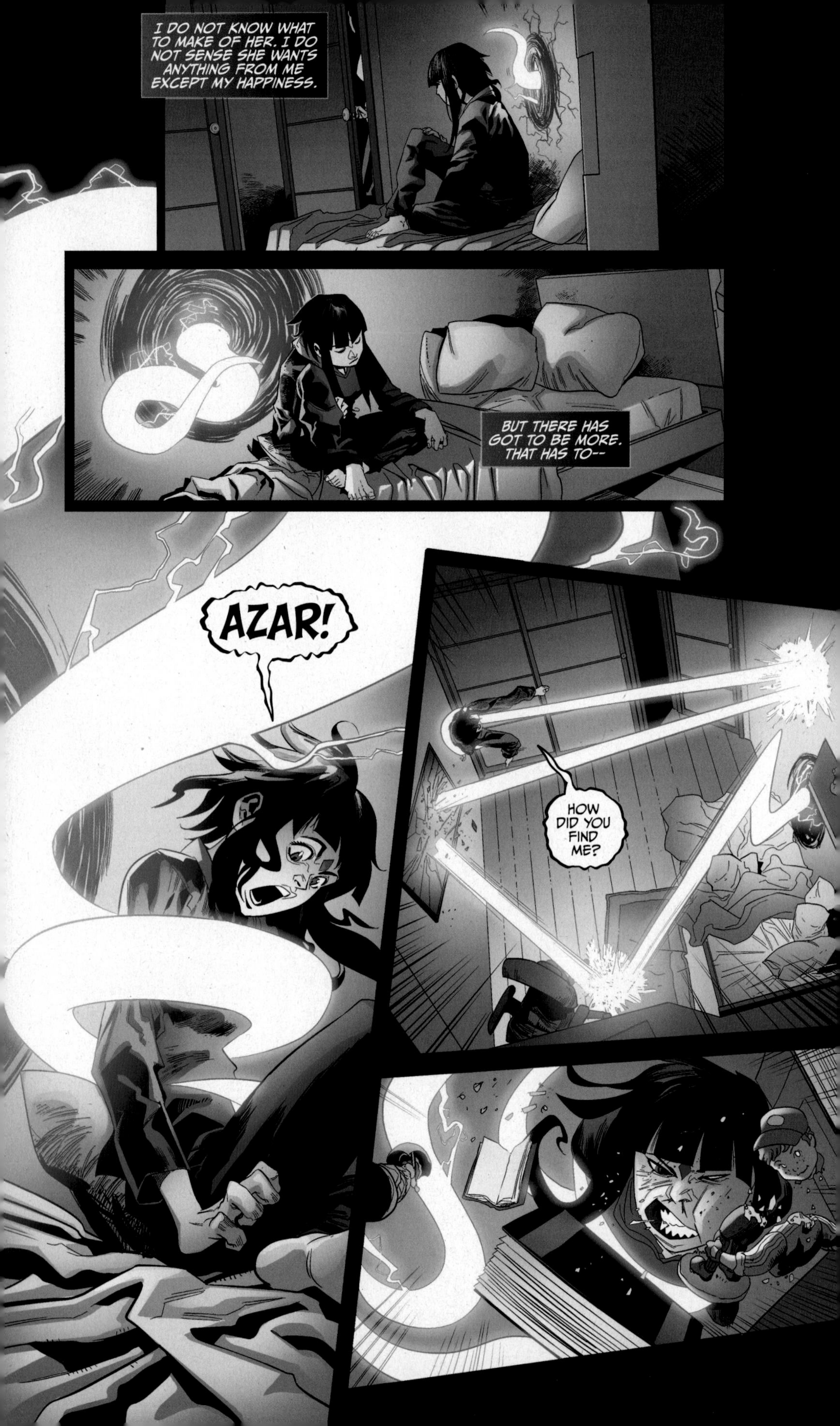
I DO NOT KNOW WHAT TO MAKE OF HER. I DO NOT SENSE SHE WANTS ANYTHING FROM ME EXCEPT MY HAPPINESS.
BUT THERE HAS GOT TO BE MORE. THAT HAS TO--
AZAR!
HOW DID YOU FIND ME?

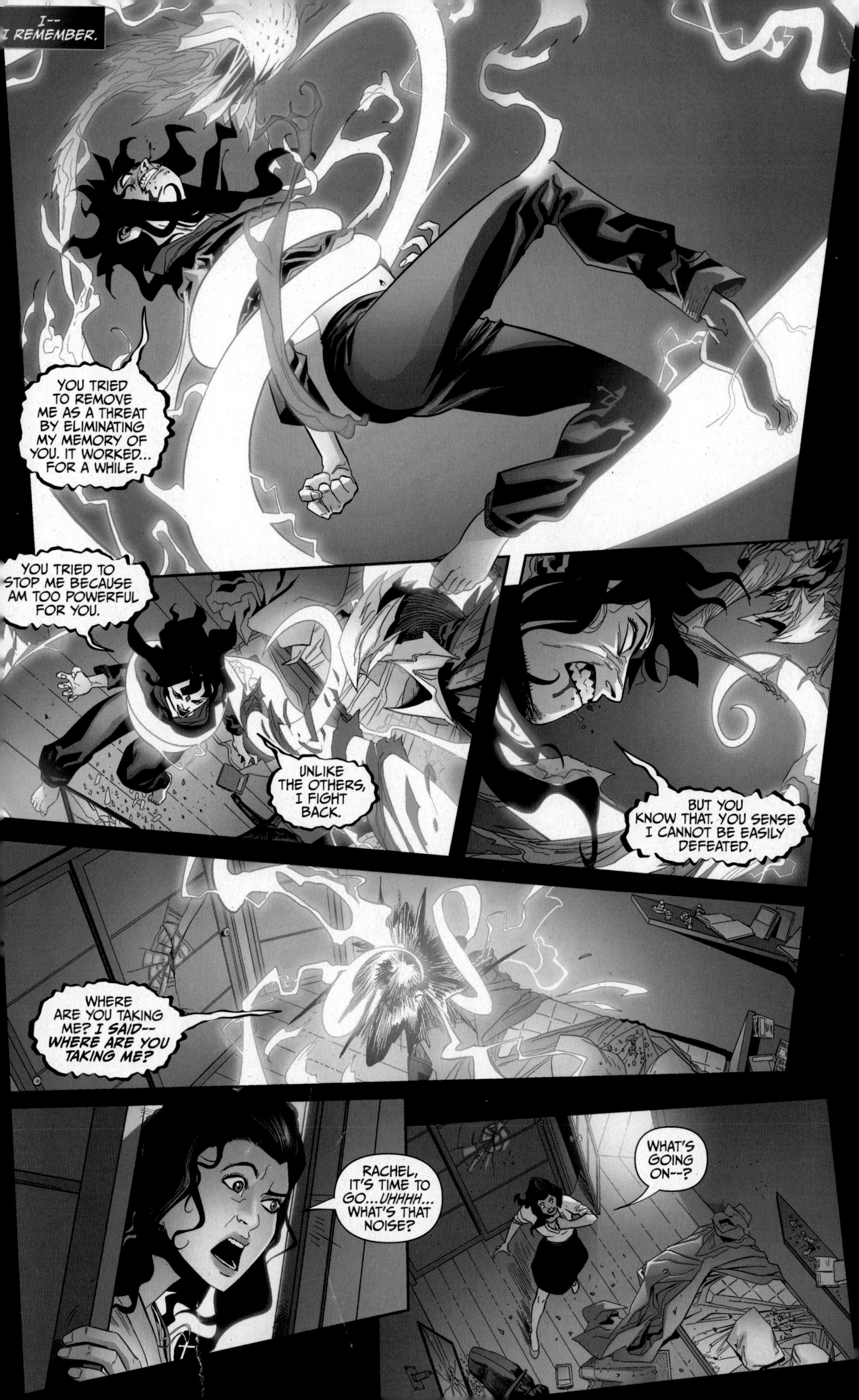
I-- I REMEMBER.
YOU TRIED TO REMOVE ME AS A THREAT BY ELIMINATING MY MEMORY OF YOU. IT WORKED... FOR A WHILE.
YOU TRIED TO STOP ME BECAUSE AM TOO POWERFUL FOR YOU.
UNLIKE THE OTHERS, I FIGHT BACK.
BUT YOU KNOW THAT. YOU SENSE I CANNOT BE EASILY DEFEATED.
WHERE ARE YOU TAKING ME? I SAID-- WHERE ARE YOU TAKING ME?
RACHEL, IT'S TIME TO GO...UHHHH... WHAT'S THAT NOISE?
WHAT'S GOING ON--?

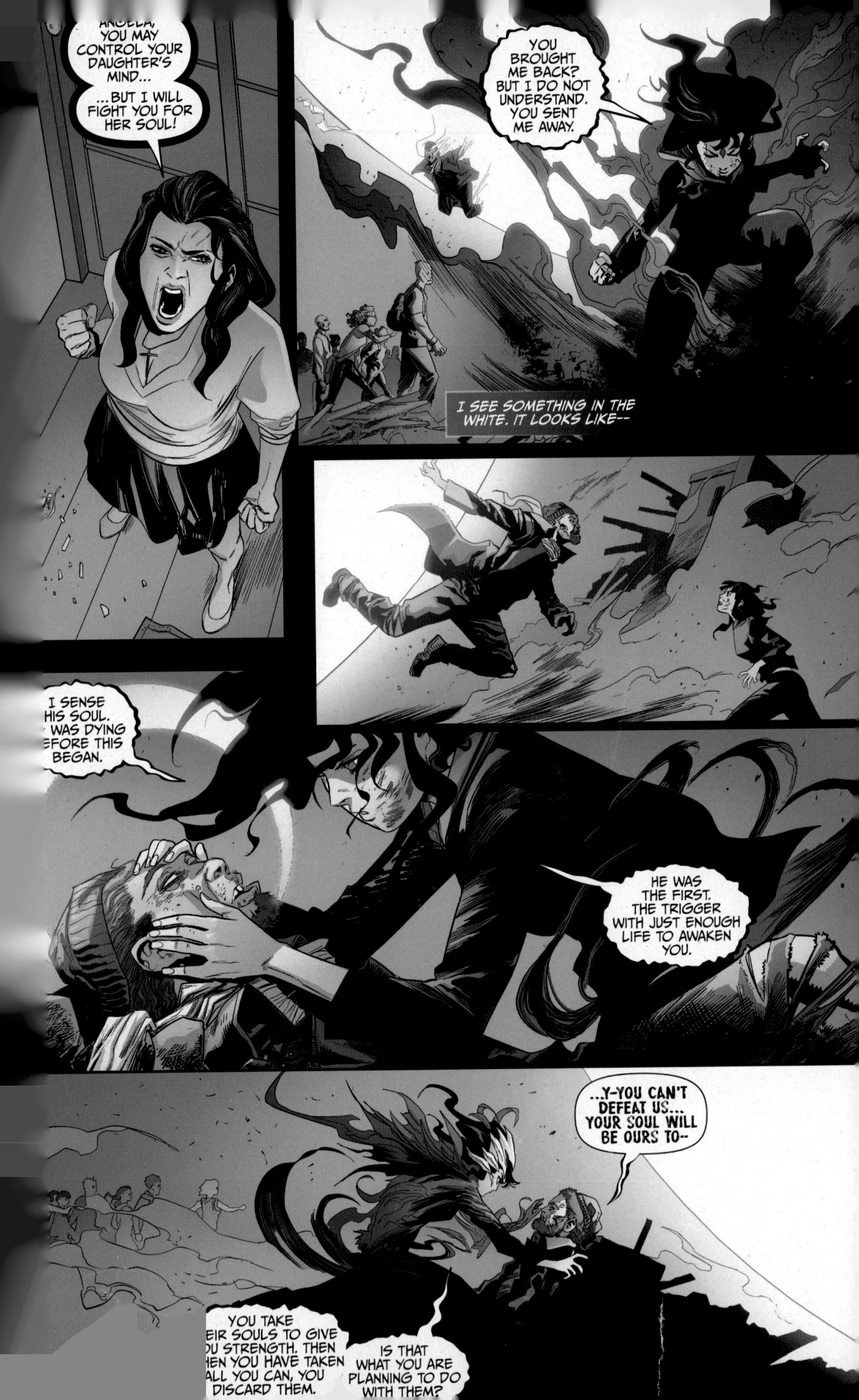
ANGELA, YOU MAY CONTROL YOUR DAUGHTER'S MIND...
...BUT I WILL FIGHT YOU FOR HER SOUL!
YOU BROUGHT ME BACK? BUT I DO NOT UNDERSTAND. YOU SENT ME AWAY.
I SEE SOMETHING IN THE WHITE. IT LOOKS LIKE--
I SENSE HIS SOUL. WAS DYING EFORE THIS BEGAN.
HE WAS THE FIRST. THE TRIGGER WITH JUST ENOUGH LIFE TO AWAKEN YOU.
...Y-YOU CAN'T DEFEAT US... YOUR SOUL WILL BE OURS TO--
YOU TAKE EIR SOULS TO GIVE OU STRENGTH. THEN HEN YOU HAVE TAKEN ALL YOU CAN, YOU DISCARD THEM.
IS THAT WHAT YOU ARE PLANNING TO DO WITH THEM?

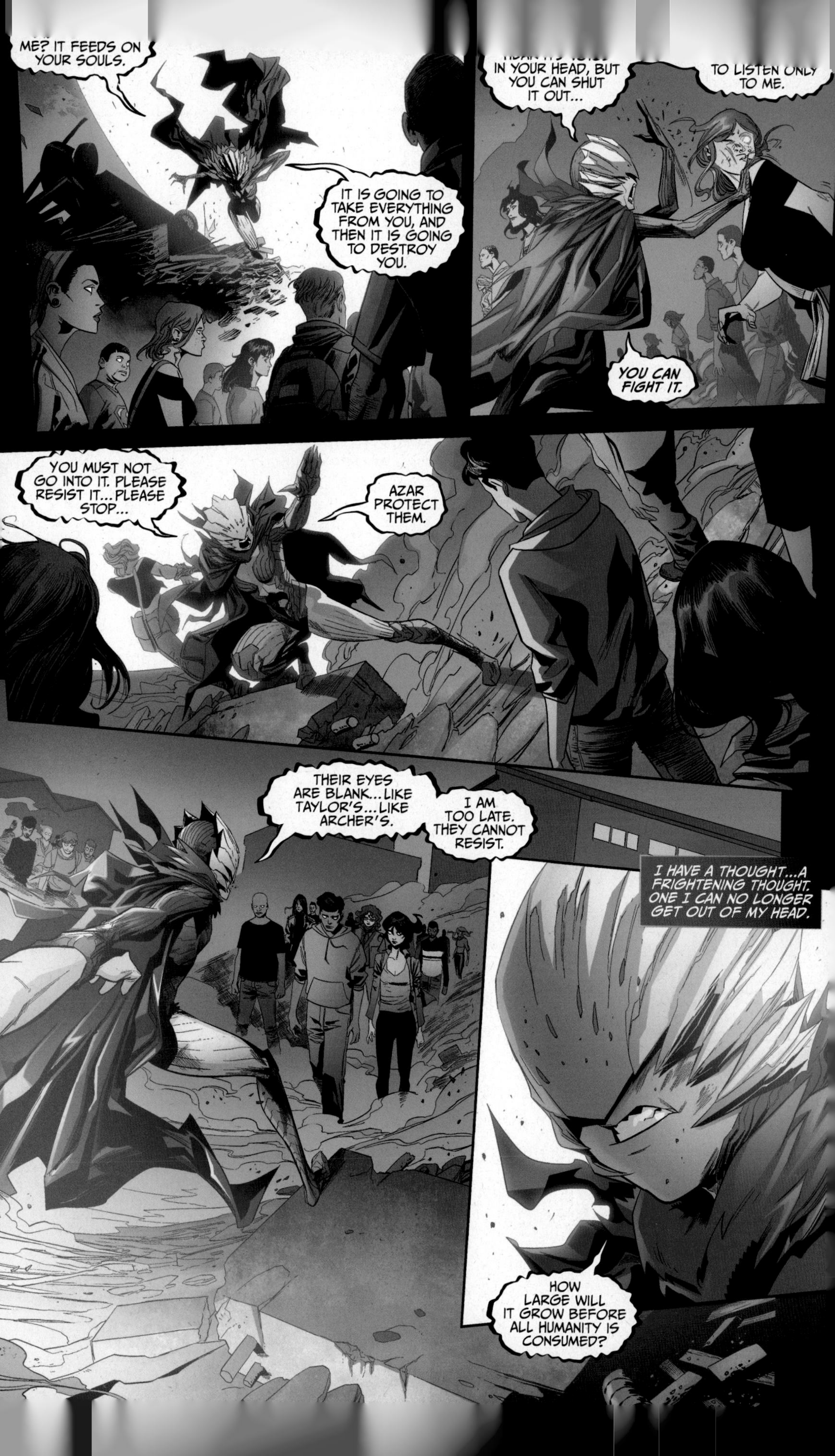
ME? IT FEEDS ON YOUR SOULS.
IT IS GOING TO TAKE EVERYTHING FROM YOU, AND THEN IT IS GOING TO DESTROY YOU.
IN YOUR HEAD, BUT YOU CAN SHUT IT OUT...
TO LISTEN ONLY TO ME.
YOU CAN FIGHT IT.
YOU MUST NOT GO INTO IT. PLEASE RESIST IT...PLEASE STOP...
AZAR PROTECT THEM.
THEIR EYES ARE BLANK...LIKE TAYLOR'S...LIKE ARCHER'S.
I AM TOO LATE. THEY CANNOT RESIST.
I HAVE A THOUGHT...A FRIGHTENING THOUGHT. ONE I CAN NO LONGER GET OUT OF MY HEAD.
HOW LARGE WILL IT GROW BEFORE ALL HUMANITY IS CONSUMED?

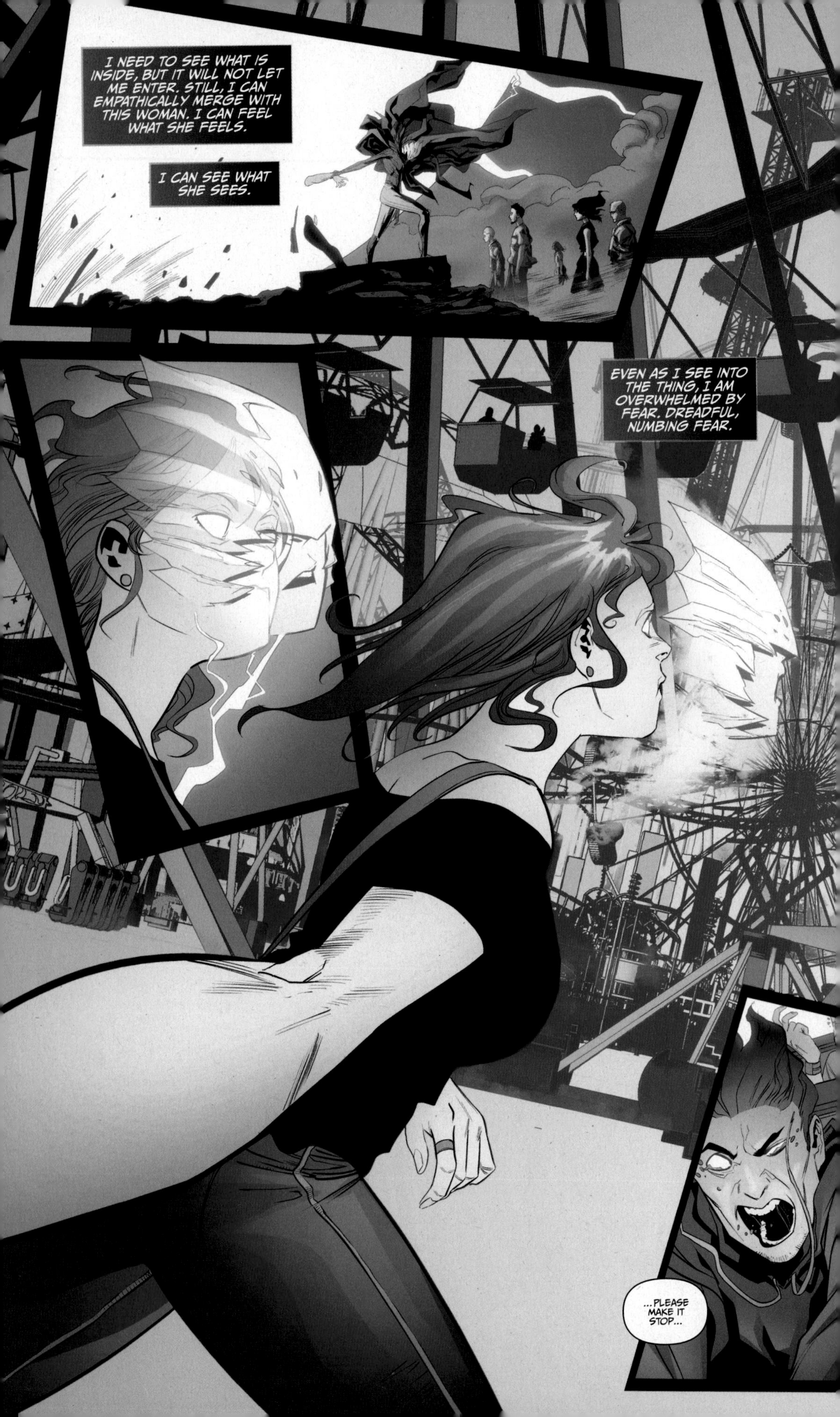
I NEED TO SEE WHAT IS INSIDE, BUT IT WILL NOT LET ME ENTER. STILL, I CAN EMPATHICALLY MERGE WITH THIS WOMAN. I CAN FEEL WHAT SHE FEELS.
I CAN SEE WHAT SHE SEES.
EVEN AS I SEE INTO THE THING, I AM OVERWHELMED BY FEAR. DREADFUL, NUMBING FEAR.
...PLEASE MAKE IT STOP...

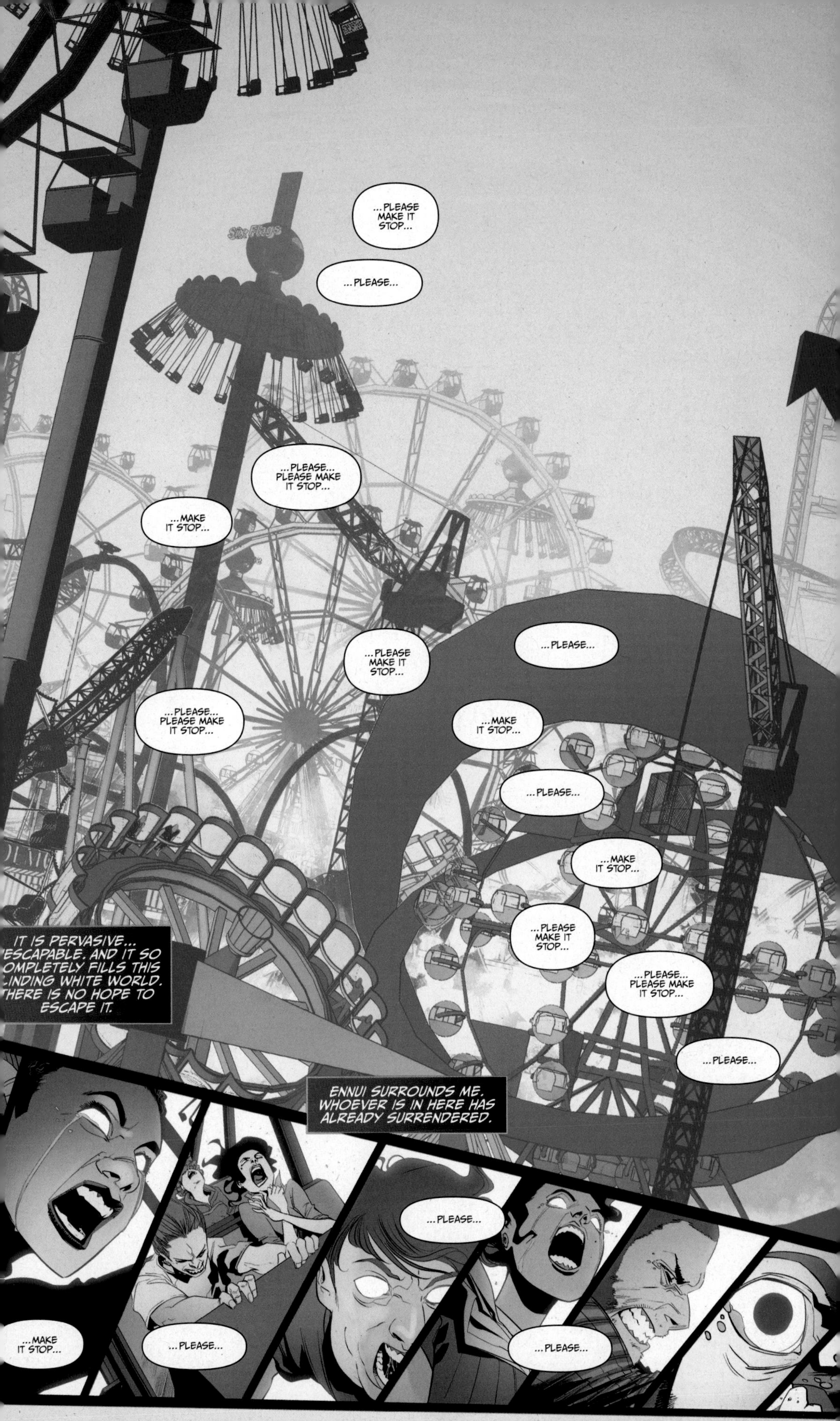

...PLEASE MAKE IT STOP...
...PLEASE...
Six Flags
...PLEASE... PLEASE MAKE IT STOP...
...MAKE IT STOP...
...PLEASE MAKE IT STOP...
...PLEASE...
...PLEASE... PLEASE MAKE IT STOP...
...MAKE IT STOP...
...PLEASE...
...MAKE IT STOP...
...PLEASE MAKE IT STOP...
...PLEASE... PLEASE MAKE IT STOP...
IT IS PERVASIVE... ESCAPABLE. AND IT SO OMPLETELY FILLS THIS LINDING WHITE WORLD. THERE IS NO HOPE TO ESCAPE IT.
...PLEASE...
ENNUI SURROUNDS ME. WHOEVER IS IN HERE HAS ALREADY SURRENDERED.
...PLEASE...
...MAKE IT STOP...
...PLEASE...
...PLEASE...

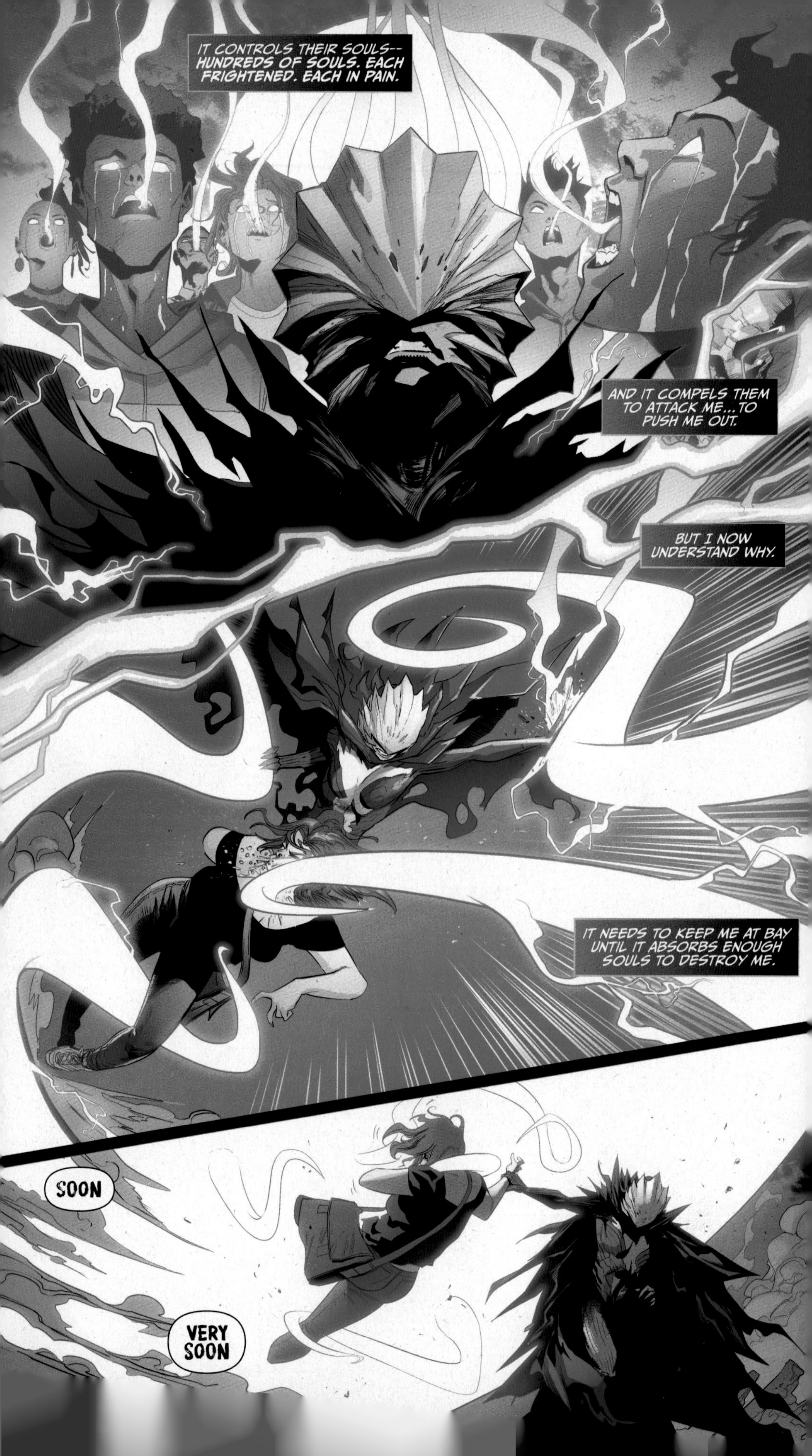
IT CONTROLS THEIR SOULS--HUNDREDS OF SOULS. EACH FRIGHTENED. EACH IN PAIN.
AND IT COMPELS THEM TO ATTACK ME...TO PUSH ME OUT.
BUT I NOW UNDERSTAND WHY.
IT NEEDS TO KEEP ME AT BAY UNTIL IT ABSORBS ENOUGH SOULS TO DESTROY ME.
SOON
VERY SOON

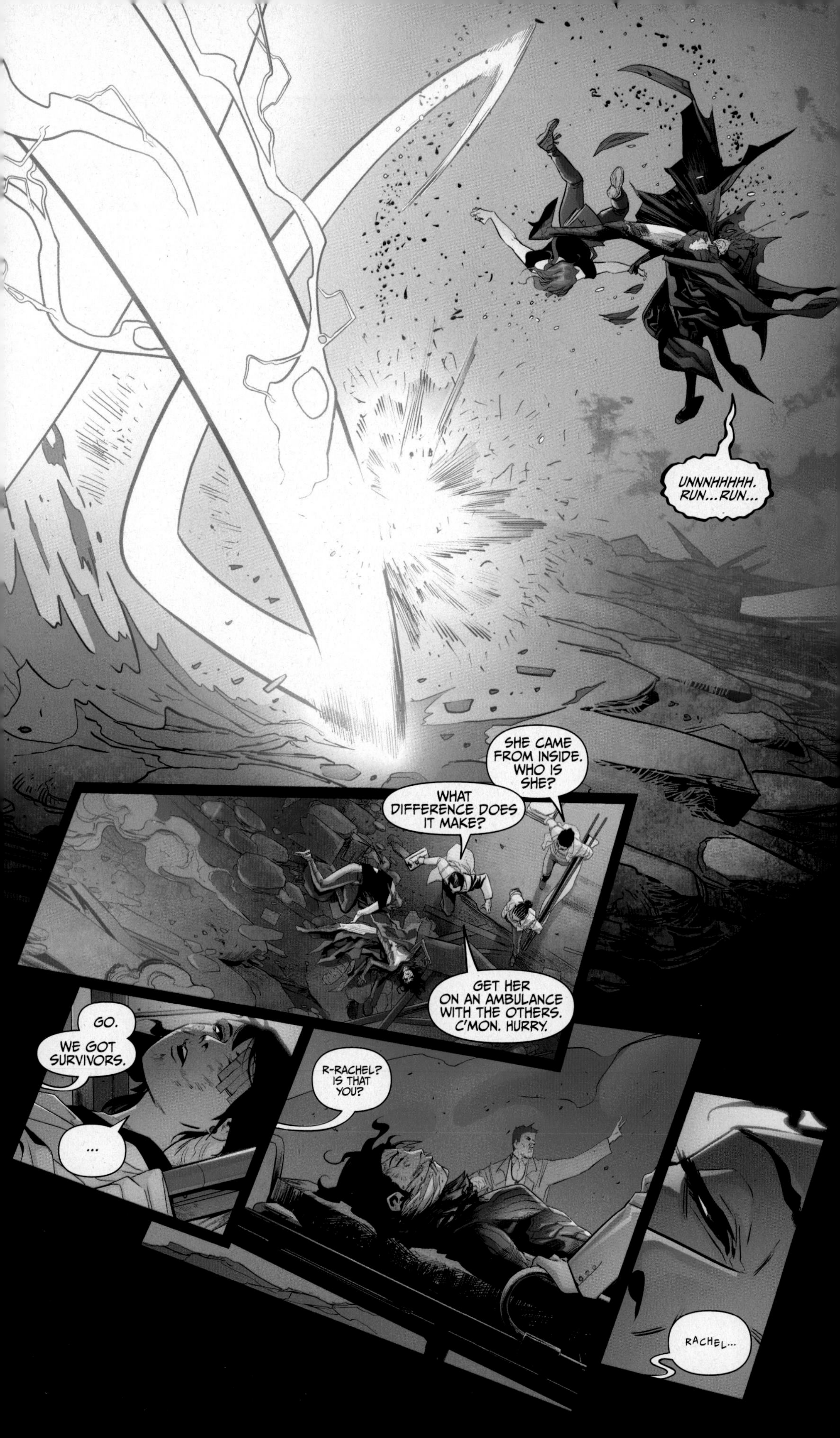
UNNNHHHHH. RUN...RUN...
SHE CAME FROM INSIDE. WHO IS SHE?
WHAT DIFFERENCE DOES IT MAKE?
GET HER ON AN AMBULANCE WITH THE OTHERS. C'MON. HURRY.
GO.
WE GOT SURVIVORS.
...
R-RACHEL? IS THAT YOU?
RACHEL...

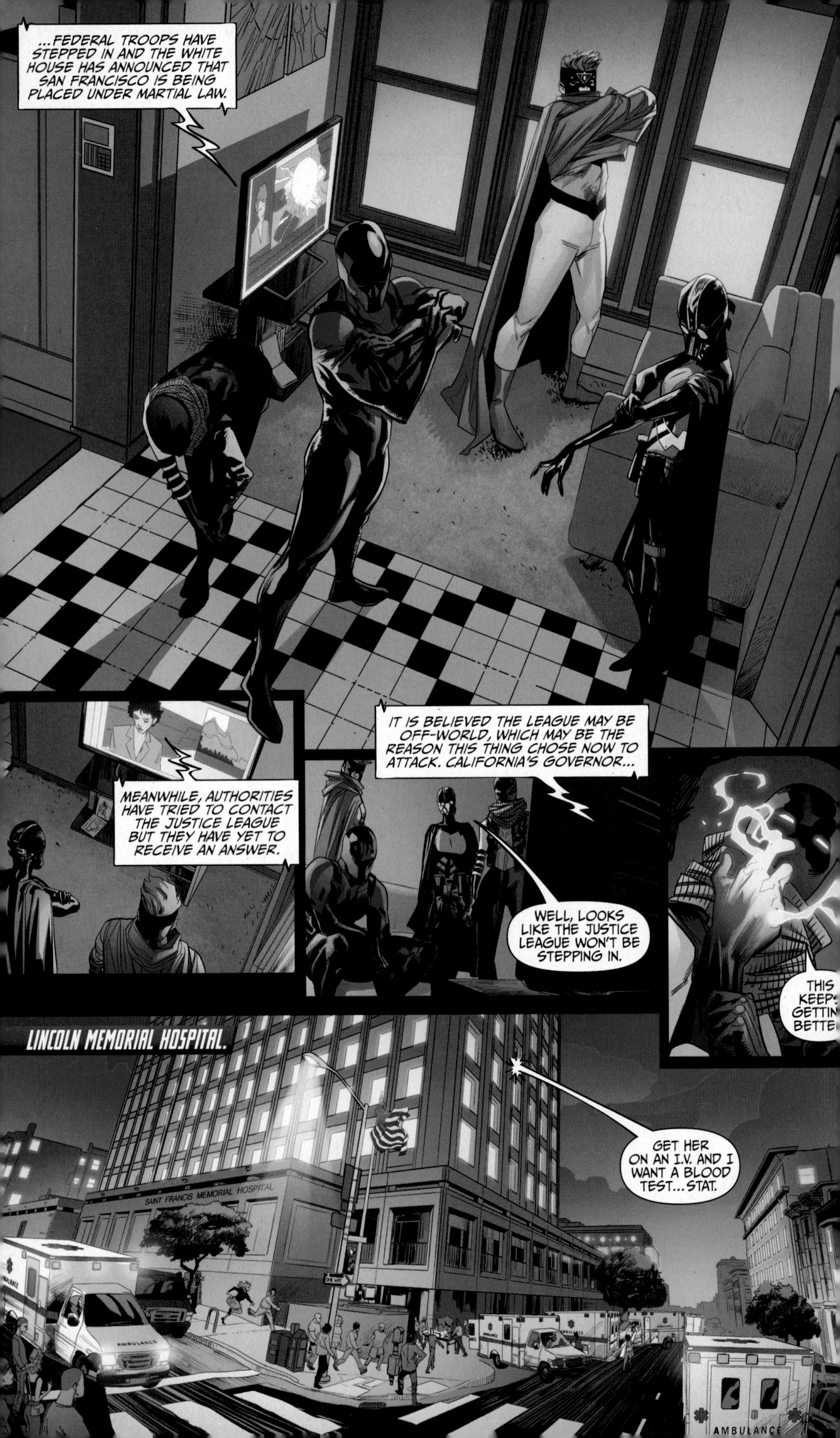
...FEDERAL TROOPS HAVE STEPPED IN AND THE WHITE HOUSE HAS ANNOUNCED THAT SAN FRANCISCO IS BEING PLACED UNDER MARTIAL LAW.
MEANWHILE, AUTHORITIES HAVE TRIED TO CONTACT THE JUSTICE LEAGUE BUT THEY HAVE YET TO RECEIVE AN ANSWER.
IT IS BELIEVED THE LEAGUE MAY BE OFF-WORLD, WHICH MAY BE THE REASON THIS THING CHOSE NOW TO ATTACK. CALIFORNIA'S GOVERNOR...
WELL, LOOKS LIKE THE JUSTICE LEAGUE WON'T BE STEPPING IN.
LINCOLN MEMORIAL HOSPITAL.
SAINT FRANCIS MEMORIAL HOSPITAL
ONE WAY
GET HER ON AN I.V. AND I WANT A BLOOD TEST...STAT.
AMBULANCE

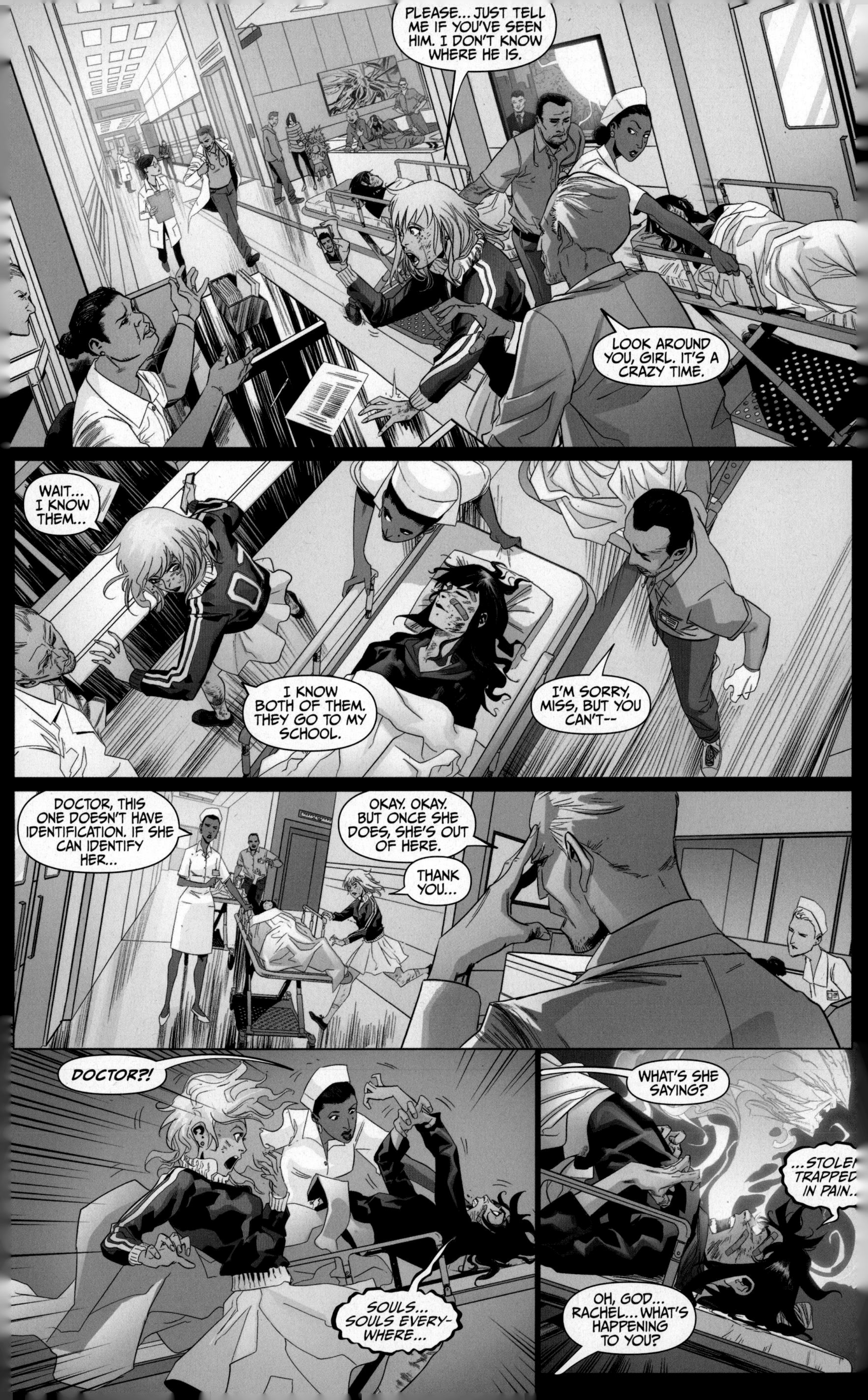
PLEASE... JUST TELL ME IF YOU'VE SEEN HIM. I DON'T KNOW WHERE HE IS.
LOOK AROUND YOU, GIRL. IT'S A CRAZY TIME.
WAIT... I KNOW THEM...
I KNOW BOTH OF THEM. THEY GO TO MY SCHOOL.
I'M SORRY, MISS, BUT YOU CAN'T--
DOCTOR, THIS ONE DOESN'T HAVE IDENTIFICATION. IF SHE CAN IDENTIFY HER...
OKAY. OKAY. BUT ONCE SHE DOES, SHE'S OUT OF HERE.
THANK YOU...
DOCTOR?!
SOULS... SOULS EVERY-WHERE...
WHAT'S SHE SAYING?
...STOLE TRAPPED IN PAIN...
OH, GOD... RACHEL... WHAT'S HAPPENING TO YOU?

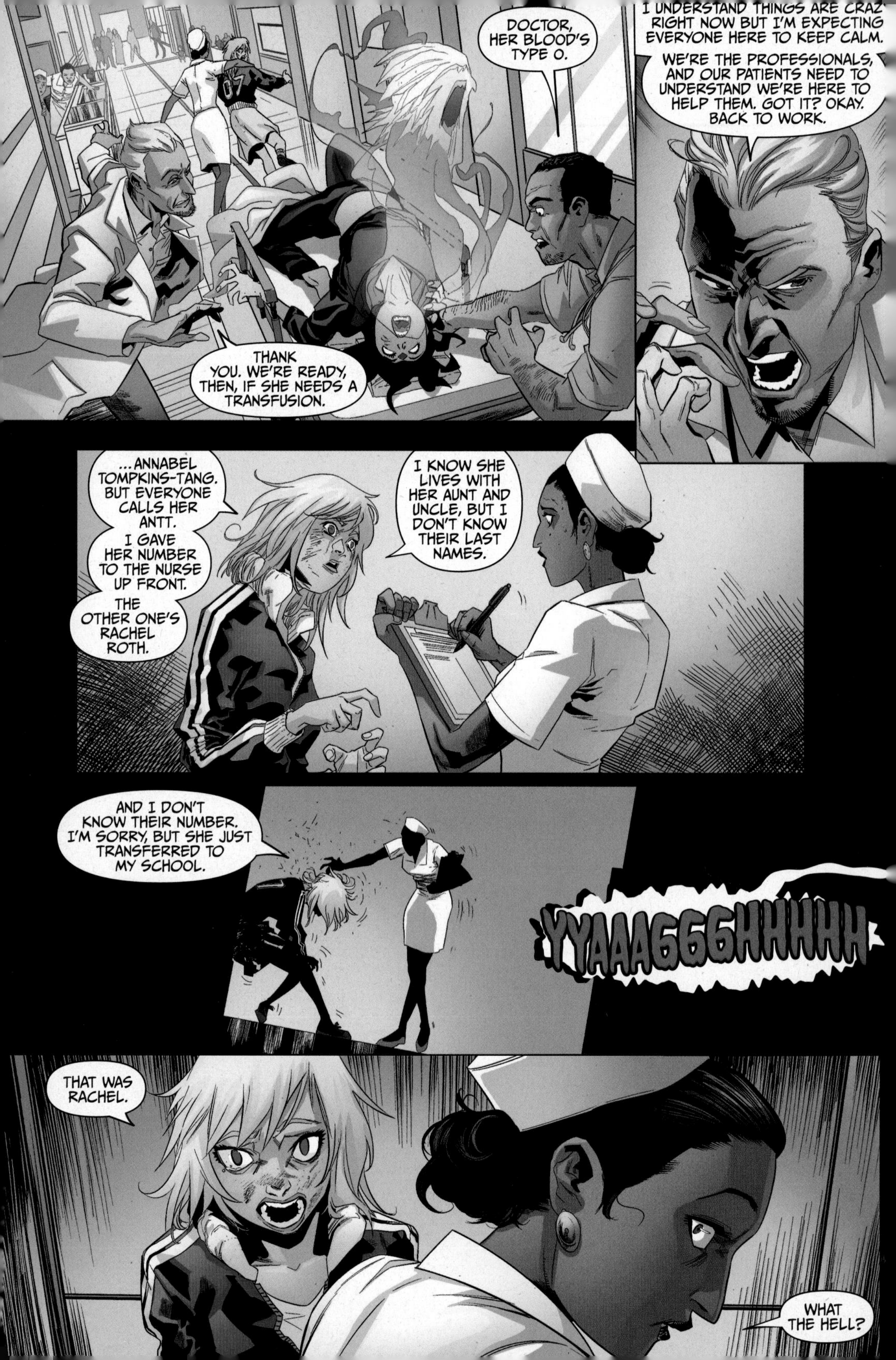
DOCTOR, HER BLOOD'S TYPE O.
THANK YOU. WE'RE READY, THEN, IF SHE NEEDS A TRANSFUSION.
I UNDERSTAND THINGS ARE CRAZ RIGHT NOW BUT I'M EXPECTING EVERYONE HERE TO KEEP CALM.
WE'RE THE PROFESSIONALS, AND OUR PATIENTS NEED TO UNDERSTAND WE'RE HERE TO HELP THEM. GOT IT? OKAY. BACK TO WORK.
...ANNABEL TOMPKINS-TANG. BUT EVERYONE CALLS HER ANTT.
I GAVE HER NUMBER TO THE NURSE UP FRONT.
THE OTHER ONE'S RACHEL ROTH.
I KNOW SHE LIVES WITH HER AUNT AND UNCLE, BUT I DON'T KNOW THEIR LAST NAMES.
AND I DON'T KNOW THEIR NUMBER. I'M SORRY, BUT SHE JUST TRANSFERRED TO MY SCHOOL.
YYAAAGGGHHHHH
THAT WAS RACHEL.
WHAT THE HELL?

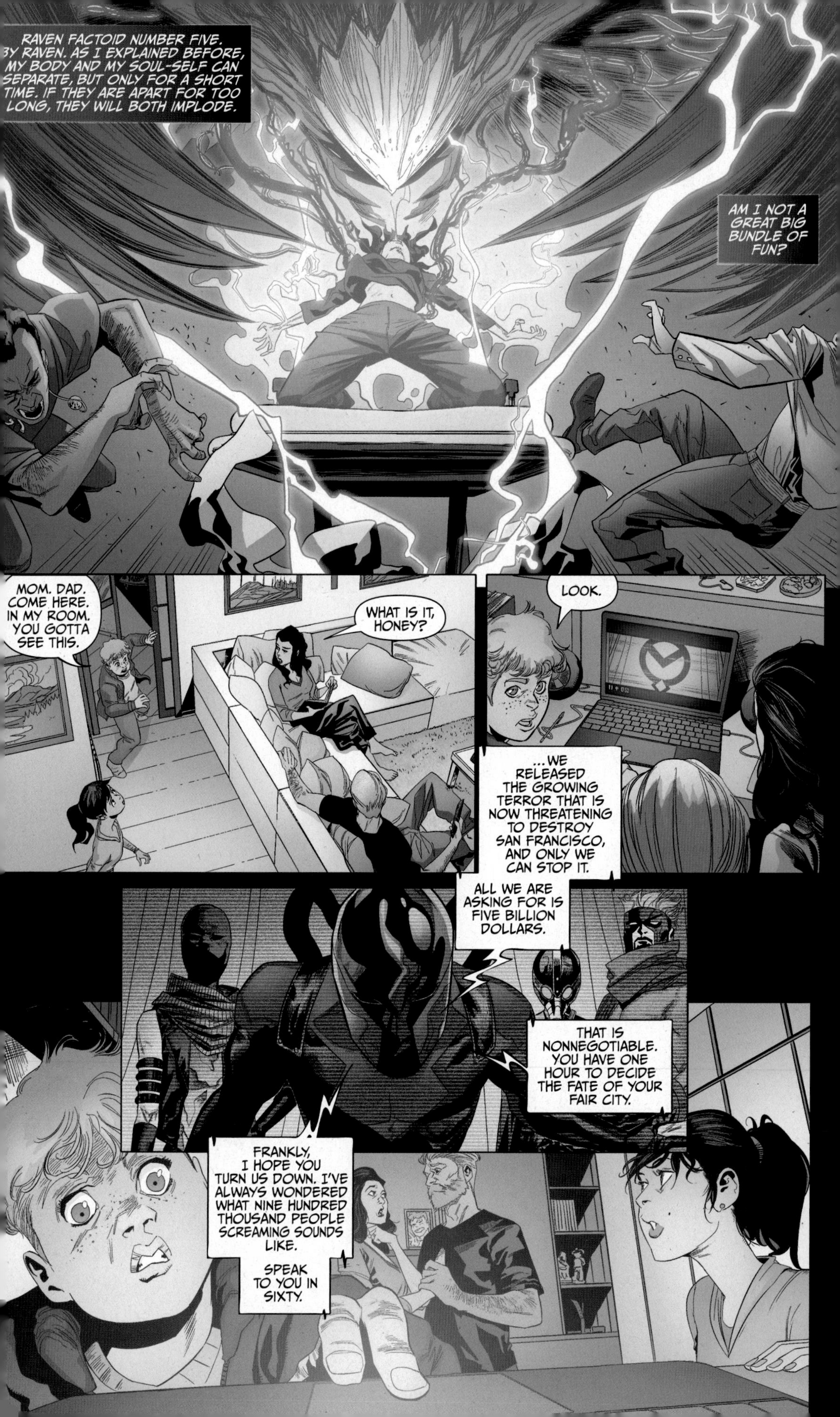
RAVEN FACTOID NUMBER FIVE. BY RAVEN. AS I EXPLAINED BEFORE, MY BODY AND MY SOUL-SELF CAN SEPARATE, BUT ONLY FOR A SHORT TIME. IF THEY ARE APART FOR TOO LONG, THEY WILL BOTH IMPLODE.
AM I NOT A GREAT BIG BUNDLE OF FUN?
MOM. DAD. COME HERE. IN MY ROOM. YOU GOTTA SEE THIS.
WHAT IS IT, HONEY?
LOOK.
...WE RELEASED THE GROWING TERROR THAT IS NOW THREATENING TO DESTROY SAN FRANCISCO, AND ONLY WE CAN STOP IT.
ALL WE ARE ASKING FOR IS FIVE BILLION DOLLARS.
THAT IS NONNEGOTIABLE. YOU HAVE ONE HOUR TO DECIDE THE FATE OF YOUR FAIR CITY.
FRANKLY, I HOPE YOU TURN US DOWN. I'VE ALWAYS WONDERED WHAT NINE HUNDRED THOUSAND PEOPLE SCREAMING SOUNDS LIKE.
SPEAK TO YOU IN SIXTY.

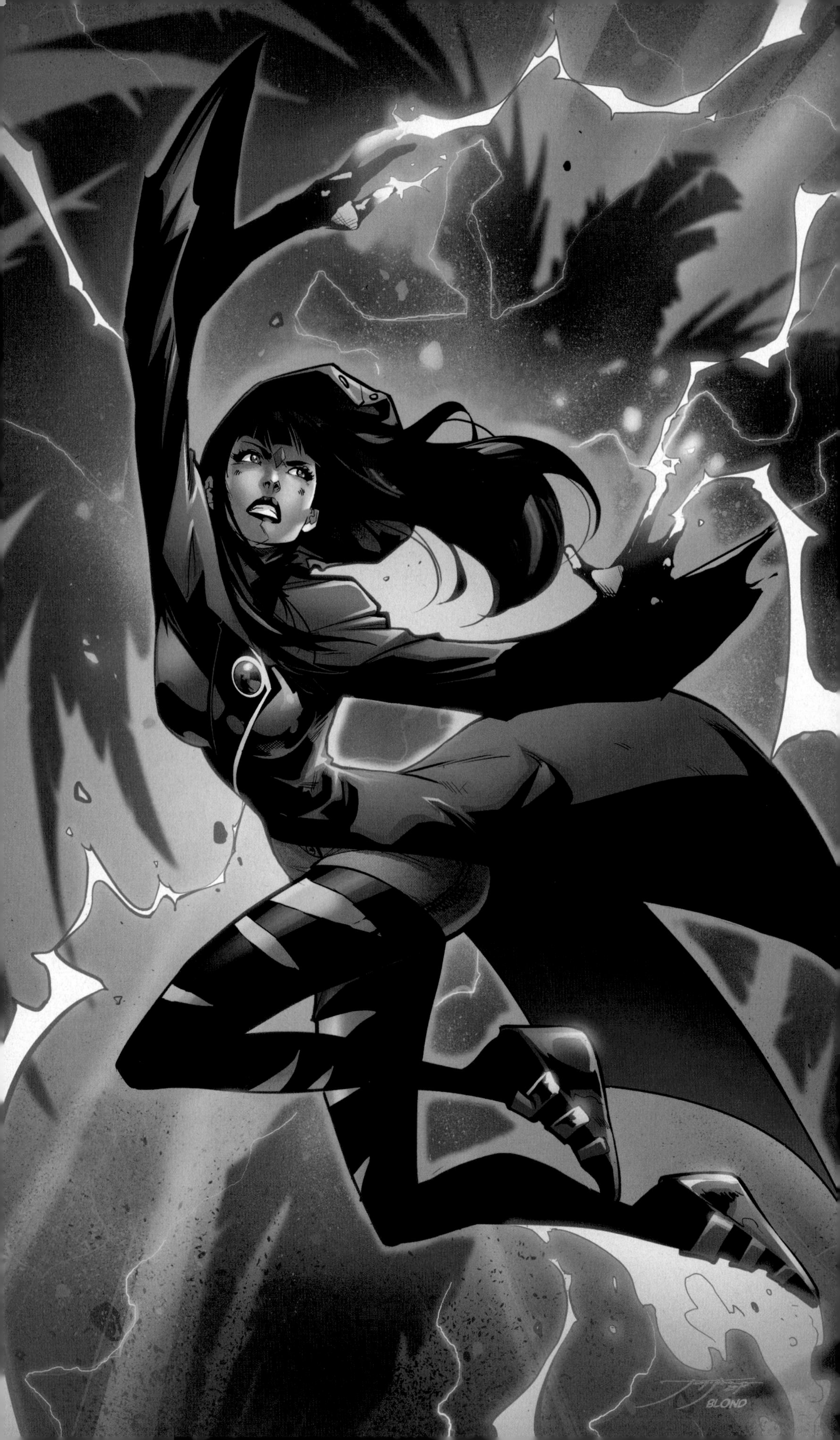
BLOND

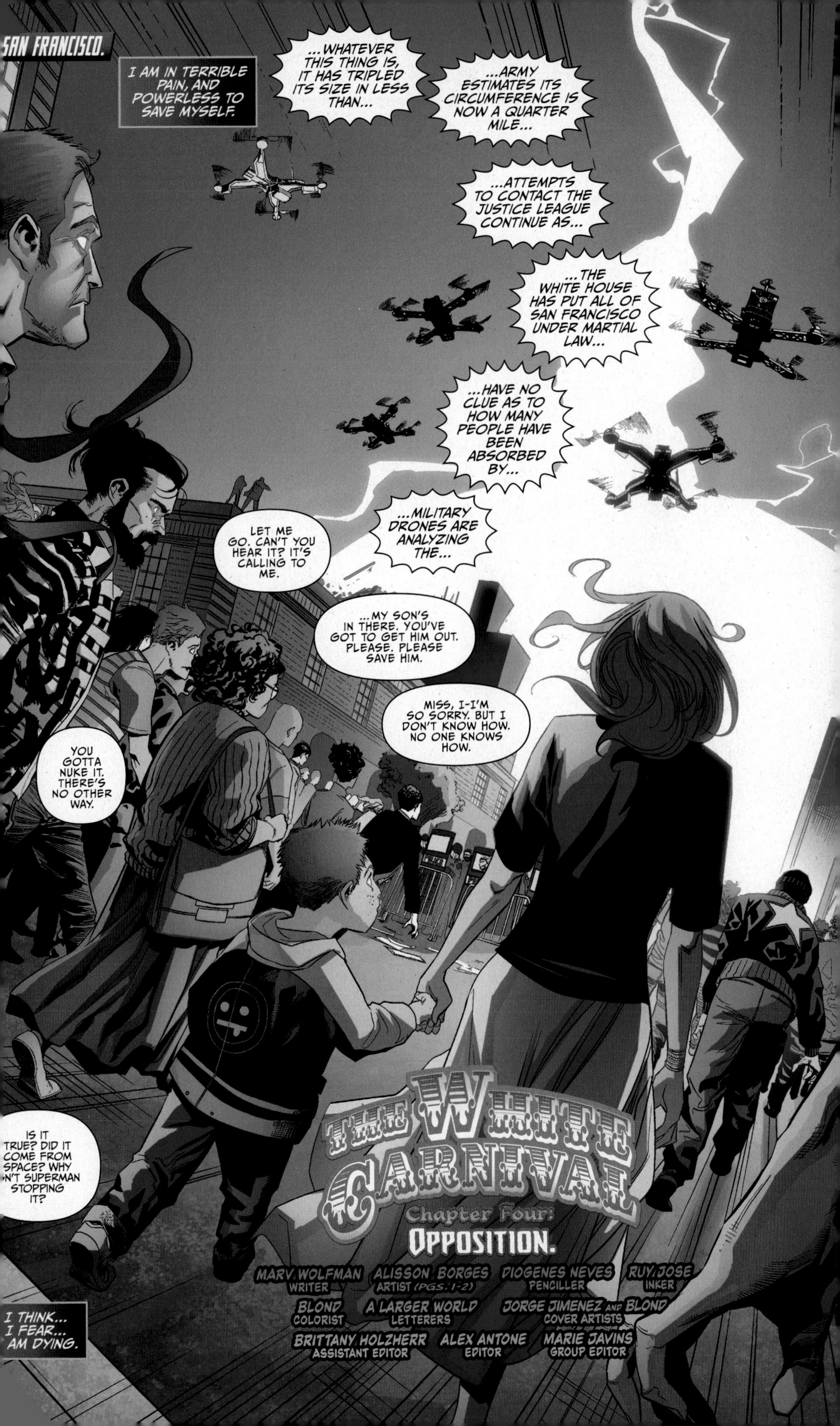
SAN FRANCISCO.
I AM IN TERRIBLE PAIN, AND POWERLESS TO SAVE MYSELF.
...WHATEVER THIS THING IS, IT HAS TRIPLED ITS SIZE IN LESS THAN...
...ARMY ESTIMATES ITS CIRCUMFERENCE IS NOW A QUARTER MILE...
...ATTEMPTS TO CONTACT THE JUSTICE LEAGUE CONTINUE AS...
...THE WHITE HOUSE HAS PUT ALL OF SAN FRANCISCO UNDER MARTIAL LAW...
...HAVE NO CLUE AS TO HOW MANY PEOPLE HAVE BEEN ABSORBED BY...
...MILITARY DRONES ARE ANALYZING THE...
LET ME GO. CAN'T YOU HEAR IT? IT'S CALLING TO ME.
...MY SON'S IN THERE. YOU'VE GOT TO GET HIM OUT. PLEASE. PLEASE SAVE HIM.
MISS, I-I'M SO SORRY. BUT I DON'T KNOW HOW. NO ONE KNOWS HOW.
YOU GOTTA NUKE IT. THERE'S NO OTHER WAY.
IS IT TRUE? DID IT COME FROM SPACE? WHY 'N'T SUPERMAN STOPPING IT?
THE WHITE CARNIVAL
Chapter Four:
OPPOSITION.
MARV WOLFMAN WRITER
ALISSON BORGES ARTIST (PGS. 1-2)
DIOGENES NEVES PENCILLER
RUY JOSE INKER
BLOND COLORIST
A LARGER WORLD LETTERERS
JORGE JIMENEZ AND BLOND COVER ARTISTS
BRITTANY HOLZHERR ASSISTANT EDITOR
ALEX ANTONE EDITOR
MARIE JAVINS GROUP EDITOR
I THINK... I FEAR... AM DYING.

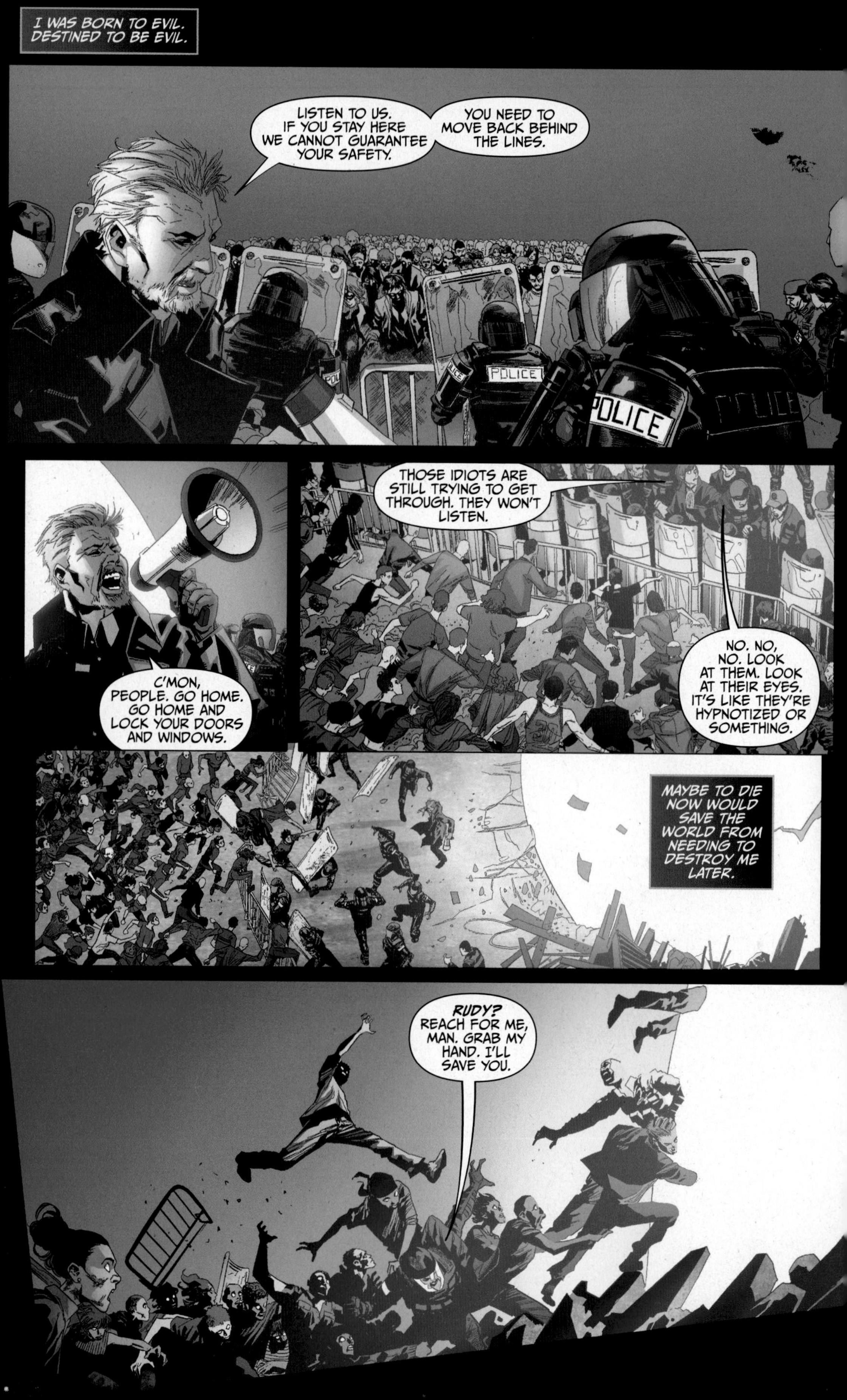
I WAS BORN TO EVIL. DESTINED TO BE EVIL.
LISTEN TO US. IF YOU STAY HERE WE CANNOT GUARANTEE YOUR SAFETY.
YOU NEED TO MOVE BACK BEHIND THE LINES.
POLICE
POLICE
POLICE
C'MON, PEOPLE. GO HOME. GO HOME AND LOCK YOUR DOORS AND WINDOWS.
THOSE IDIOTS ARE STILL TRYING TO GET THROUGH. THEY WON'T LISTEN.
NO. NO, NO. LOOK AT THEM. LOOK AT THEIR EYES. IT'S LIKE THEY'RE HYPNOTIZED OR SOMETHING.
MAYBE TO DIE NOW WOULD SAVE THE WORLD FROM NEEDING TO DESTROY ME LATER.
RUDY? REACH FOR ME, MAN. GRAB MY HAND. I'LL SAVE YOU.

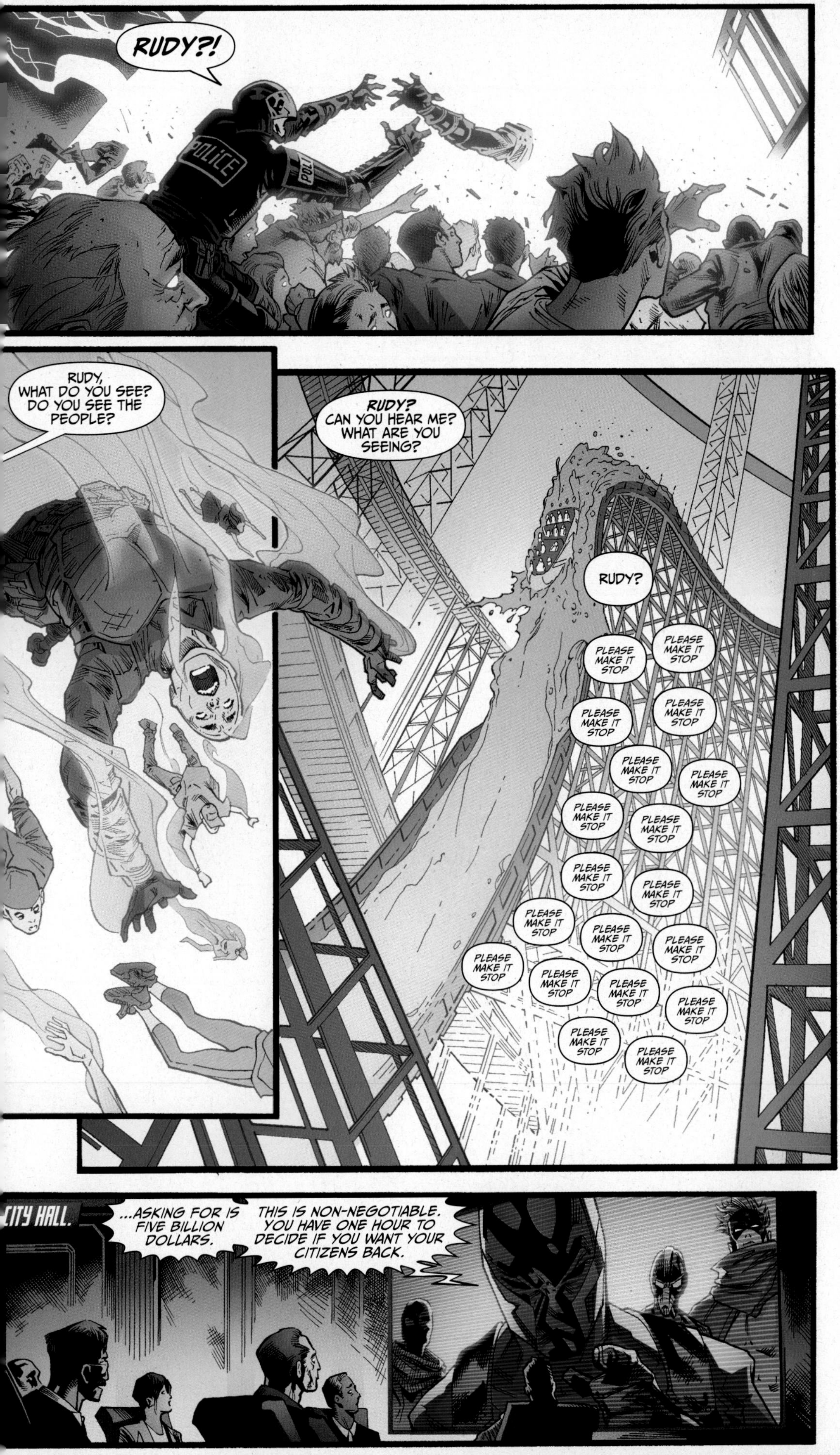
RUDY?!
RUDY, WHAT DO YOU SEE? DO YOU SEE THE PEOPLE?
RUDY? CAN YOU HEAR ME? WHAT ARE YOU SEEING?
RUDY?
PLEASE MAKE IT STOP
PLEASE MAKE IT STOP
PLEASE MAKE IT STOP
PLEASE MAKE IT STOP
PLEASE MAKE IT STOP
PLEASE MAKE IT STOP
PLEASE MAKE IT STOP
PLEASE MAKE IT STOP
PLEASE MAKE IT STOP
PLEASE MAKE IT STOP
PLEASE MAKE IT STOP
PLEASE MAKE IT STOP
PLEASE MAKE IT STOP
PLEASE MAKE IT STOP
PLEASE MAKE IT STOP
PLEASE MAKE IT STOP
PLEASE MAKE IT STOP
PLEASE MAKE IT STOP
PLEASE MAKE IT STOP
CITY HALL.
...ASKING FOR IS FIVE BILLION DOLLARS.
THIS IS NON-NEGOTIABLE. YOU HAVE ONE HOUR TO DECIDE IF YOU WANT YOUR CITIZENS BACK.

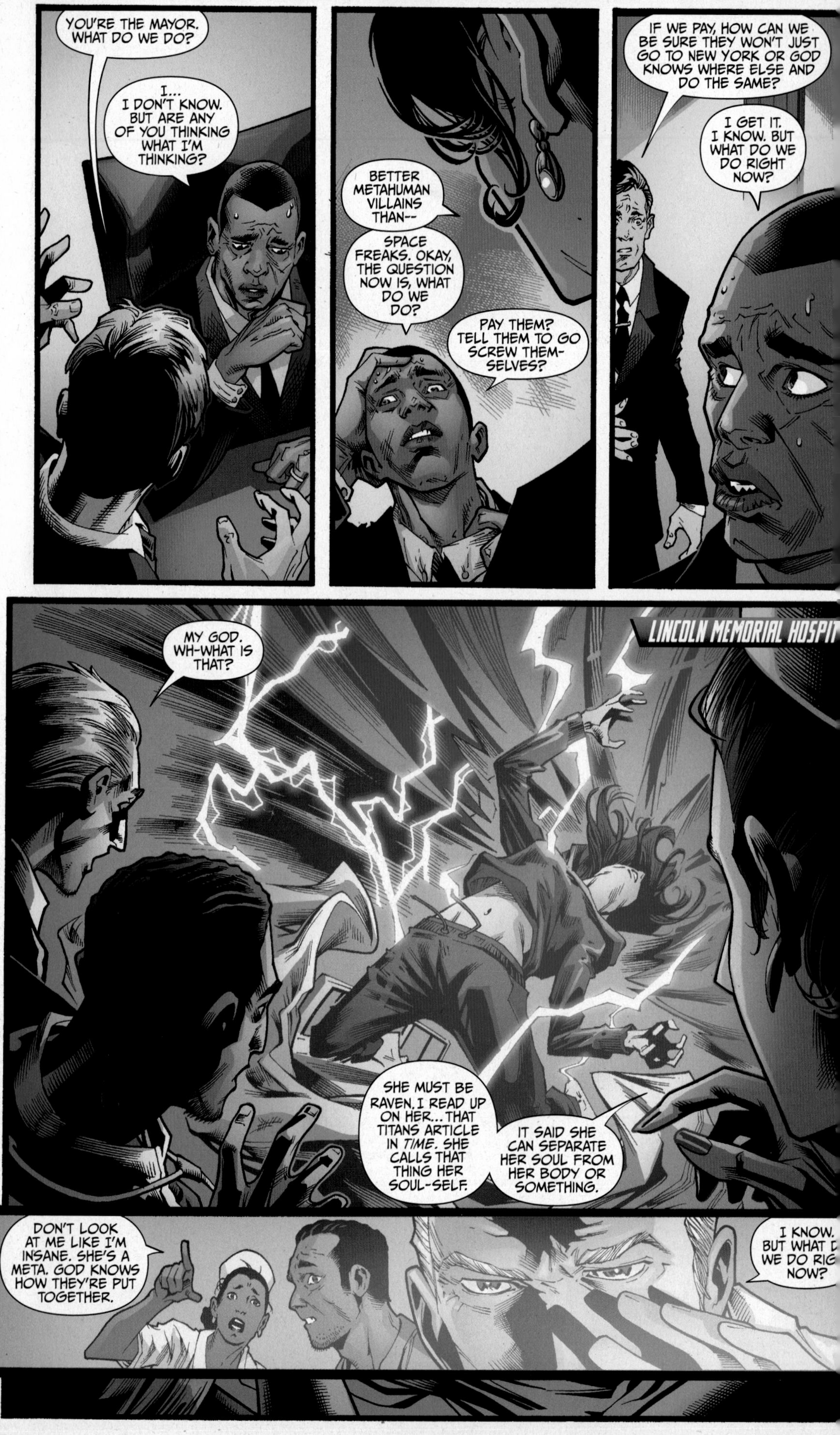
YOU'RE THE MAYOR. WHAT DO WE DO?
I... I DON'T KNOW. BUT ARE ANY OF YOU THINKING WHAT I'M THINKING?
BETTER METAHUMAN VILLAINS THAN--
SPACE FREAKS. OKAY, THE QUESTION NOW IS, WHAT DO WE DO?
PAY THEM? TELL THEM TO GO SCREW THEM-SELVES?
IF WE PAY, HOW CAN WE BE SURE THEY WON'T JUST GO TO NEW YORK OR GOD KNOWS WHERE ELSE AND DO THE SAME?
I GET IT. I KNOW. BUT WHAT DO WE DO RIGHT NOW?
LINCOLN MEMORIAL HOSPIT
MY GOD. WH-WHAT IS THAT?
SHE MUST BE RAVEN. I READ UP ON HER... THAT TITANS ARTICLE IN *TIME*. SHE CALLS THAT THING HER SOUL-SELF.
IT SAID SHE CAN SEPARATE HER SOUL FROM HER BODY OR SOMETHING.
DON'T LOOK AT ME LIKE I'M INSANE. SHE'S A META. GOD KNOWS HOW THEY'RE PUT TOGETHER.
I KNOW. BUT WHAT D WE DO RIG NOW?

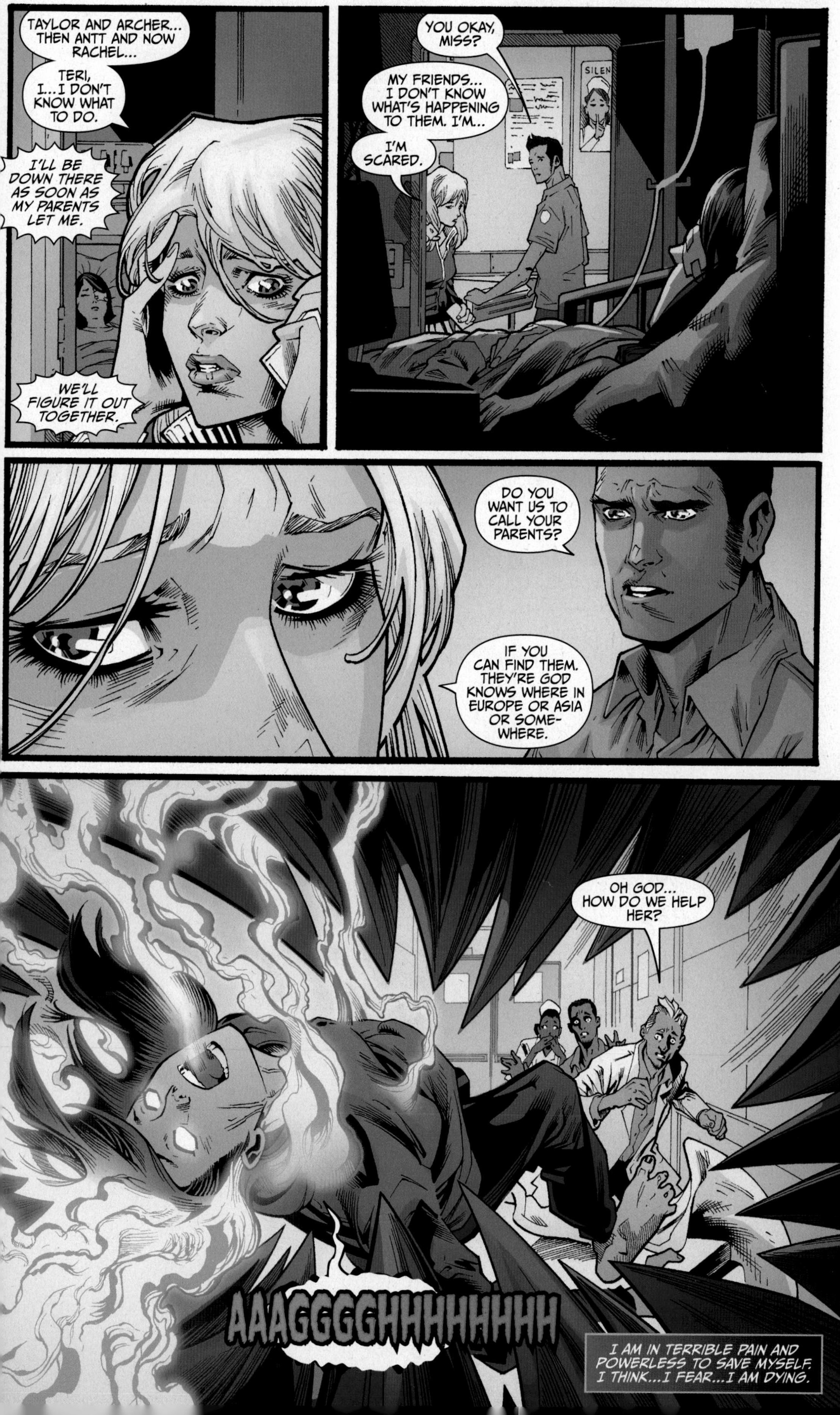
TAYLOR AND ARCHER... THEN ANTT AND NOW RACHEL...
TERI, I...I DON'T KNOW WHAT TO DO.
I'LL BE DOWN THERE AS SOON AS MY PARENTS LET ME.
WE'LL FIGURE IT OUT TOGETHER.
YOU OKAY, MISS?
MY FRIENDS... I DON'T KNOW WHAT'S HAPPENING TO THEM. I'M...
I'M SCARED.
SILEN
DO YOU WANT US TO CALL YOUR PARENTS?
IF YOU CAN FIND THEM. THEY'RE GOD KNOWS WHERE IN EUROPE OR ASIA OR SOME-WHERE.
OH GOD... HOW DO WE HELP HER?
AAAGGGGHHHHHHH
I AM IN TERRIBLE PAIN AND POWERLESS TO SAVE MYSELF. I THINK...I FEAR...I AM DYING.

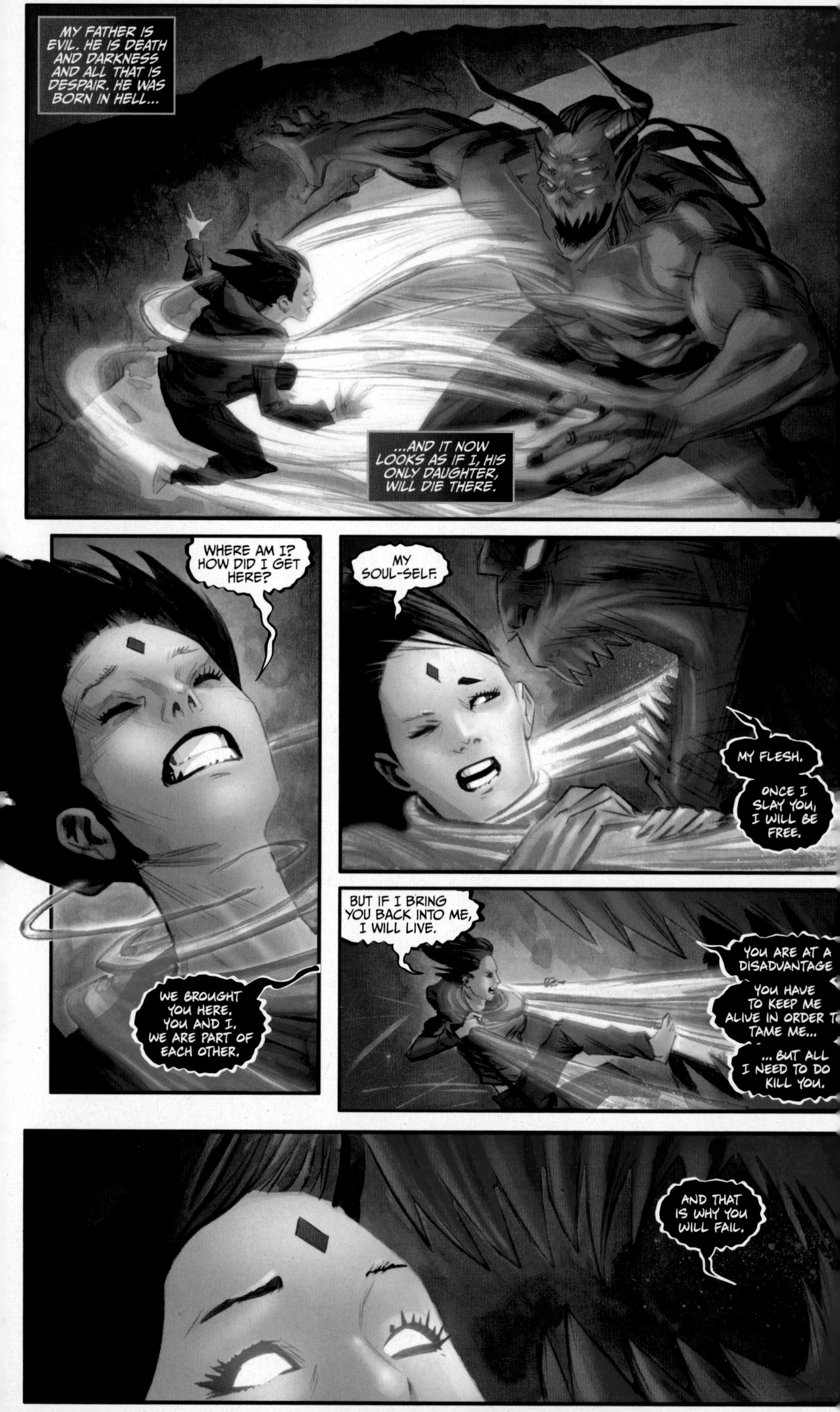

MY FATHER IS EVIL. HE IS DEATH AND DARKNESS AND ALL THAT IS DESPAIR. HE WAS BORN IN HELL...
...AND IT NOW LOOKS AS IF I, HIS ONLY DAUGHTER, WILL DIE THERE.
WHERE AM I? HOW DID I GET HERE?
WE BROUGHT YOU HERE. YOU AND I. WE ARE PART OF EACH OTHER.
MY SOUL-SELF.
MY FLESH.
ONCE I SLAY YOU, I WILL BE FREE.
BUT IF I BRING YOU BACK INTO ME, I WILL LIVE.
YOU ARE AT A DISADVANTAGE
YOU HAVE TO KEEP ME ALIVE IN ORDER TO TAME ME...
...BUT ALL I NEED TO DO KILL YOU.
AND THAT IS WHY YOU WILL FAIL.

RACHEL. YOU HAVE TO FIGHT IT.

ANTT?

NO. SHE IS NOT MY CLASSMATE. SHE IS A MANIFESTATION FORMED FROM MY MEMORIES. BUT WHY HER?

I FEEL HOW GOOD YOU ARE. HOW STRONG YOU ARE. R, YOU WANT TO SAVE EVERYONE AND I KNOW YOU CAN.

BUT YOU HAVE TO FIGHT YOUR DARKNESS.

ANTT IS ALWAYS POSITIVE. SHE SEES ONLY THE GOOD. I KNOW I NEED TO THINK LIKE SHE DOES. I NEED TO BELIEVE. IN MYSELF. BUT I CANNOT.

SURE YOU CAN, R. YOU CAN DO ANYTHING 'CAUSE YOU'RE THE BEST.

BUT YOU HAVE TO DO IT FAST. THE DOCTORS WANT TO OPERATE ON YOU. AND IF THEY DO WHILE RAVEN'S BIG-BAD IS STILL OUT THERE...

...YOU, RAVEN, THE LITTLE BUT GOOD, WILL LOSE THE REAL WAR. SO YOU GOTTA FIGHT BACK.

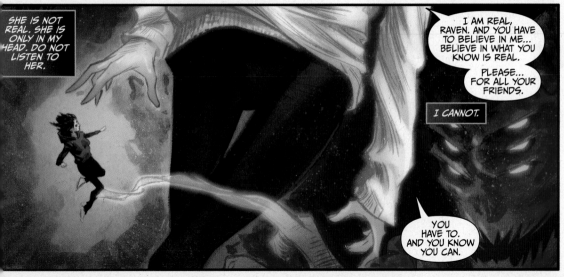

SHE IS NOT REAL. SHE IS ONLY IN MY HEAD. DO NOT LISTEN TO HER.

I AM REAL, RAVEN. AND YOU HAVE TO BELIEVE IN ME... BELIEVE IN WHAT YOU KNOW IS REAL.

PLEASE... FOR ALL YOUR FRIENDS.

I CANNOT.

YOU HAVE TO. AND YOU KNOW YOU CAN.

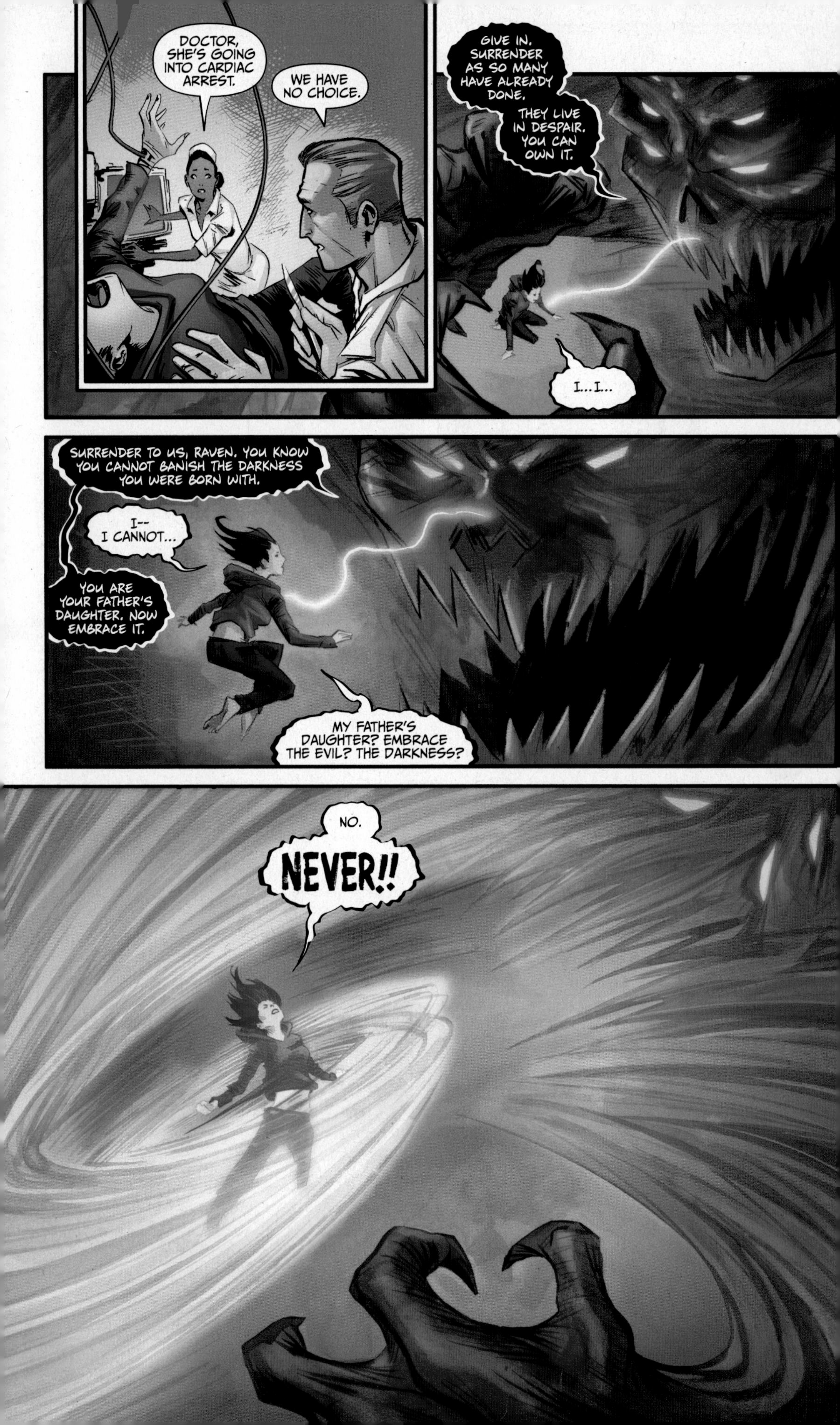
DOCTOR, SHE'S GOING INTO CARDIAC ARREST.
WE HAVE NO CHOICE.
GIVE IN. SURRENDER AS SO MANY HAVE ALREADY DONE.
THEY LIVE IN DESPAIR. YOU CAN OWN IT.
I... I...
SURRENDER TO US, RAVEN. YOU KNOW YOU CANNOT BANISH THE DARKNESS YOU WERE BORN WITH.
I-- I CANNOT...
YOU ARE YOUR FATHER'S DAUGHTER. NOW EMBRACE IT.
MY FATHER'S DAUGHTER? EMBRACE THE EVIL? THE DARKNESS?
NO.
NEVER!!

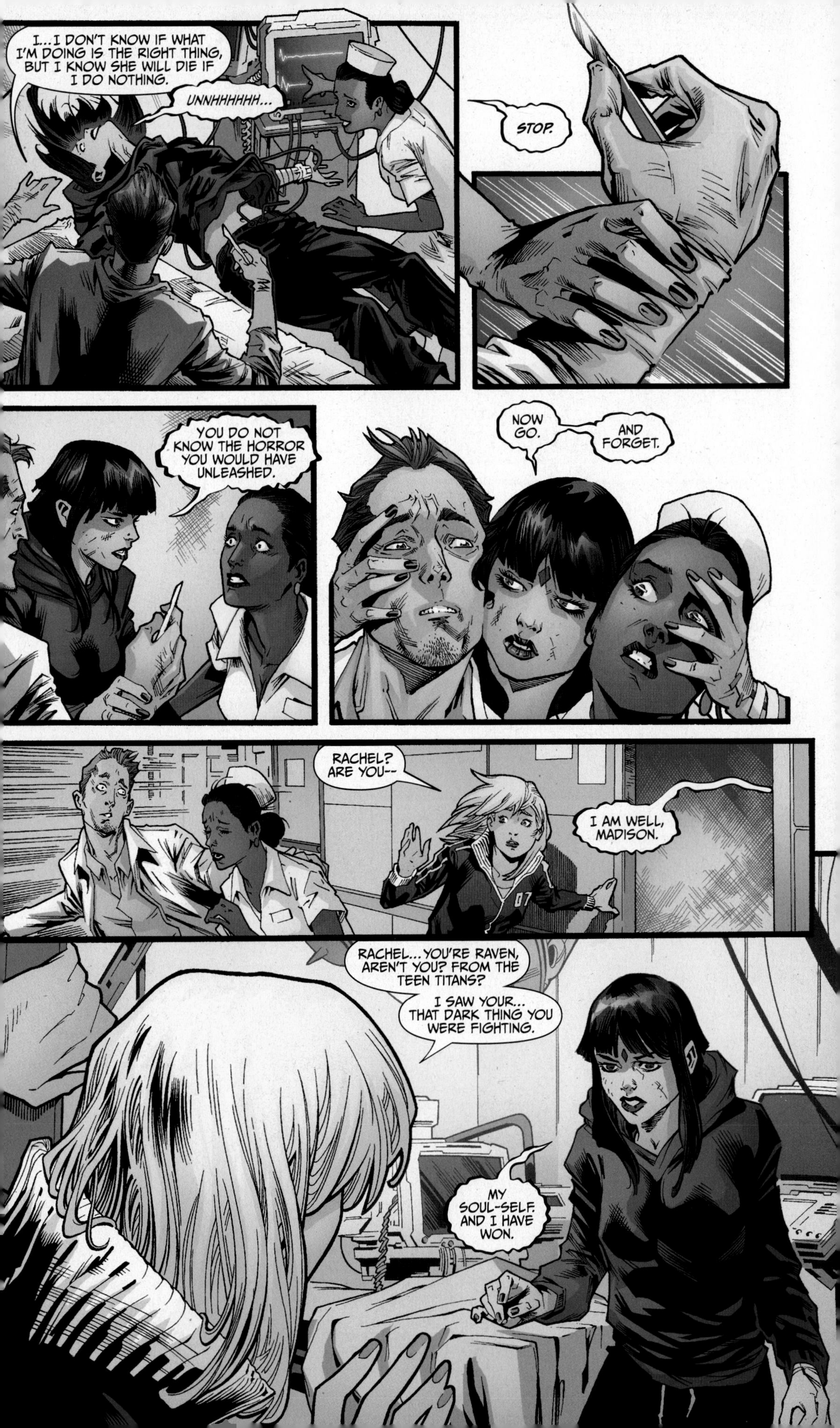
I...I DON'T KNOW IF WHAT I'M DOING IS THE RIGHT THING, BUT I KNOW SHE WILL DIE IF I DO NOTHING.
UNNHHHHHH...
STOP.
YOU DO NOT KNOW THE HORROR YOU WOULD HAVE UNLEASHED.
NOW GO.
AND FORGET.
RACHEL? ARE YOU--
I AM WELL, MADISON.
RACHEL...YOU'RE RAVEN, AREN'T YOU? FROM THE TEEN TITANS?
I SAW YOUR... THAT DARK THING YOU WERE FIGHTING.
MY SOUL-SELF. AND I HAVE WON.

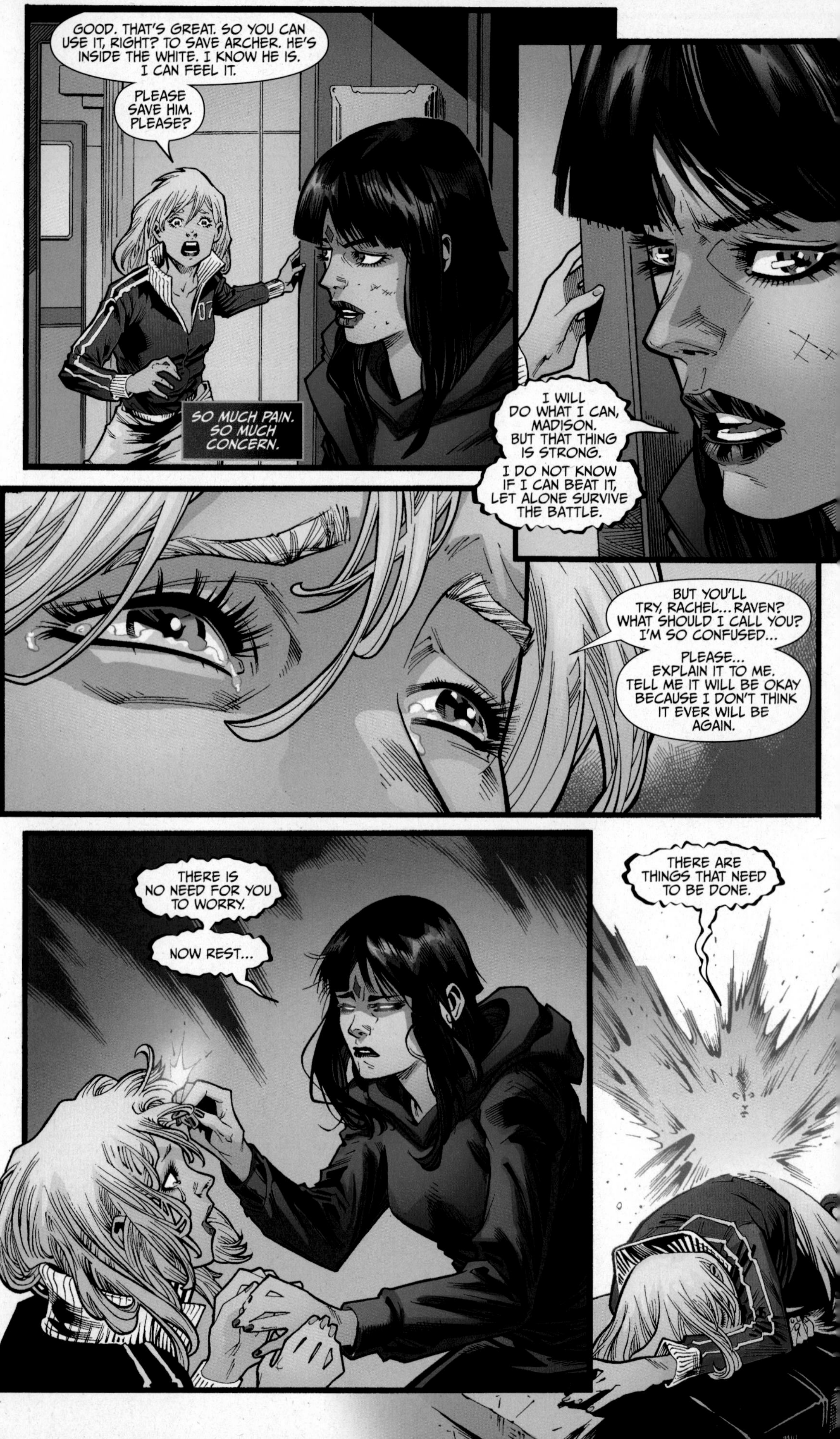
GOOD. THAT'S GREAT. SO YOU CAN USE IT, RIGHT? TO SAVE ARCHER. HE'S INSIDE THE WHITE. I KNOW HE IS. I CAN FEEL IT.
PLEASE SAVE HIM. PLEASE?
SO MUCH PAIN. SO MUCH CONCERN.
I WILL DO WHAT I CAN, MADISON. BUT THAT THING IS STRONG.
I DO NOT KNOW IF I CAN BEAT IT, LET ALONE SURVIVE THE BATTLE.
BUT YOU'LL TRY, RACHEL... RAVEN? WHAT SHOULD I CALL YOU? I'M SO CONFUSED...
PLEASE... EXPLAIN IT TO ME. TELL ME IT WILL BE OKAY BECAUSE I DON'T THINK IT EVER WILL BE AGAIN.
THERE IS NO NEED FOR YOU TO WORRY.
NOW REST...
THERE ARE THINGS THAT NEED TO BE DONE.

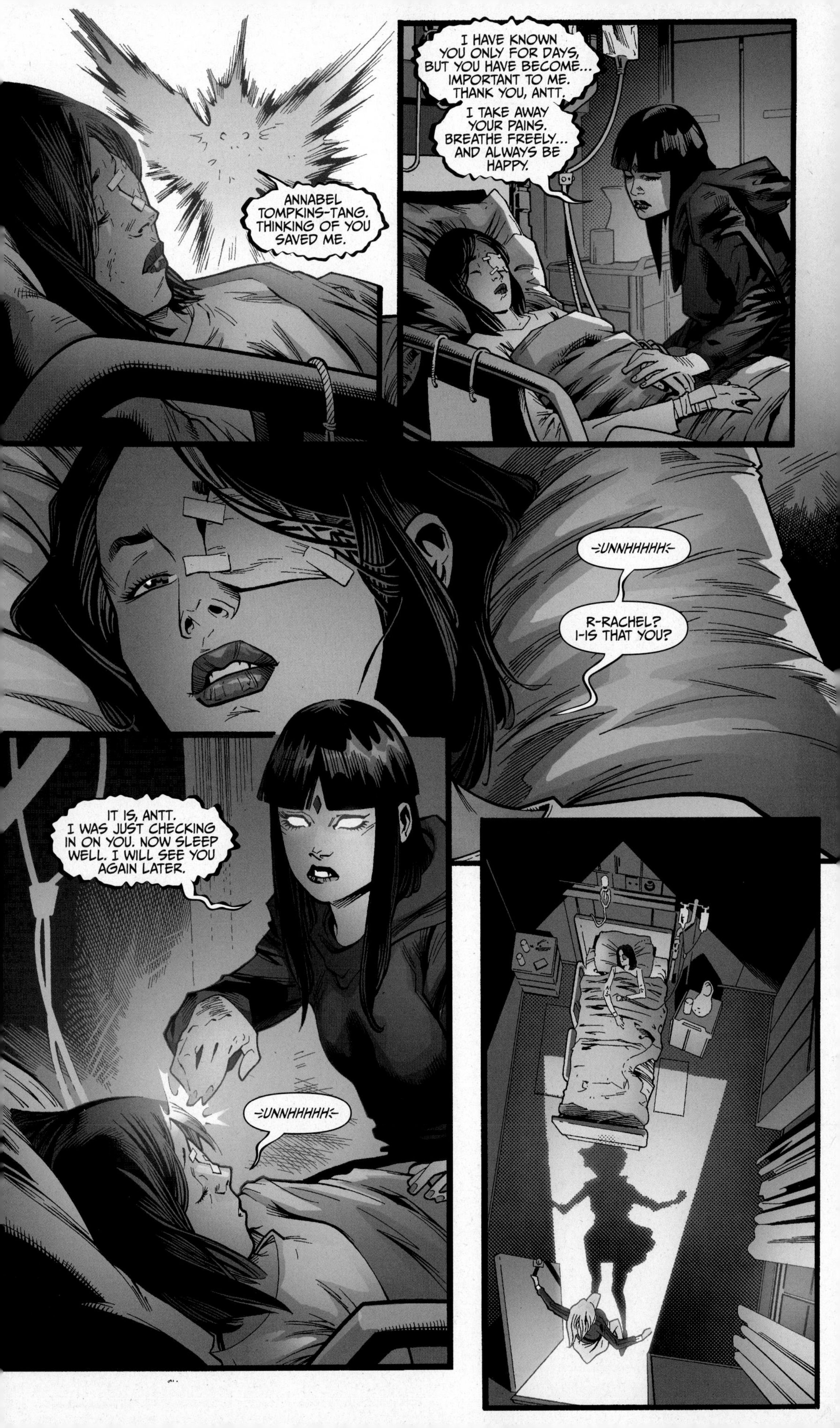
ANNABEL TOMPKINS-TANG. THINKING OF YOU SAVED ME.
I HAVE KNOWN YOU ONLY FOR DAYS, BUT YOU HAVE BECOME... IMPORTANT TO ME. THANK YOU, ANTT.
I TAKE AWAY YOUR PAINS. BREATHE FREELY... AND ALWAYS BE HAPPY.
UNNHHHHH
R-RACHEL? I-IS THAT YOU?
IT IS, ANTT. I WAS JUST CHECKING IN ON YOU. NOW SLEEP WELL. I WILL SEE YOU AGAIN LATER.
UNNHHHHH

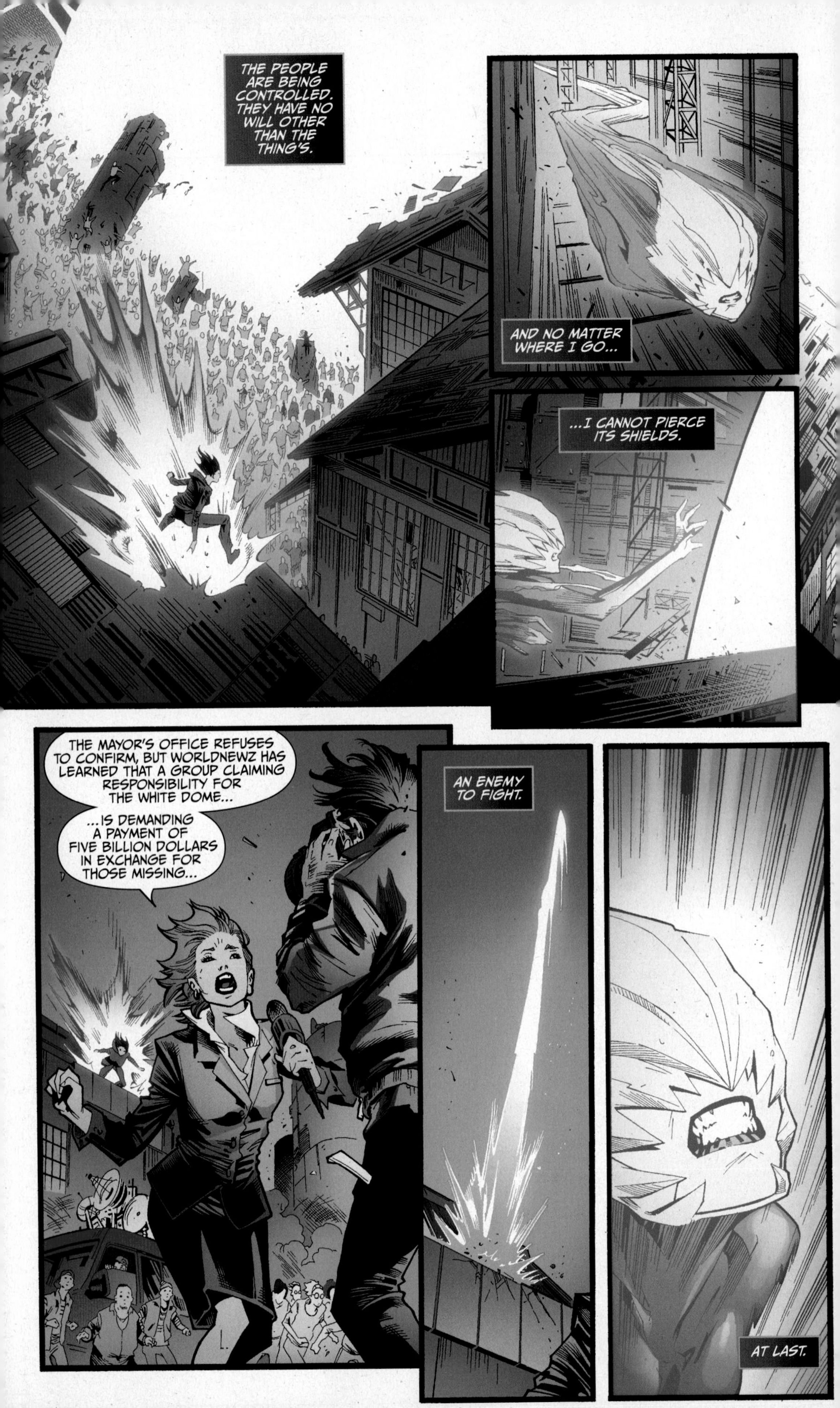

THE PEOPLE ARE BEING CONTROLLED. THEY HAVE NO WILL OTHER THAN THE THING'S.
AND NO MATTER WHERE I GO...
...I CANNOT PIERCE ITS SHIELDS.
THE MAYOR'S OFFICE REFUSES TO CONFIRM, BUT WORLDNEWZ HAS LEARNED THAT A GROUP CLAIMING RESPONSIBILITY FOR THE WHITE DOME...
...IS DEMANDING A PAYMENT OF FIVE BILLION DOLLARS IN EXCHANGE FOR THOSE MISSING...
AN ENEMY TO FIGHT.
AT LAST.

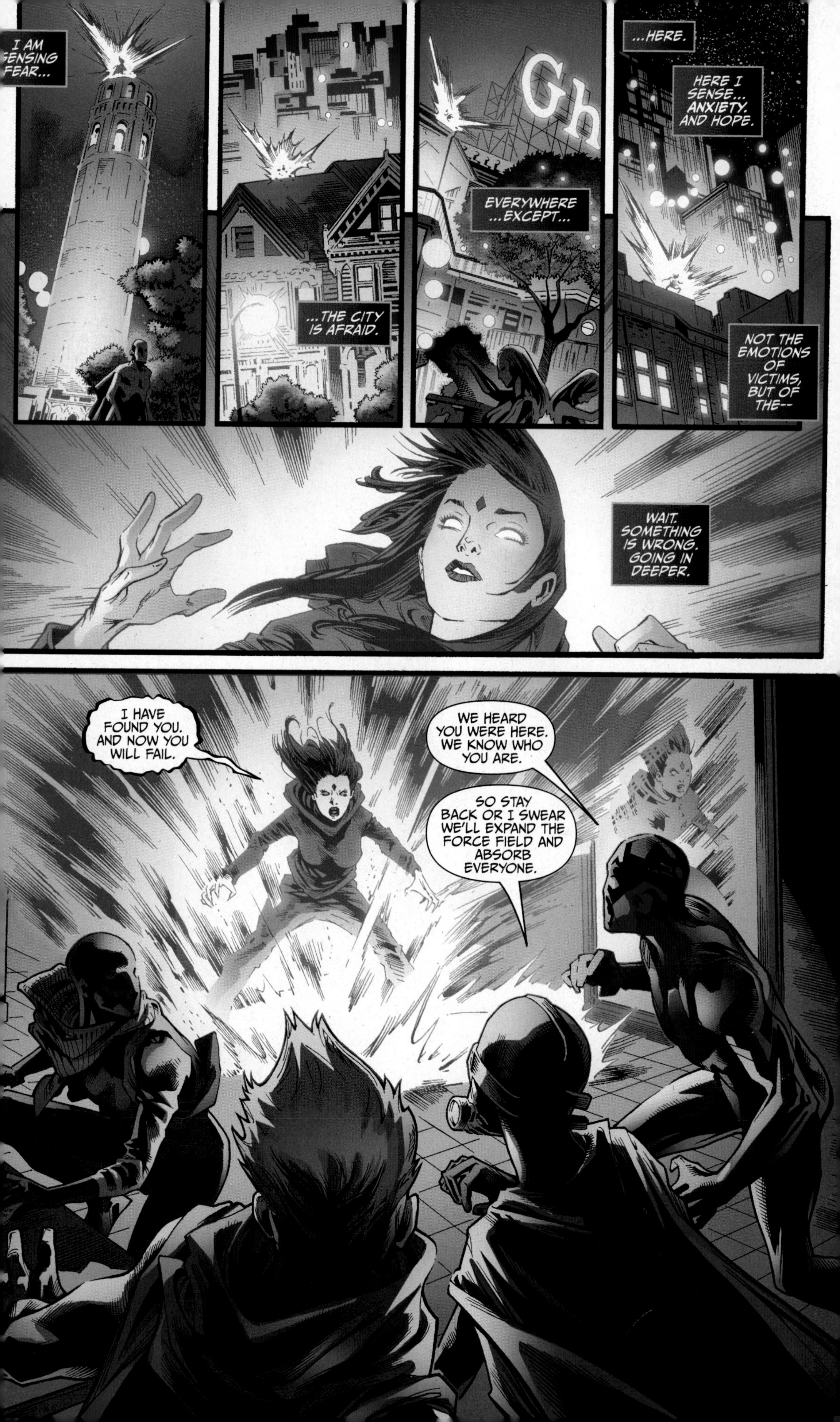
I AM SENSING FEAR...
...THE CITY IS AFRAID.
EVERYWHERE ...EXCEPT...
...HERE.
HERE I SENSE... ANXIETY. AND HOPE.
NOT THE EMOTIONS OF VICTIMS, BUT OF THE--
WAIT. SOMETHING IS WRONG. GOING IN DEEPER.
I HAVE FOUND YOU. AND NOW YOU WILL FAIL.
WE HEARD YOU WERE HERE. WE KNOW WHO YOU ARE.
SO STAY BACK OR I SWEAR WE'LL EXPAND THE FORCE FIELD AND ABSORB EVERYONE.

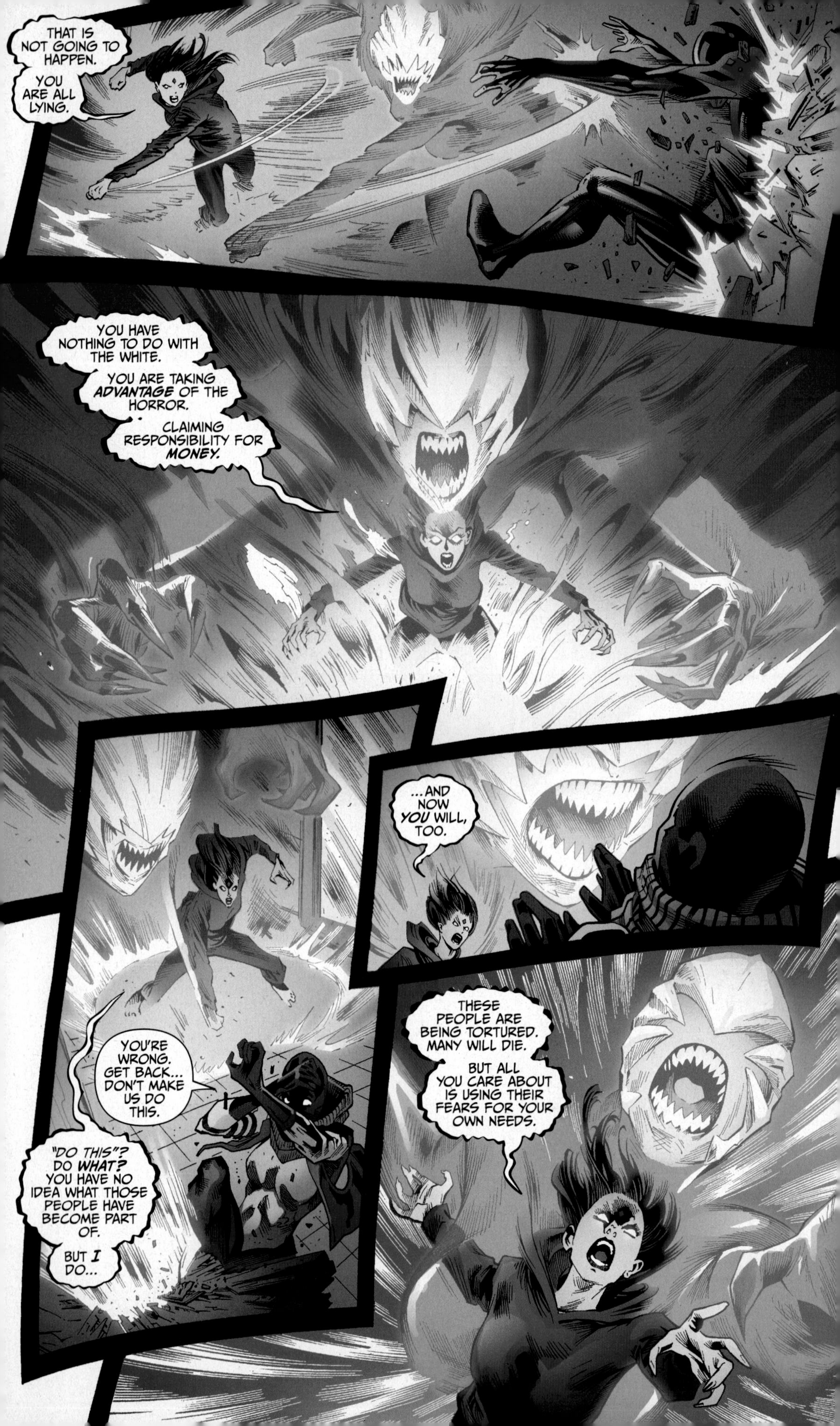
THAT IS NOT GOING TO HAPPEN.
YOU ARE ALL LYING.
YOU HAVE NOTHING TO DO WITH THE WHITE.
YOU ARE TAKING ADVANTAGE OF THE HORROR.
CLAIMING RESPONSIBILITY FOR MONEY.
YOU'RE WRONG. GET BACK... DON'T MAKE US DO THIS.
"DO THIS"? DO WHAT? YOU HAVE NO IDEA WHAT THOSE PEOPLE HAVE BECOME PART OF.
BUT I DO...
...AND NOW YOU WILL, TOO.
THESE PEOPLE ARE BEING TORTURED. MANY WILL DIE.
BUT ALL YOU CARE ABOUT IS USING THEIR FEARS FOR YOUR OWN NEEDS.

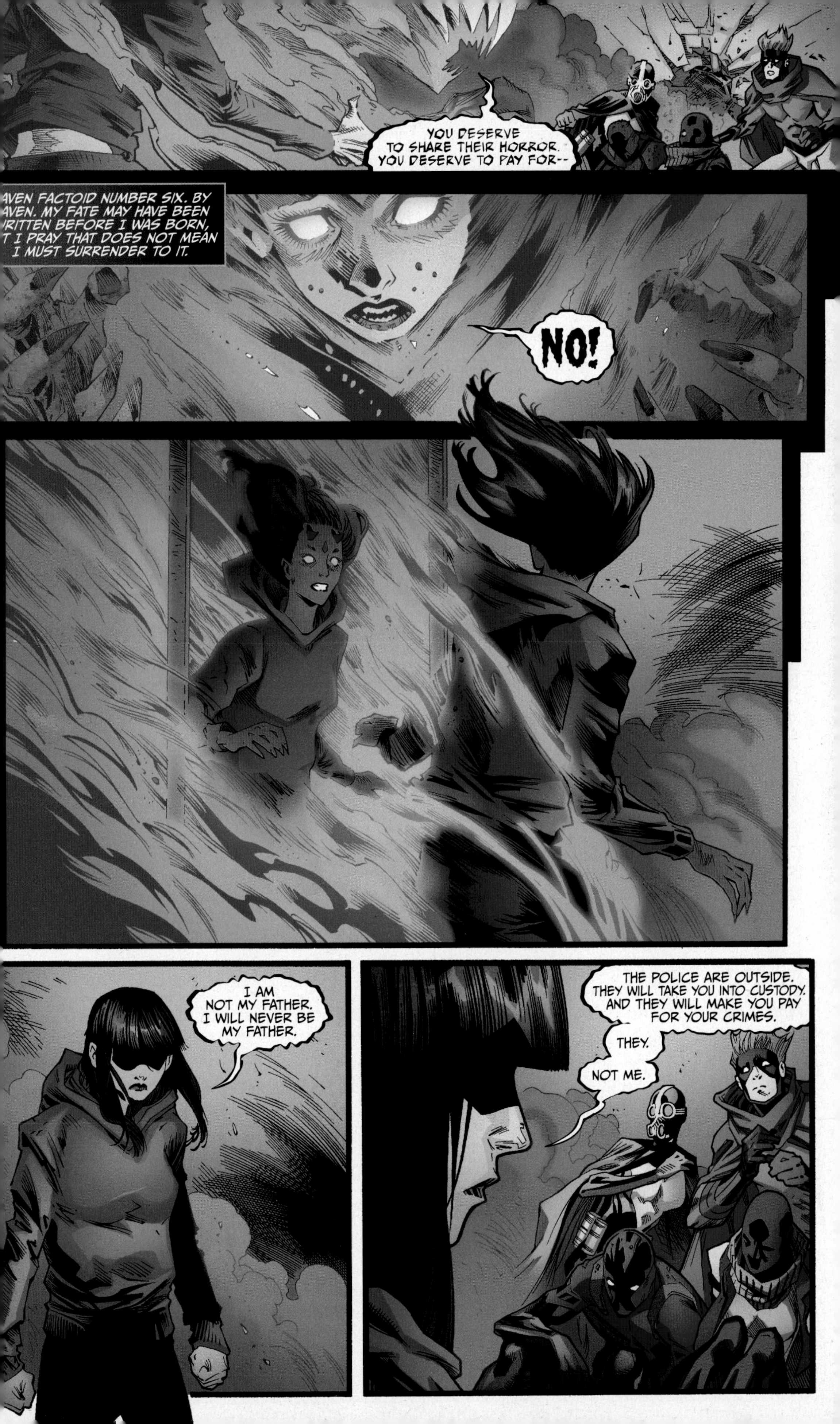
YOU DESERVE TO SHARE THEIR HORROR. YOU DESERVE TO PAY FOR--
AVEN FACTOID NUMBER SIX. BY AVEN. MY FATE MAY HAVE BEEN RITTEN BEFORE I WAS BORN, T I PRAY THAT DOES NOT MEAN I MUST SURRENDER TO IT.
NO!
I AM NOT MY FATHER. I WILL NEVER BE MY FATHER.
THE POLICE ARE OUTSIDE. THEY WILL TAKE YOU INTO CUSTODY. AND THEY WILL MAKE YOU PAY FOR YOUR CRIMES.
THEY.
NOT ME.

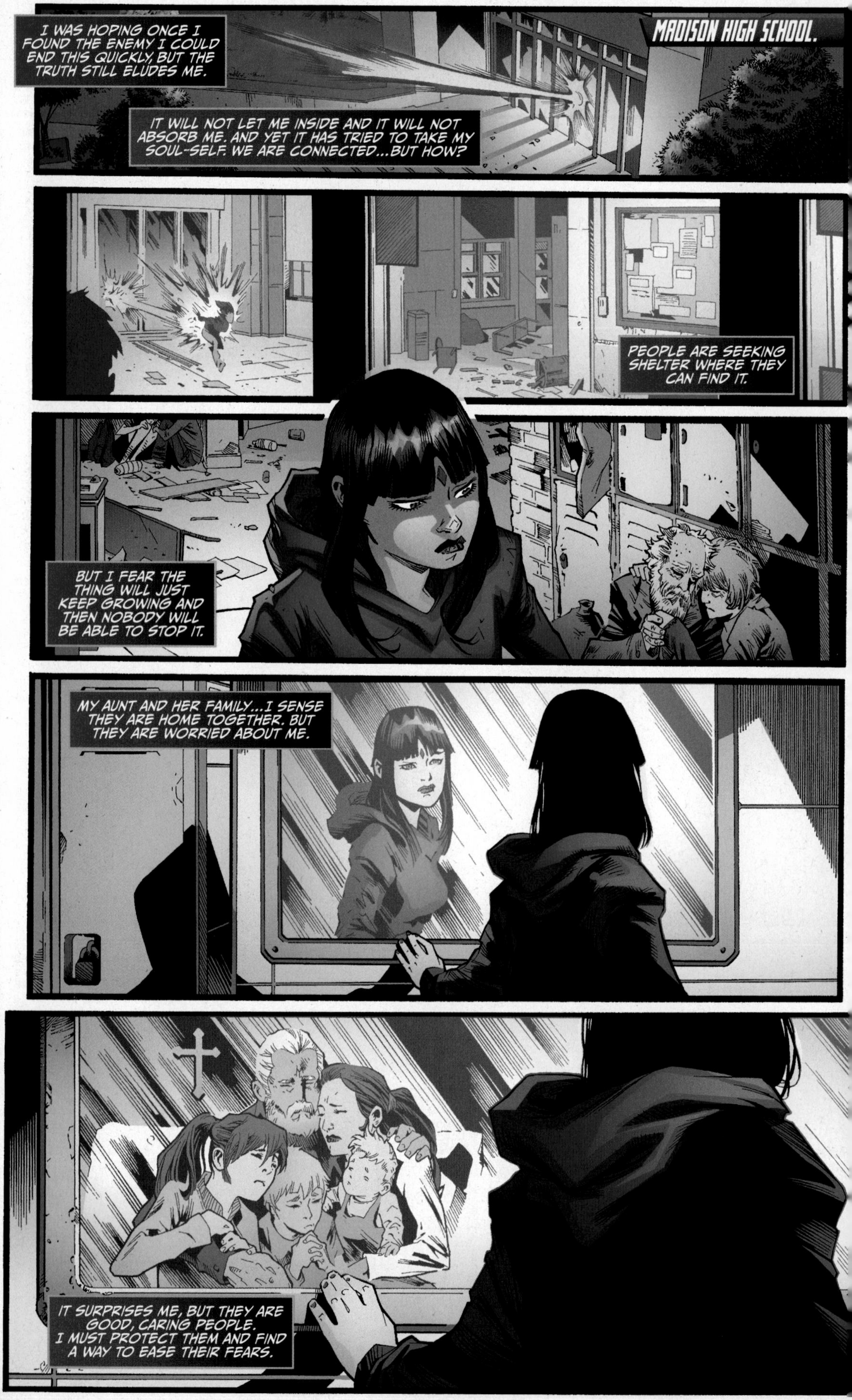
I WAS HOPING ONCE I FOUND THE ENEMY I COULD END THIS QUICKLY, BUT THE TRUTH STILL ELUDES ME.
MADISON HIGH SCHOOL.
IT WILL NOT LET ME INSIDE AND IT WILL NOT ABSORB ME. AND YET IT HAS TRIED TO TAKE MY SOUL-SELF. WE ARE CONNECTED...BUT HOW?
PEOPLE ARE SEEKING SHELTER WHERE THEY CAN FIND IT.
BUT I FEAR THE THING WILL JUST KEEP GROWING AND THEN NOBODY WILL BE ABLE TO STOP IT.
MY AUNT AND HER FAMILY...I SENSE THEY ARE HOME TOGETHER. BUT THEY ARE WORRIED ABOUT ME.
IT SURPRISES ME, BUT THEY ARE GOOD, CARING PEOPLE. I MUST PROTECT THEM AND FIND A WAY TO EASE THEIR FEARS.

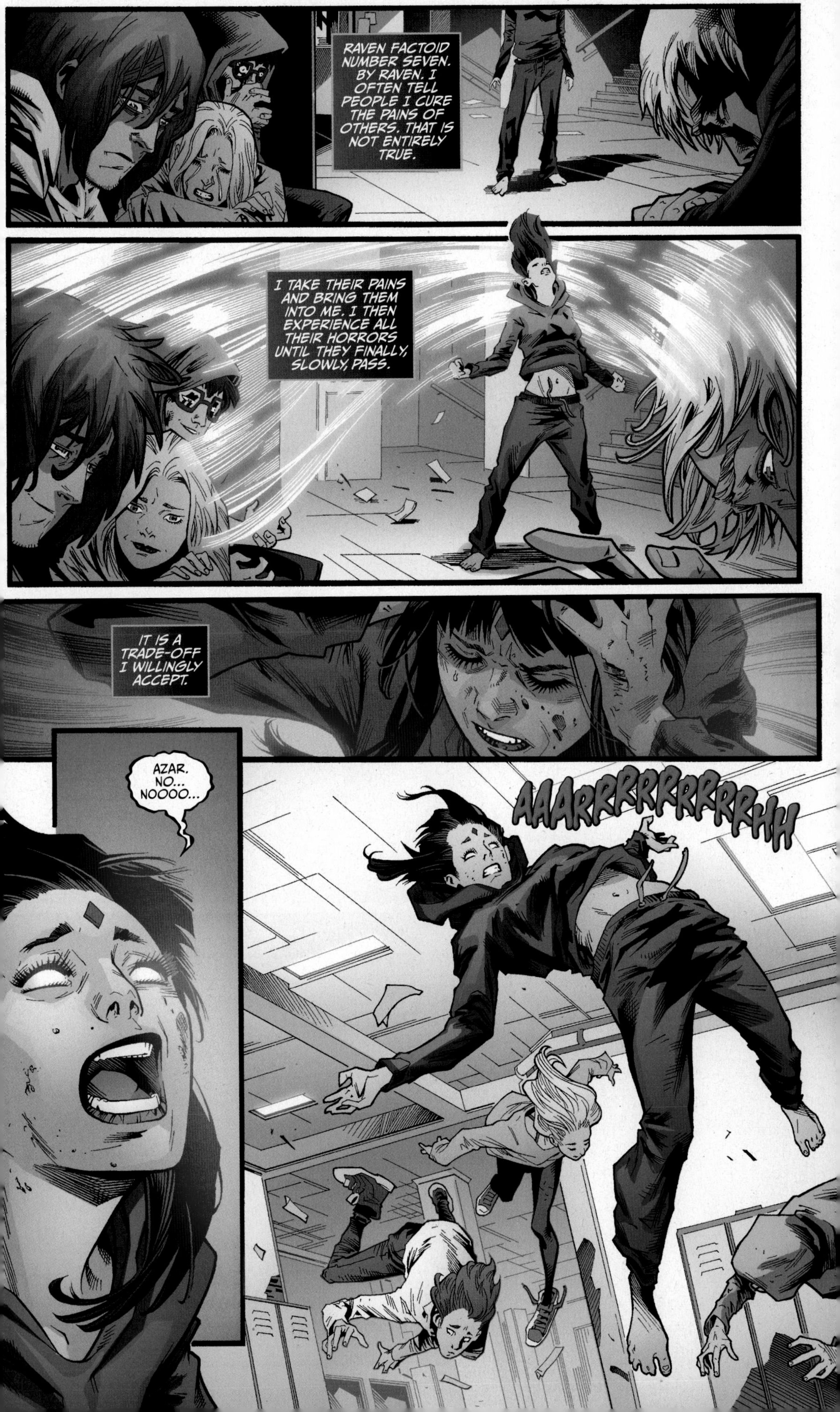

RAVEN FACTOID NUMBER SEVEN. BY RAVEN. I OFTEN TELL PEOPLE I CURE THE PAINS OF OTHERS. THAT IS NOT ENTIRELY TRUE.
I TAKE THEIR PAINS AND BRING THEM INTO ME. I THEN EXPERIENCE ALL THEIR HORRORS UNTIL THEY FINALLY, SLOWLY, PASS.
IT IS A TRADE-OFF I WILLINGLY ACCEPT.
AZAR. NO... NOOOO...
AAARRRRRRRRRRHH

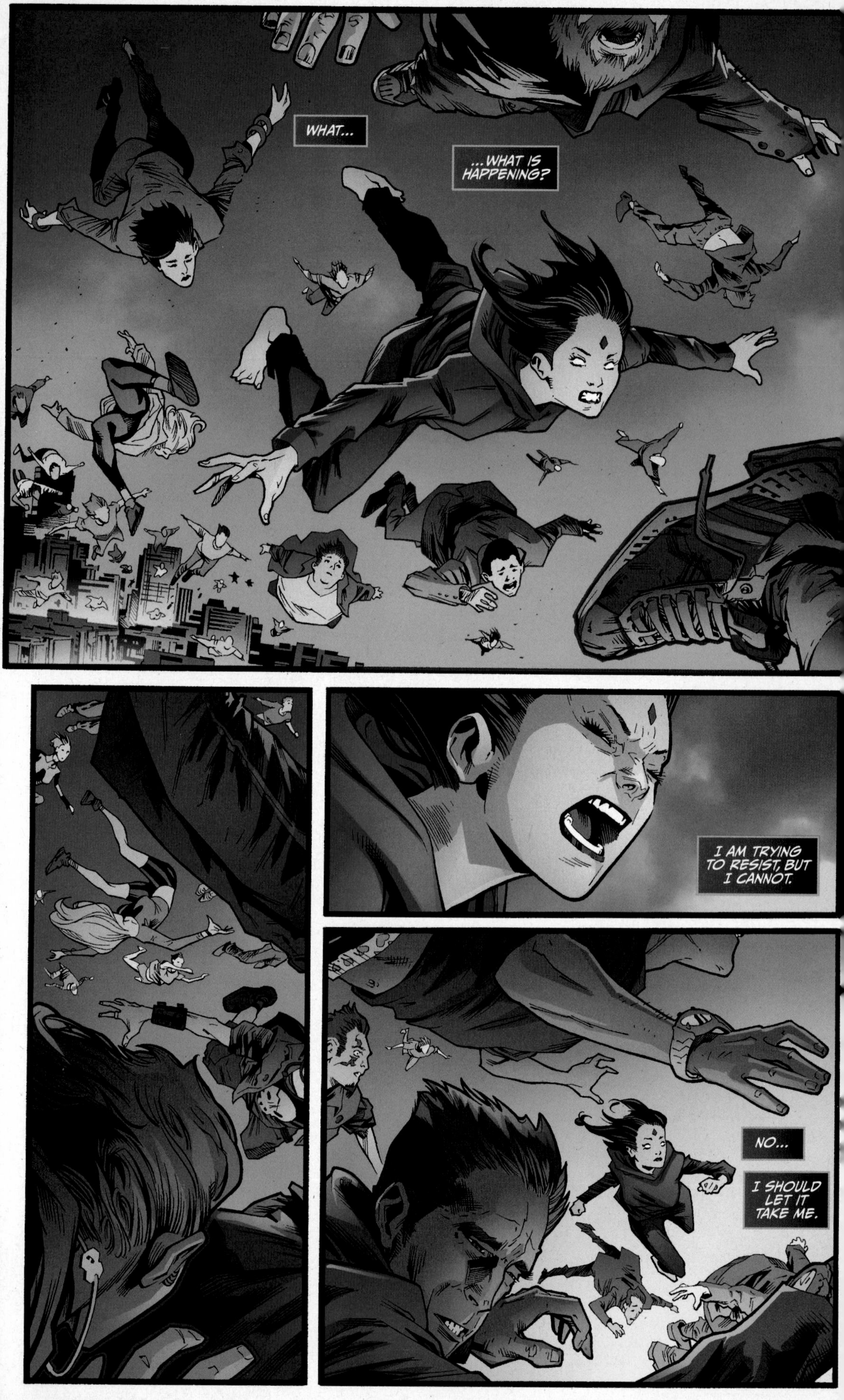
WHAT...
...WHAT IS HAPPENING?
I AM TRYING TO RESIST, BUT I CANNOT.
NO...
I SHOULD LET IT TAKE ME.

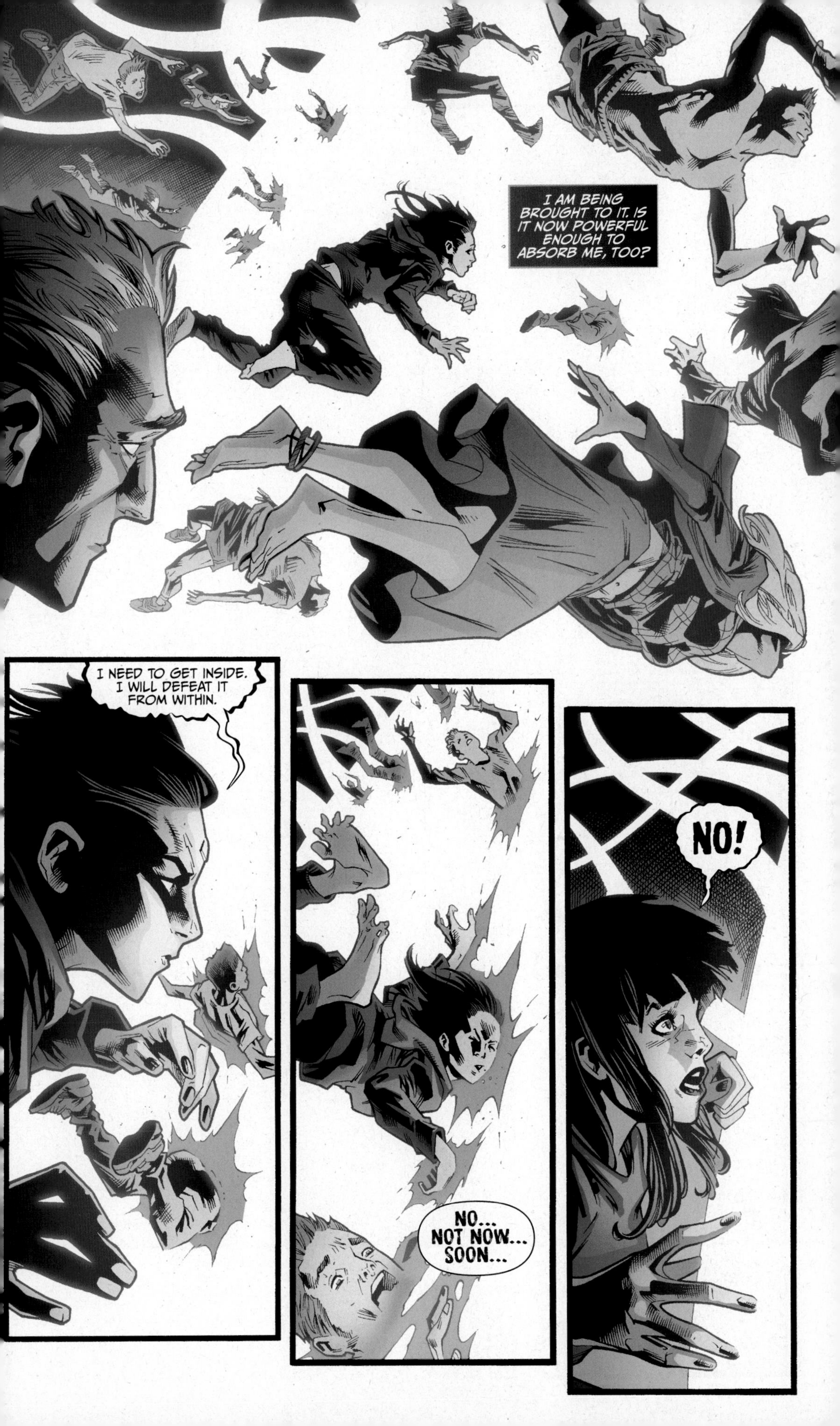
I AM BEING BROUGHT TO IT. IS IT NOW POWERFUL ENOUGH TO ABSORB ME, TOO?
I NEED TO GET INSIDE. I WILL DEFEAT IT FROM WITHIN.
NO... NOT NOW... SOON...
NO!

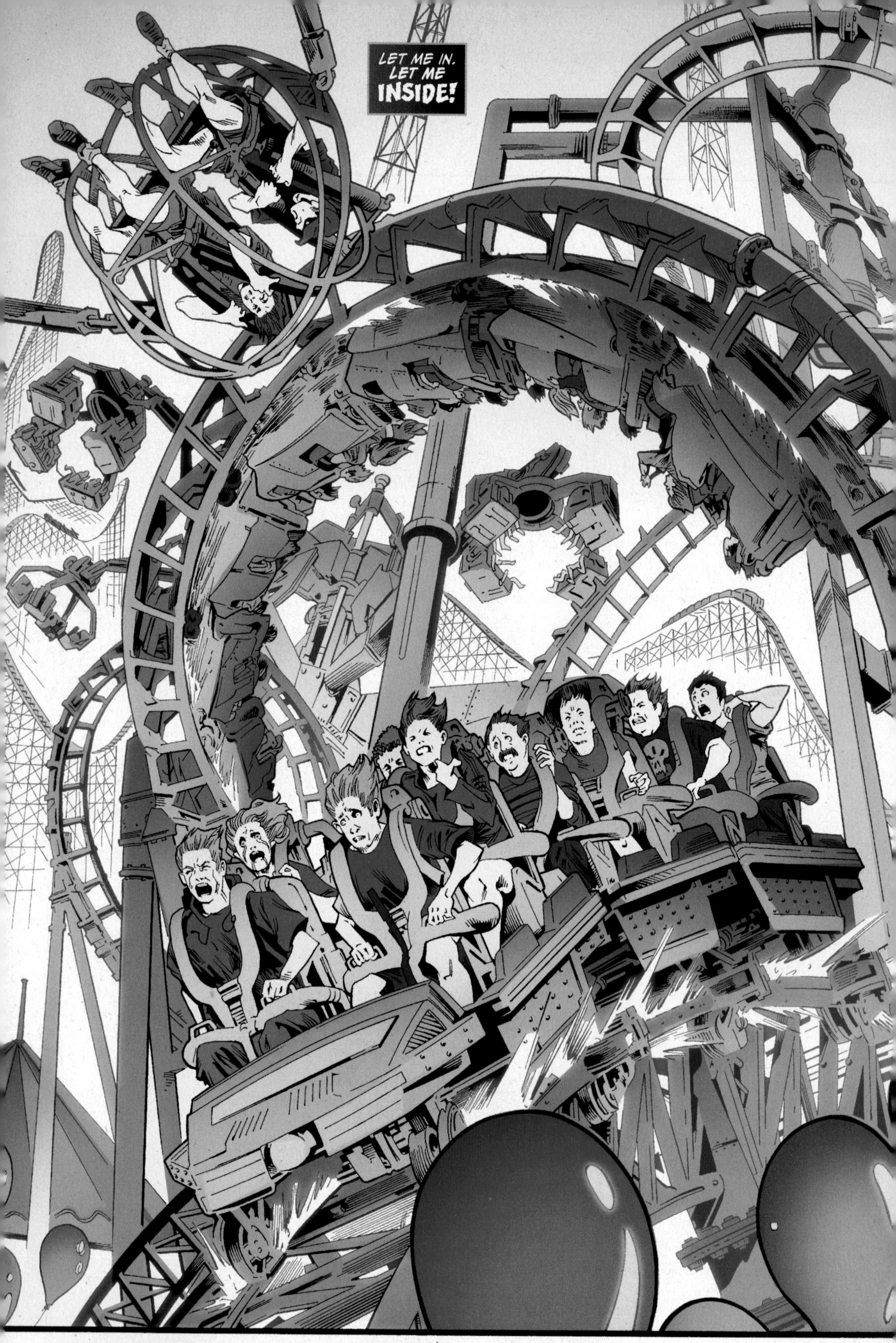
LET ME IN.
LET ME
INSIDE!

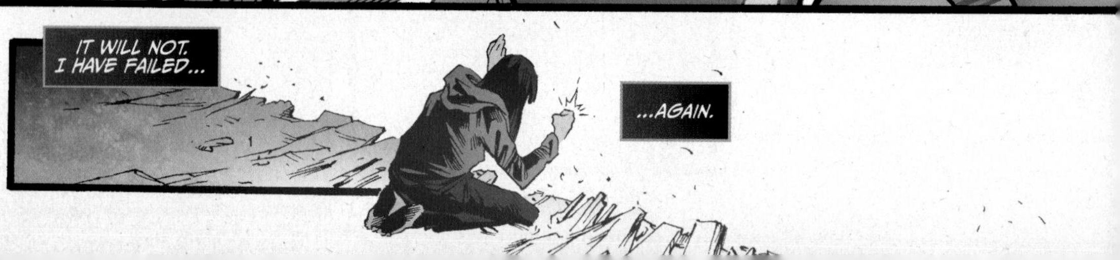
IT WILL NOT.
I HAVE FAILED...
...AGAIN.

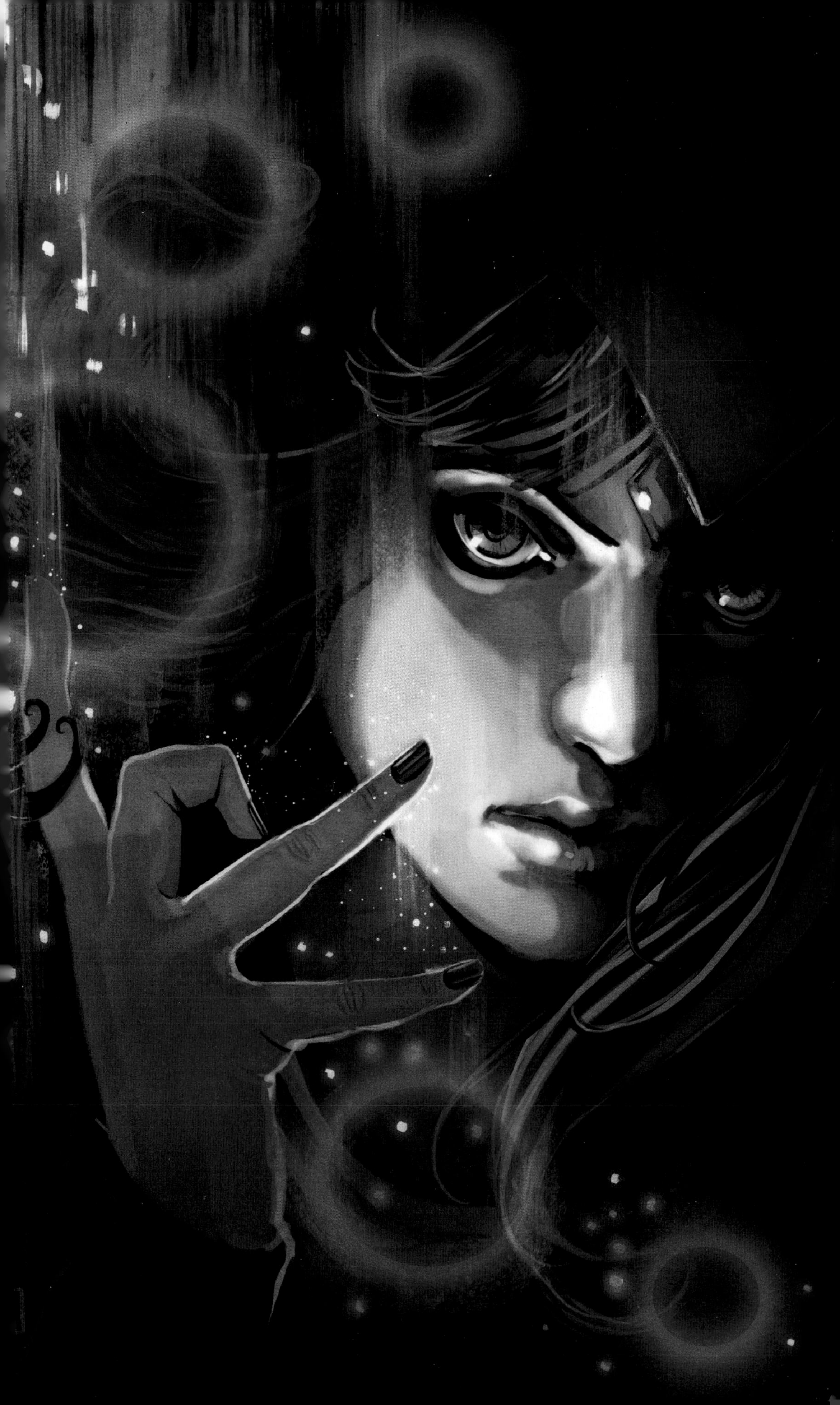

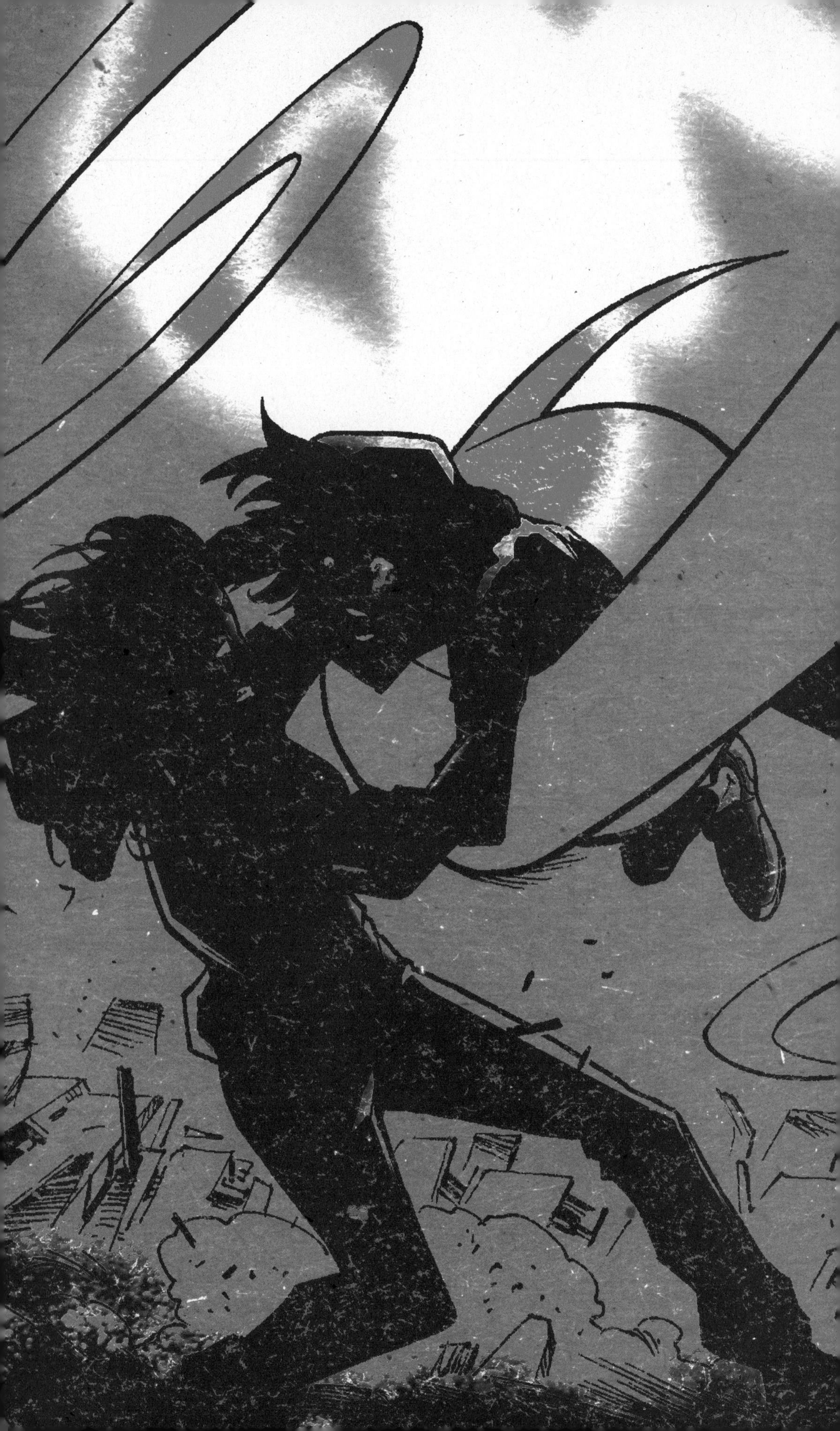

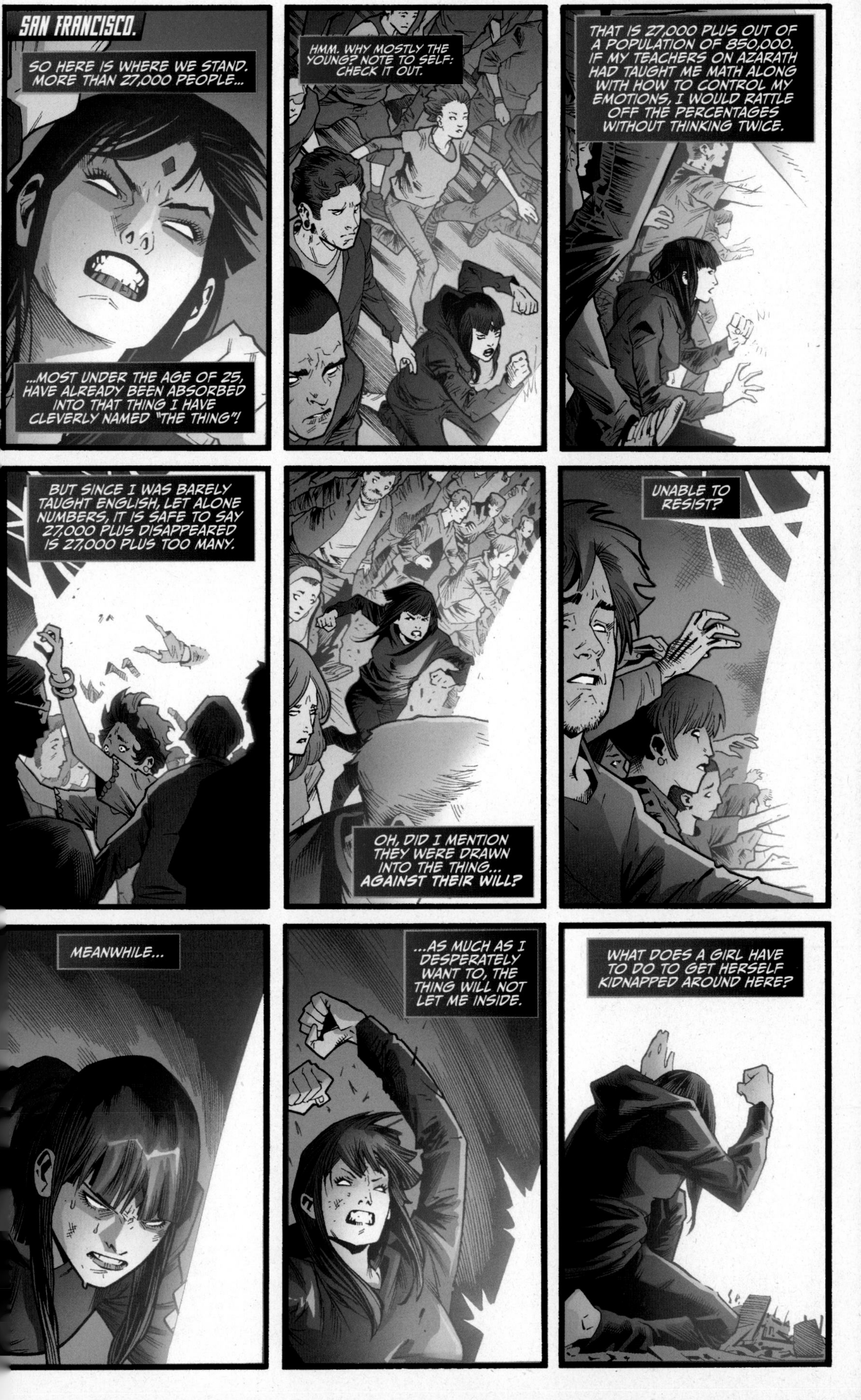
SAN FRANCISCO.
SO HERE IS WHERE WE STAND. MORE THAN 27,000 PEOPLE...
...MOST UNDER THE AGE OF 25, HAVE ALREADY BEEN ABSORBED INTO THAT THING I HAVE CLEVERLY NAMED "THE THING"!
HMM. WHY MOSTLY THE YOUNG? NOTE TO SELF: CHECK IT OUT.
THAT IS 27,000 PLUS OUT OF A POPULATION OF 850,000. IF MY TEACHERS ON AZARATH HAD TAUGHT ME MATH ALONG WITH HOW TO CONTROL MY EMOTIONS, I WOULD RATTLE OFF THE PERCENTAGES WITHOUT THINKING TWICE.
BUT SINCE I WAS BARELY TAUGHT ENGLISH, LET ALONE NUMBERS, IT IS SAFE TO SAY 27,000 PLUS DISAPPEARED IS 27,000 PLUS TOO MANY.
OH, DID I MENTION THEY WERE DRAWN INTO THE THING... AGAINST THEIR WILL?
UNABLE TO RESIST?
MEANWHILE...
...AS MUCH AS I DESPERATELY WANT TO, THE THING WILL NOT LET ME INSIDE.
WHAT DOES A GIRL HAVE TO DO TO GET HERSELF KIDNAPPED AROUND HERE?

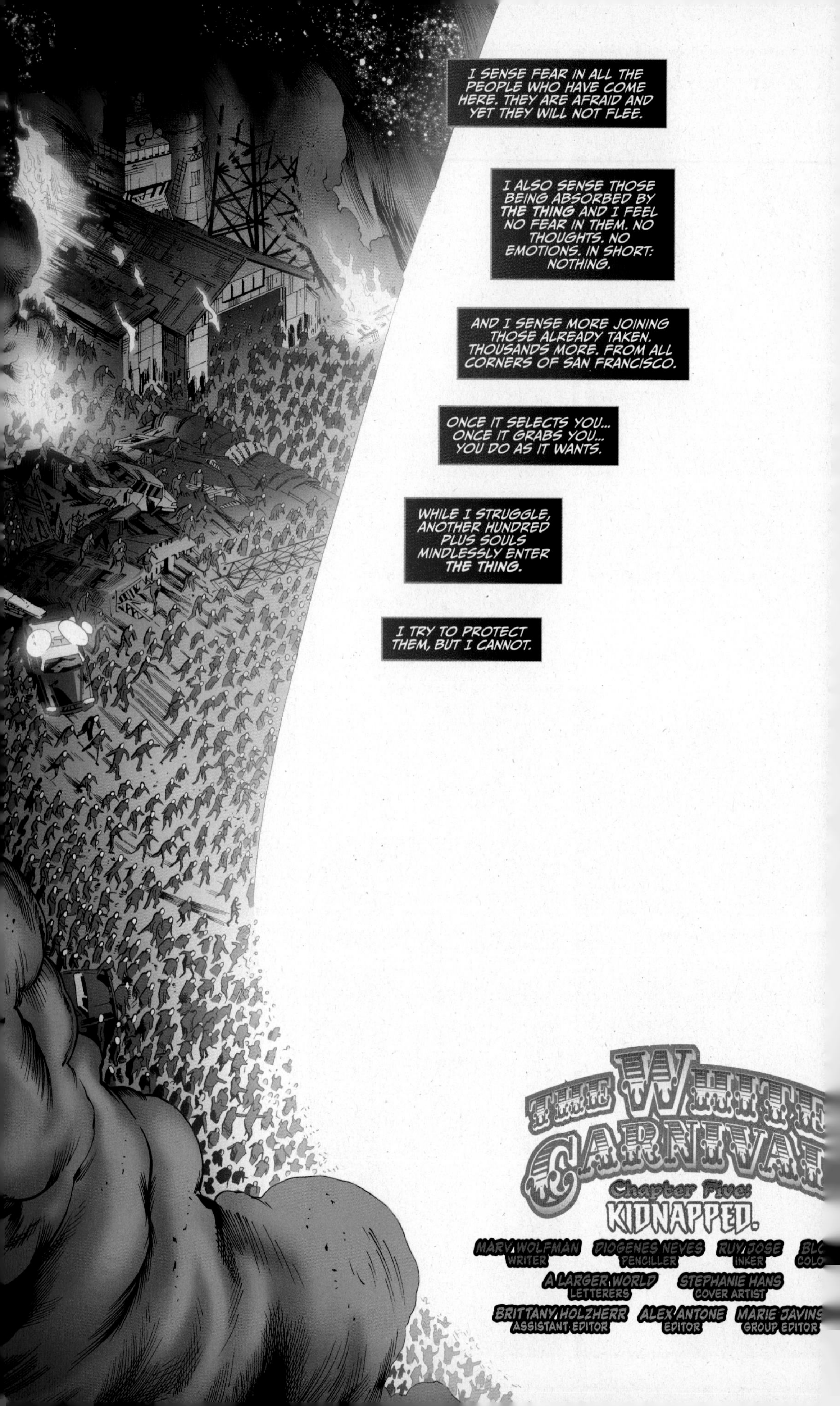

I SENSE FEAR IN ALL THE PEOPLE WHO HAVE COME HERE. THEY ARE AFRAID AND YET THEY WILL NOT FLEE.
I ALSO SENSE THOSE BEING ABSORBED BY **THE THING** AND I FEEL NO FEAR IN THEM. NO THOUGHTS. NO EMOTIONS. IN SHORT: NOTHING.
AND I SENSE MORE JOINING THOSE ALREADY TAKEN. THOUSANDS MORE. FROM ALL CORNERS OF SAN FRANCISCO.
ONCE IT SELECTS YOU... ONCE IT GRABS YOU... YOU DO AS IT WANTS.
WHILE I STRUGGLE, ANOTHER HUNDRED PLUS SOULS MINDLESSLY ENTER **THE THING.**
I TRY TO PROTECT THEM, BUT I CANNOT.
THE WHITE CARNIVAL
Chapter Five:
KIDNAPPED.
MARV WOLFMAN WRITER
DIOGENES NEVES PENCILLER
RUY JOSE INKER
A LARGER WORLD LETTERERS
STEPHANIE HANS COVER ARTIST
BRITTANY HOLZHERR ASSISTANT EDITOR
ALEX ANTONE EDITOR
MARIE JAVINS GROUP EDITOR

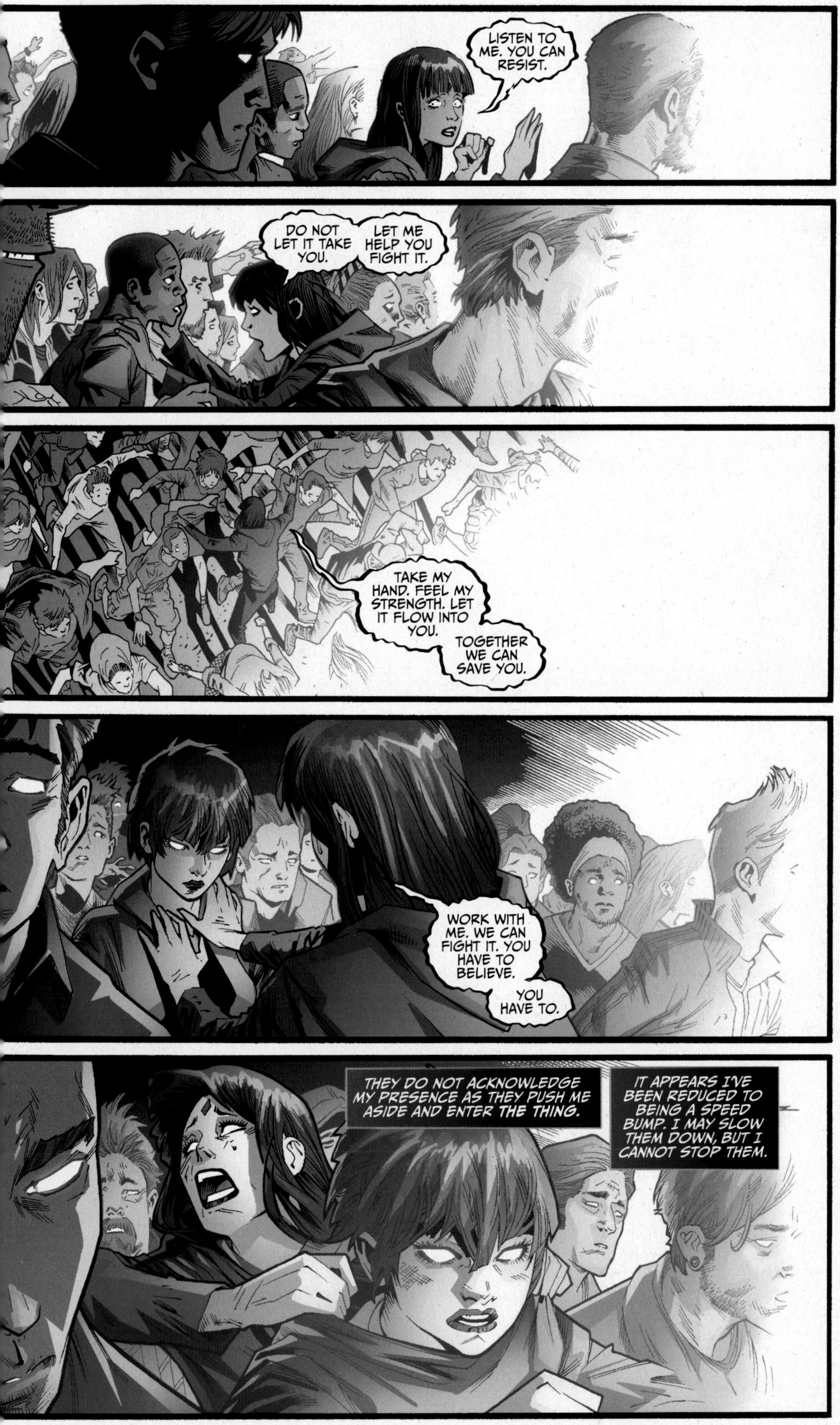

LISTEN TO ME. YOU CAN RESIST.
DO NOT LET IT TAKE YOU.
LET ME HELP YOU FIGHT IT.
TAKE MY HAND. FEEL MY STRENGTH. LET IT FLOW INTO YOU.
TOGETHER WE CAN SAVE YOU.
WORK WITH ME. WE CAN FIGHT IT. YOU HAVE TO BELIEVE.
YOU HAVE TO.
THEY DO NOT ACKNOWLEDGE MY PRESENCE AS THEY PUSH ME ASIDE AND ENTER THE THING.
IT APPEARS I'VE BEEN REDUCED TO BEING A SPEED BUMP. I MAY SLOW THEM DOWN, BUT I CANNOT STOP THEM.

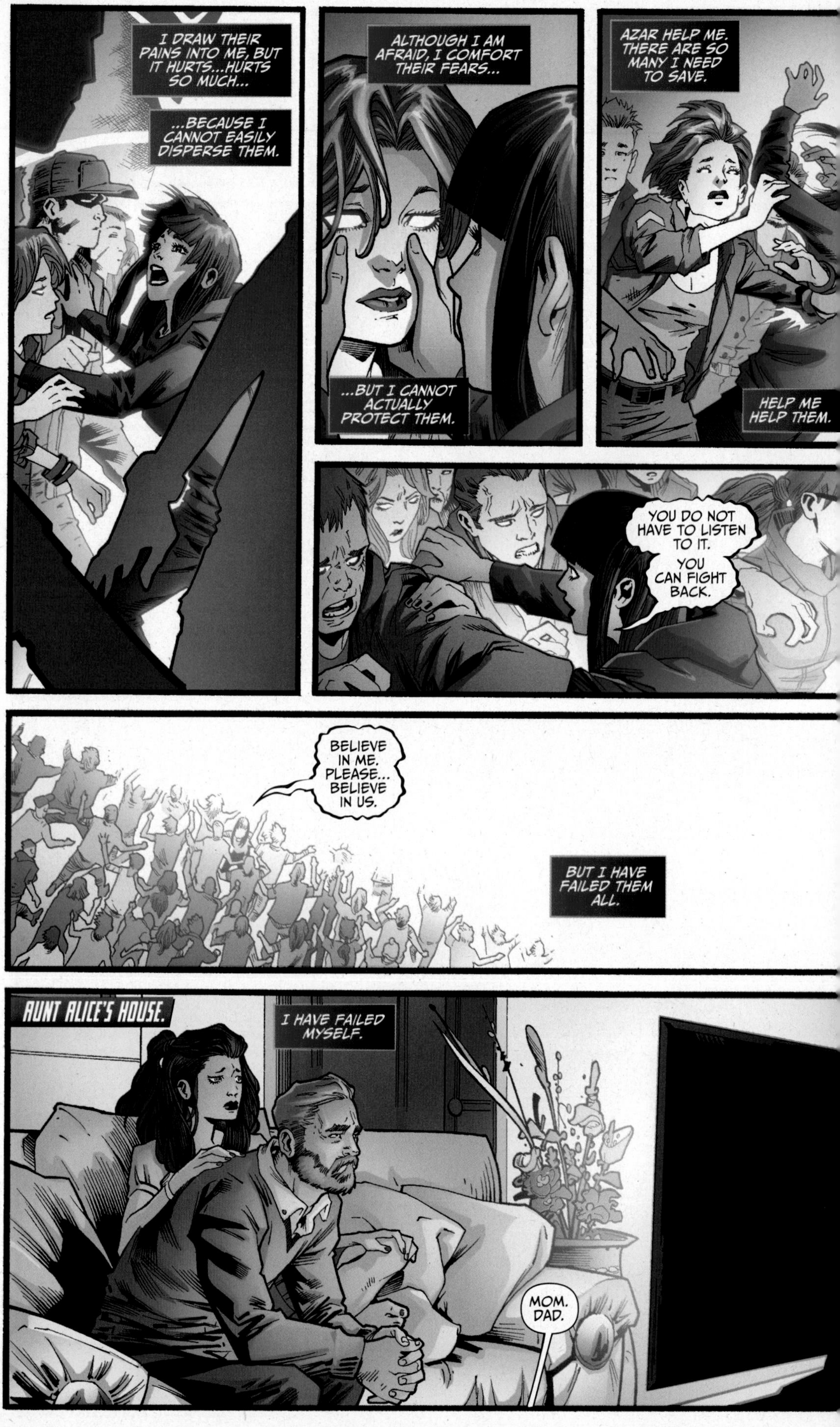
I DRAW THEIR PAINS INTO ME, BUT IT HURTS...HURTS SO MUCH...
...BECAUSE I CANNOT EASILY DISPERSE THEM.
ALTHOUGH I AM AFRAID, I COMFORT THEIR FEARS...
...BUT I CANNOT ACTUALLY PROTECT THEM.
AZAR HELP ME. THERE ARE SO MANY I NEED TO SAVE.
HELP ME HELP THEM.
YOU DO NOT HAVE TO LISTEN TO IT.
YOU CAN FIGHT BACK.
BELIEVE IN ME. PLEASE... BELIEVE IN US.
BUT I HAVE FAILED THEM ALL.
AUNT ALICE'S HOUSE.
I HAVE FAILED MYSELF.
MOM. DAD.

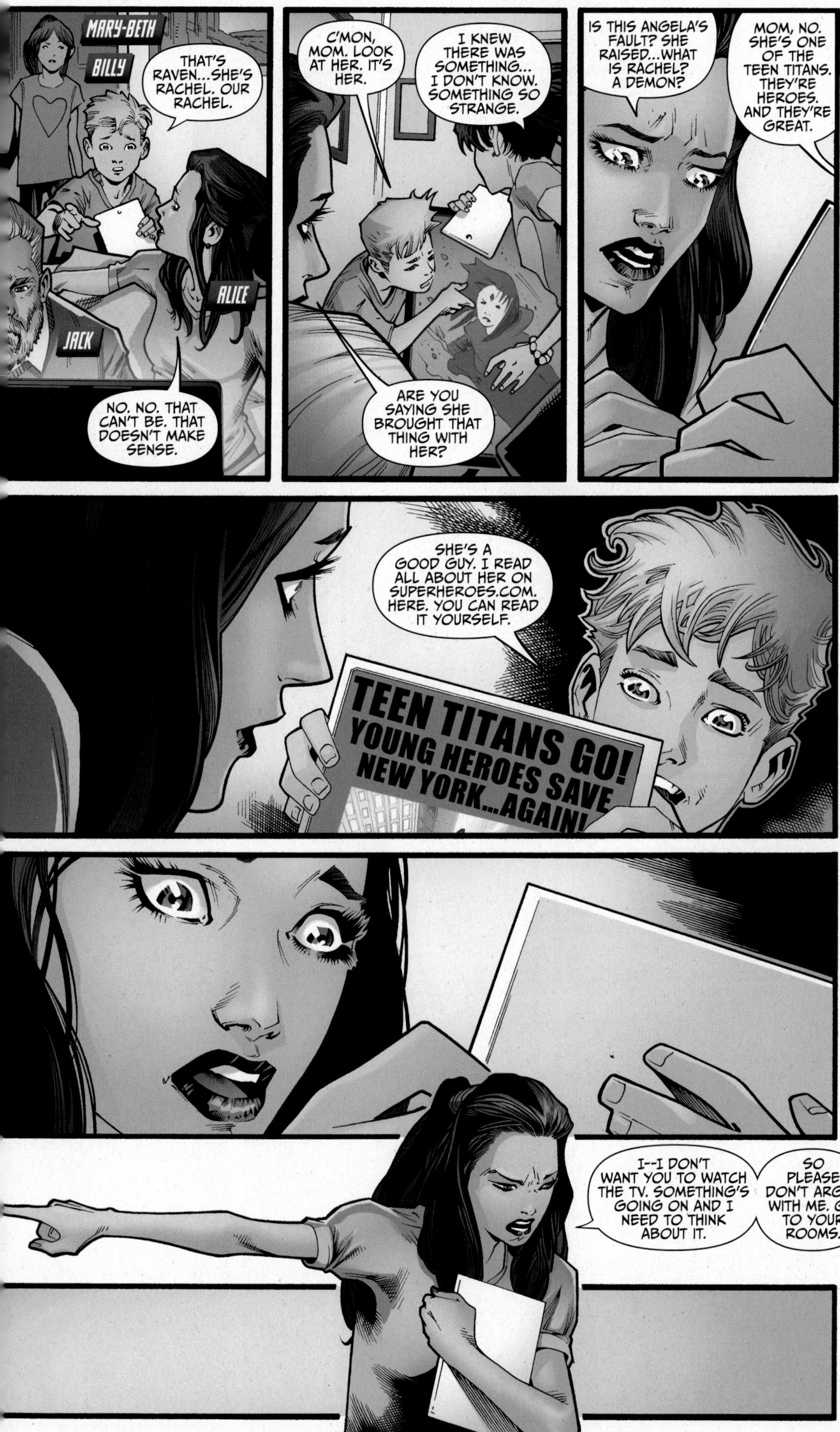
MARY-BETH
BILLY
THAT'S RAVEN...SHE'S RACHEL. OUR RACHEL.
ALICE
JACK
NO. NO. THAT CAN'T BE. THAT DOESN'T MAKE SENSE.
C'MON, MOM. LOOK AT HER. IT'S HER.
I KNEW THERE WAS SOMETHING... I DON'T KNOW. SOMETHING SO STRANGE.
ARE YOU SAYING SHE BROUGHT THAT THING WITH HER?
IS THIS ANGELA'S FAULT? SHE RAISED...WHAT IS RACHEL? A DEMON?
MOM, NO. SHE'S ONE OF THE TEEN TITANS. THEY'RE HEROES. AND THEY'RE GREAT.
SHE'S A GOOD GUY. I READ ALL ABOUT HER ON SUPERHEROES.COM. HERE. YOU CAN READ IT YOURSELF.
TEEN TITANS GO! YOUNG HEROES SAVE NEW YORK...AGAIN!
I--I DON'T WANT YOU TO WATCH THE TV. SOMETHING'S GOING ON AND I NEED TO THINK ABOUT IT.
SO PLEASE DON'T ARGUE WITH ME. GO TO YOUR ROOMS.

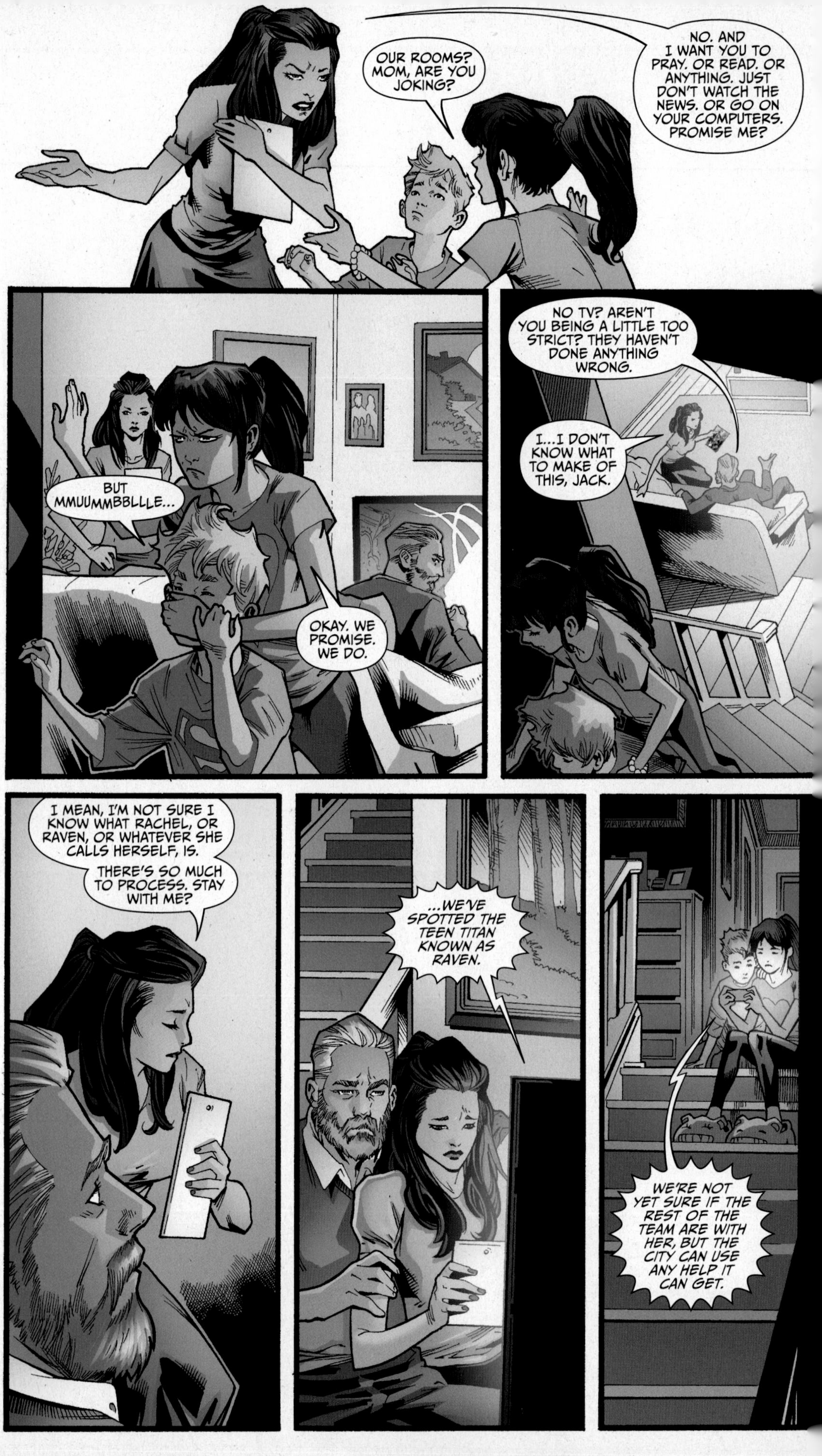

OUR ROOMS? MOM, ARE YOU JOKING?
NO. AND I WANT YOU TO PRAY. OR READ. OR ANYTHING. JUST DON'T WATCH THE NEWS. OR GO ON YOUR COMPUTERS. PROMISE ME?
BUT MMUUMMBBLLLE...
OKAY. WE PROMISE. WE DO.
NO TV? AREN'T YOU BEING A LITTLE TOO STRICT? THEY HAVEN'T DONE ANYTHING WRONG.
I...I DON'T KNOW WHAT TO MAKE OF THIS, JACK.
I MEAN, I'M NOT SURE I KNOW WHAT RACHEL, OR RAVEN, OR WHATEVER SHE CALLS HERSELF, IS.
THERE'S SO MUCH TO PROCESS. STAY WITH ME?
...WE'VE SPOTTED THE TEEN TITAN KNOWN AS RAVEN.
WE'RE NOT YET SURE IF THE REST OF THE TEAM ARE WITH HER, BUT THE CITY CAN USE ANY HELP IT CAN GET.

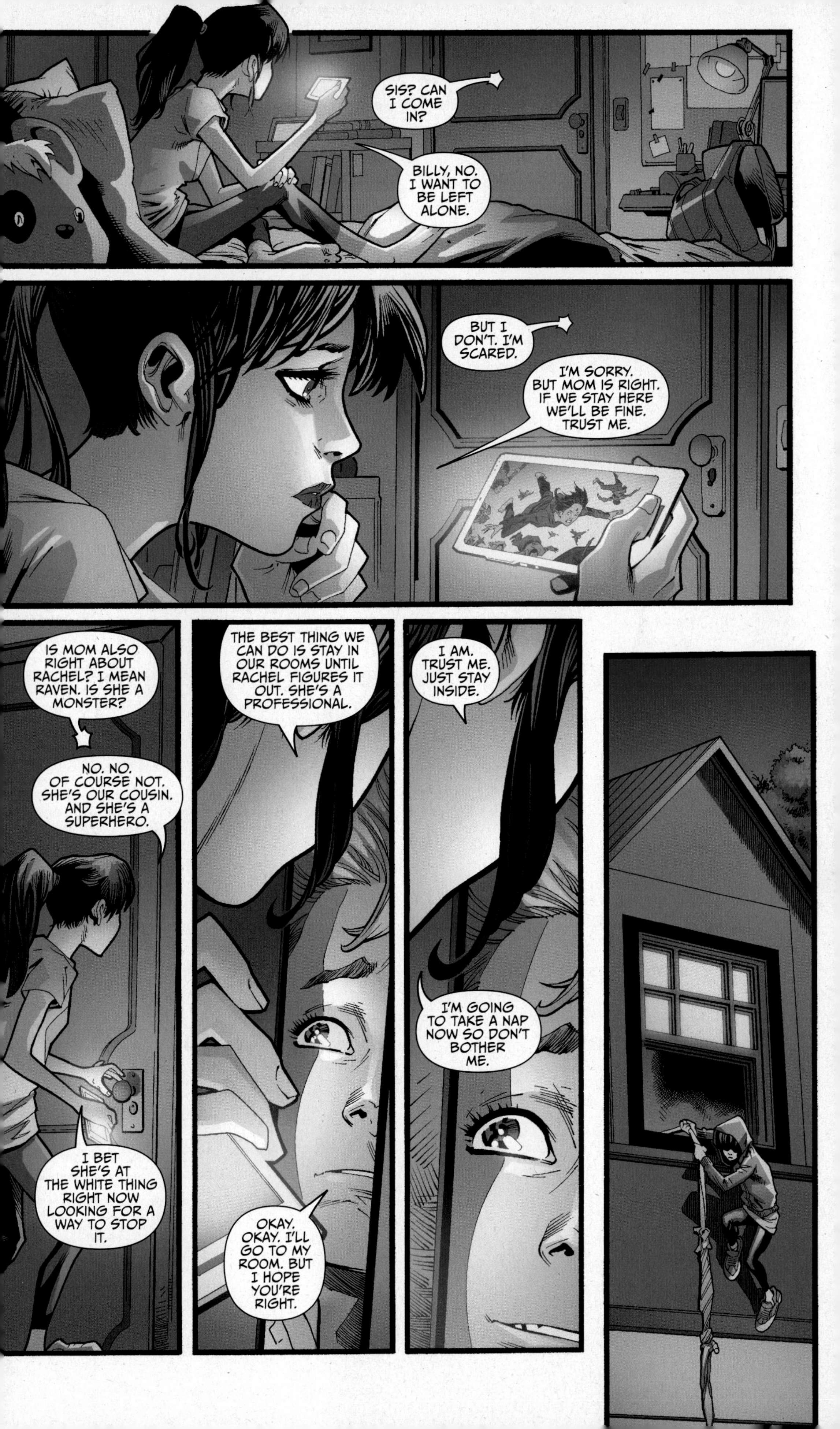
SIS? CAN I COME IN?
BILLY, NO. I WANT TO BE LEFT ALONE.
BUT I DON'T. I'M SCARED.
I'M SORRY. BUT MOM IS RIGHT. IF WE STAY HERE WE'LL BE FINE. TRUST ME.
IS MOM ALSO RIGHT ABOUT RACHEL? I MEAN RAVEN. IS SHE A MONSTER?
NO. NO. OF COURSE NOT. SHE'S OUR COUSIN. AND SHE'S A SUPERHERO.
I BET SHE'S AT THE WHITE THING RIGHT NOW LOOKING FOR A WAY TO STOP IT.
THE BEST THING WE CAN DO IS STAY IN OUR ROOMS UNTIL RACHEL FIGURES IT OUT. SHE'S A PROFESSIONAL.
OKAY. OKAY. I'LL GO TO MY ROOM. BUT I HOPE YOU'RE RIGHT.
I AM. TRUST ME. JUST STAY INSIDE.
I'M GOING TO TAKE A NAP NOW SO DON'T BOTHER ME.

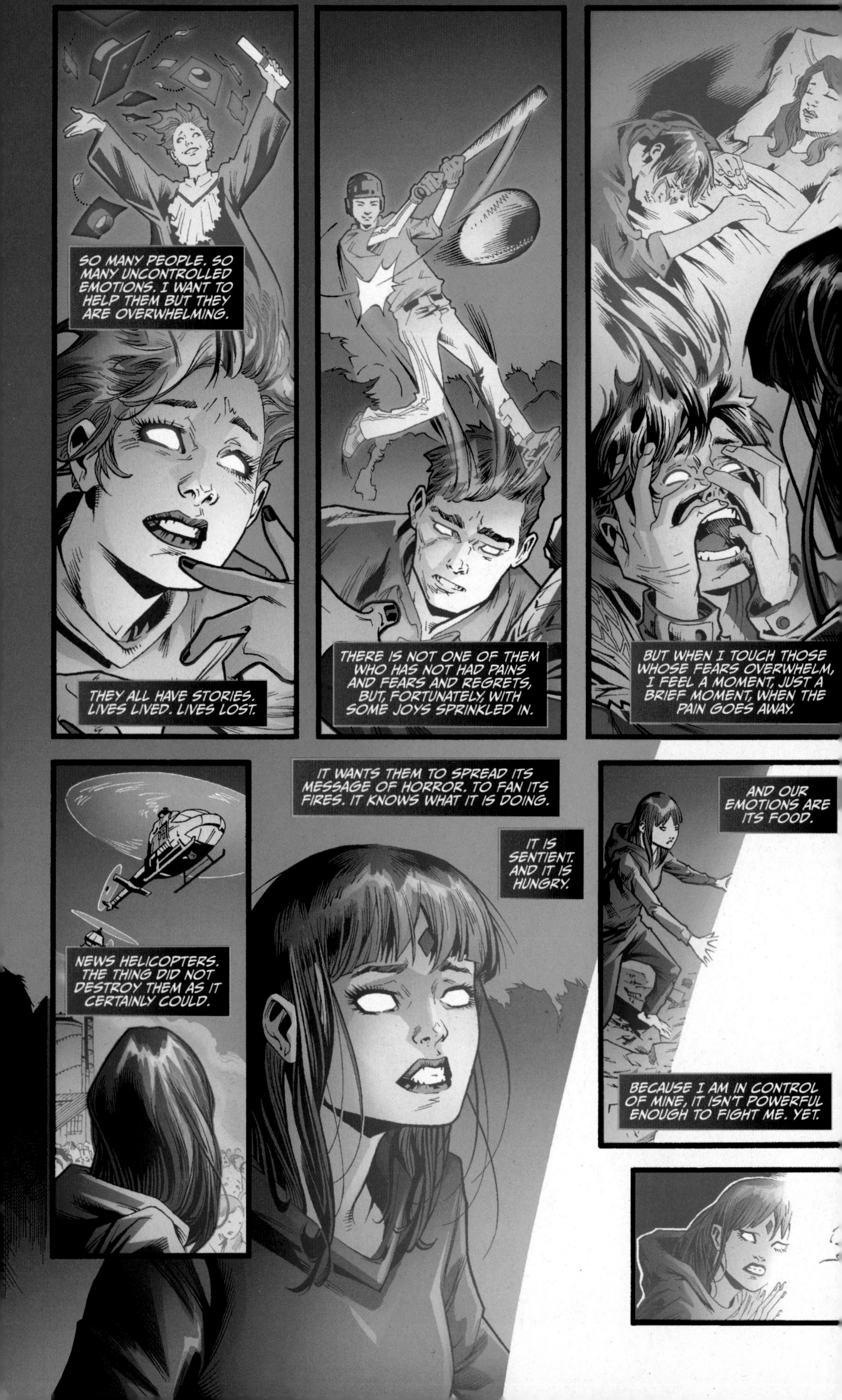
SO MANY PEOPLE. SO MANY UNCONTROLLED EMOTIONS. I WANT TO HELP THEM BUT THEY ARE OVERWHELMING.
THEY ALL HAVE STORIES. LIVES LIVED. LIVES LOST.
THERE IS NOT ONE OF THEM WHO HAS NOT HAD PAINS AND FEARS AND REGRETS, BUT, FORTUNATELY, WITH SOME JOYS SPRINKLED IN.
BUT WHEN I TOUCH THOSE WHOSE FEARS OVERWHELM, I FEEL A MOMENT, JUST A BRIEF MOMENT, WHEN THE PAIN GOES AWAY.
NEWS HELICOPTERS. THE THING DID NOT DESTROY THEM AS IT CERTAINLY COULD.
IT WANTS THEM TO SPREAD ITS MESSAGE OF HORROR. TO FAN ITS FIRES. IT KNOWS WHAT IT IS DOING.
IT IS SENTIENT. AND IT IS HUNGRY.
AND OUR EMOTIONS ARE ITS FOOD.
BECAUSE I AM IN CONTROL OF MINE, IT ISN'T POWERFUL ENOUGH TO FIGHT ME. YET.

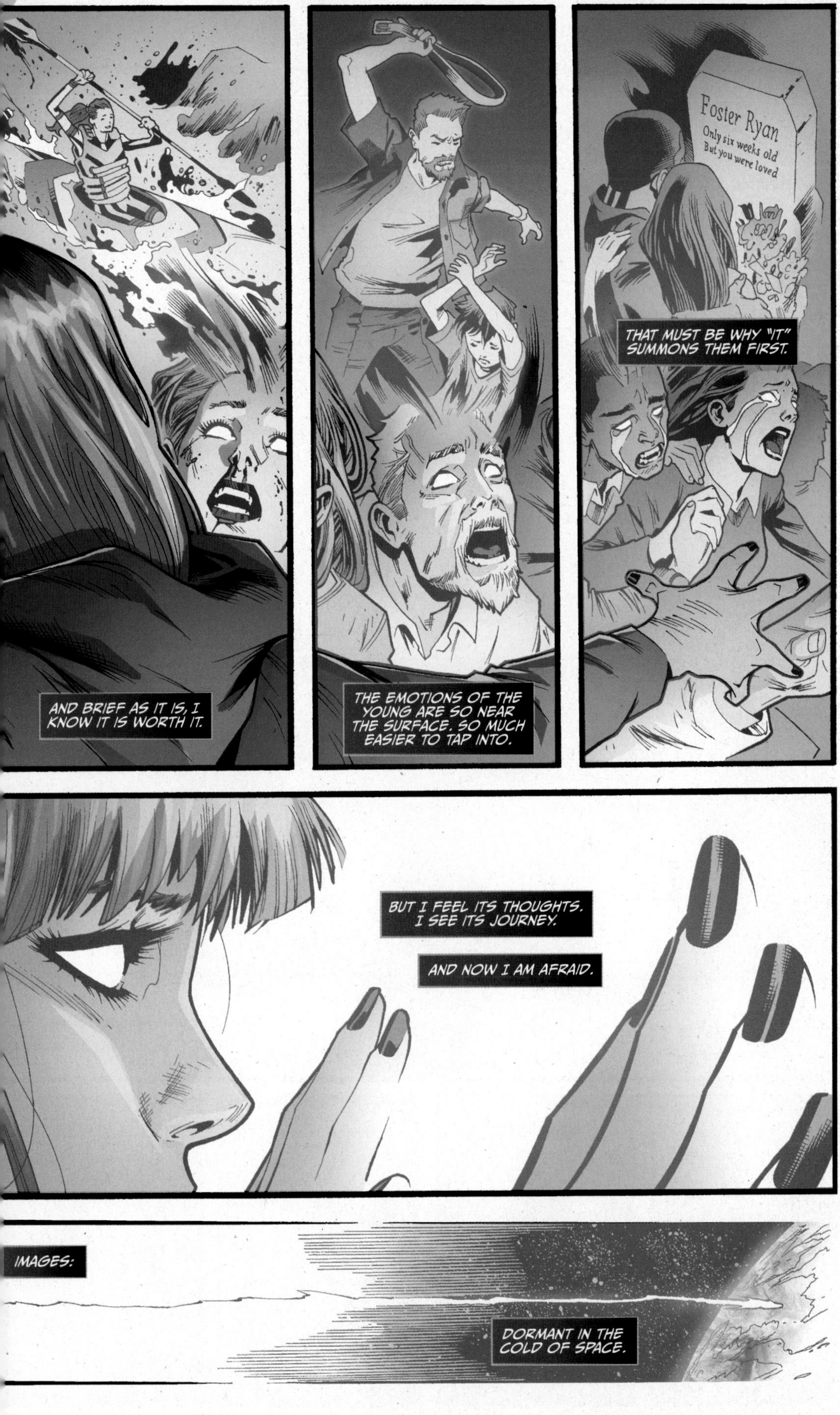
AND BRIEF AS IT IS, I KNOW IT IS WORTH IT.
THE EMOTIONS OF THE YOUNG ARE SO NEAR THE SURFACE. SO MUCH EASIER TO TAP INTO.
Foster Ryan
Only six weeks old
But you were loved
THAT MUST BE WHY "IT" SUMMONS THEM FIRST.
BUT I FEEL ITS THOUGHTS. I SEE ITS JOURNEY.
AND NOW I AM AFRAID.
IMAGES:
DORMANT IN THE COLD OF SPACE.

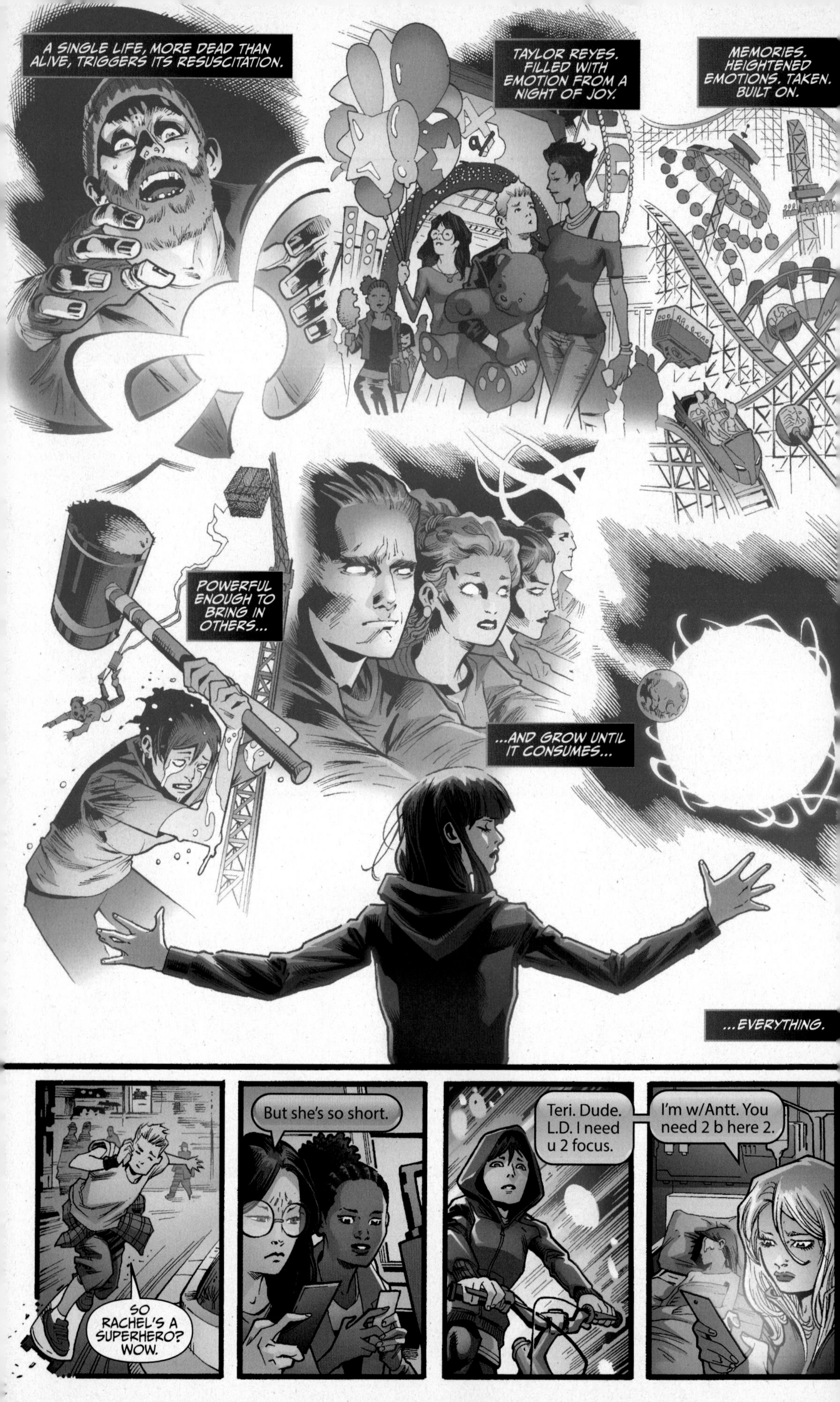
A SINGLE LIFE, MORE DEAD THAN ALIVE, TRIGGERS ITS RESUSCITATION.
TAYLOR REYES. FILLED WITH EMOTION FROM A NIGHT OF JOY.
MEMORIES. HEIGHTENED EMOTIONS. TAKEN. BUILT ON.
POWERFUL ENOUGH TO BRING IN OTHERS...
...AND GROW UNTIL IT CONSUMES...
...EVERYTHING.
SO RACHEL'S A SUPERHERO? WOW.
But she's so short.
Teri. Dude. L.D. I need u 2 focus.
I'm w/Antt. You need 2 b here 2.

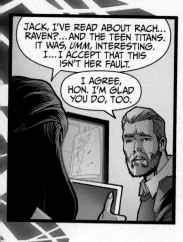

JACK, I'VE READ ABOUT RACH... RAVEN?...AND THE TEEN TITANS. IT WAS, *UMM*, INTERESTING. I...I ACCEPT THAT THIS ISN'T HER FAULT.

I AGREE, HON. I'M GLAD YOU DO, TOO.

YEAH. AND IT'S PROBABLY NOT ANGELA'S FAULT EITHER, OR THE WAY SHE RAISED THAT GIRL.

I'VE SPOKEN A LOT WITH RACHEL. I'VE LOOKED INTO HER EYES. SHE IS GOOD AND I BELIEVE IN HER.

SO WHAT DO WE DO?

HELP HER. SHE'S OUR FAMILY. SO WE LET HER KNOW SHE'S LOVED. WE LET HER KNOW SHE SHOULD BE HERE WITH US...

...NOT OUT THERE WITH THAT... THAT THING.

I COULD DRIVE THERE AND BRING HER BACK.

NO. NO, NO. THE POLICE AREN'T LETTING ANY CARS NEAR THE SITE.

...YESTERDAY SAN FRANCISCANS WITNESSED THIS *UNEXPLAINABLE* SIGHT.

EXPERTS HAVE GONE OVER THE VIDEOS TAKEN AND...

BESIDES, IF RACHEL IS THE PERSON I WANT TO BELIEVE SHE IS, SHE'LL COME BACK TO US ON HER OWN. UNTIL THEN WE PRAY FOR--

OH NO.

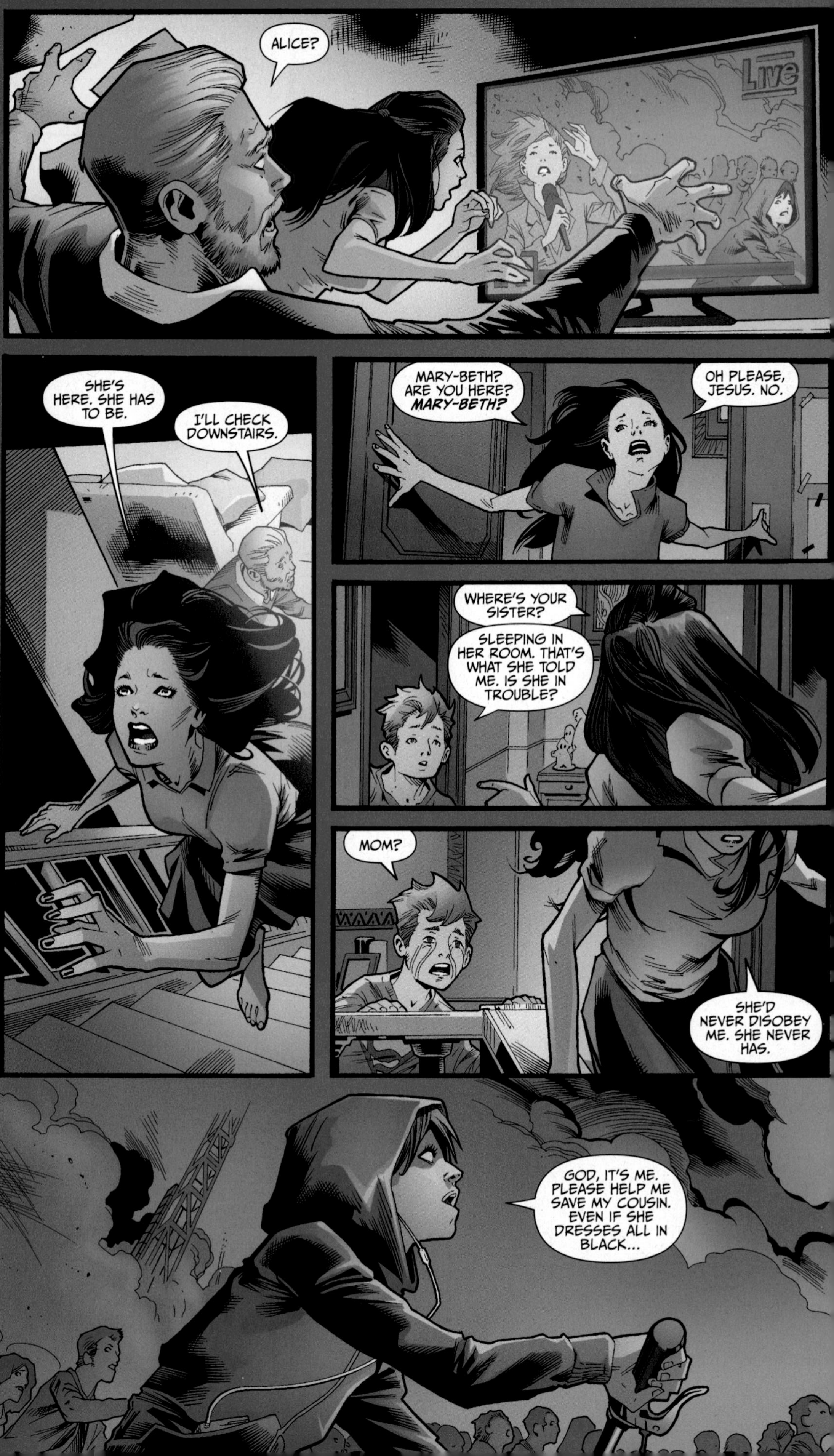
ALICE?
SHE'S HERE. SHE HAS TO BE.
I'LL CHECK DOWNSTAIRS.
MARY-BETH? ARE YOU HERE? *MARY-BETH?*
OH PLEASE, JESUS. NO.
WHERE'S YOUR SISTER?
SLEEPING IN HER ROOM. THAT'S WHAT SHE TOLD ME. IS SHE IN TROUBLE?
MOM?
SHE'D NEVER DISOBEY ME. SHE NEVER HAS.
GOD, IT'S ME. PLEASE HELP ME SAVE MY COUSIN. EVEN IF SHE DRESSES ALL IN BLACK...

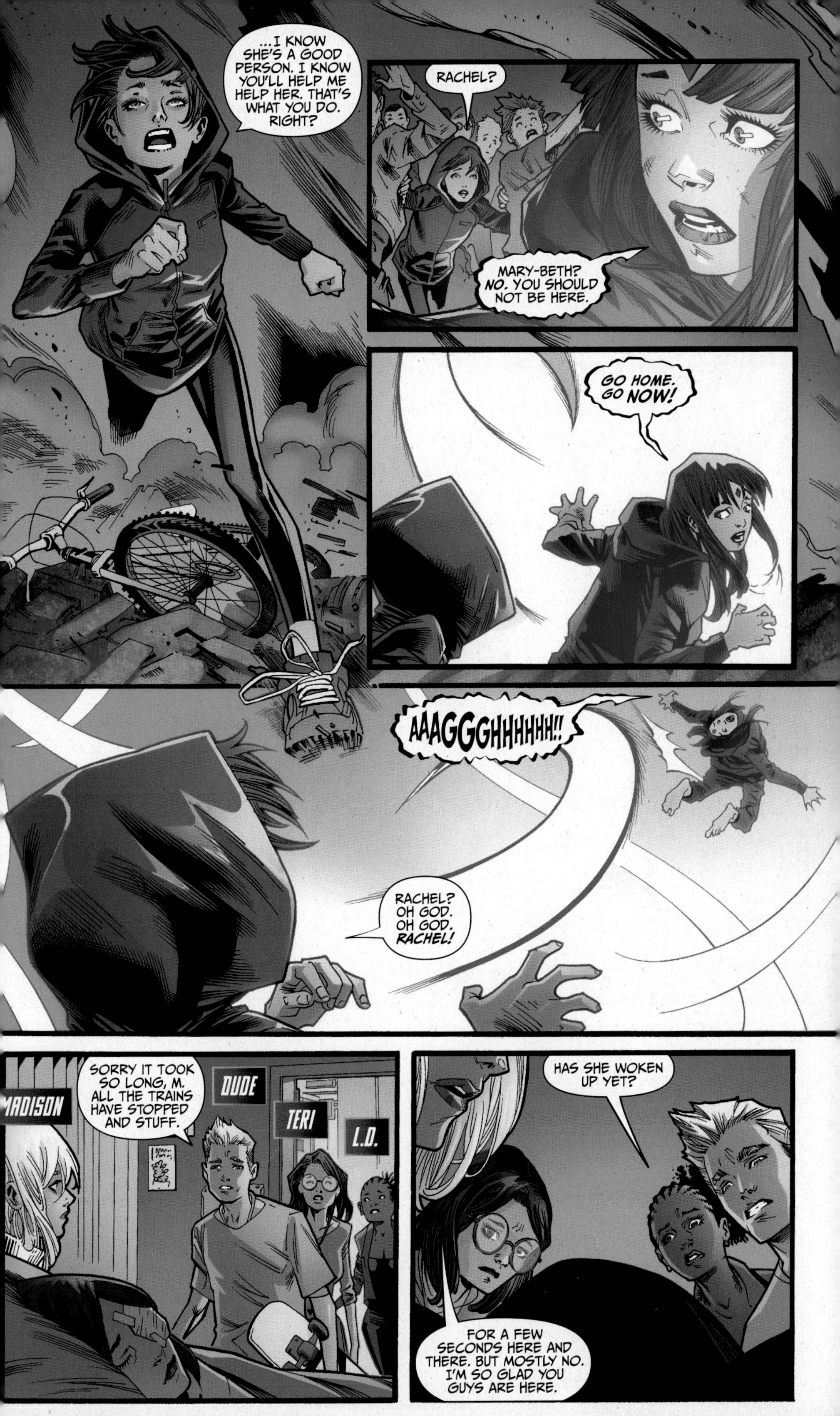
...I KNOW SHE'S A GOOD PERSON. I KNOW YOU'LL HELP ME HELP HER. THAT'S WHAT YOU DO. RIGHT?
RACHEL?
MARY-BETH? NO. YOU SHOULD NOT BE HERE.
GO HOME. GO NOW!
AAAGGGHHHHHH!!
RACHEL? OH GOD. OH GOD. RACHEL!
MADISON
DUDE
TERI
L.D.
SORRY IT TOOK SO LONG, M. ALL THE TRAINS HAVE STOPPED AND STUFF.
HAS SHE WOKEN UP YET?
FOR A FEW SECONDS HERE AND THERE. BUT MOSTLY NO. I'M SO GLAD YOU GUYS ARE HERE.

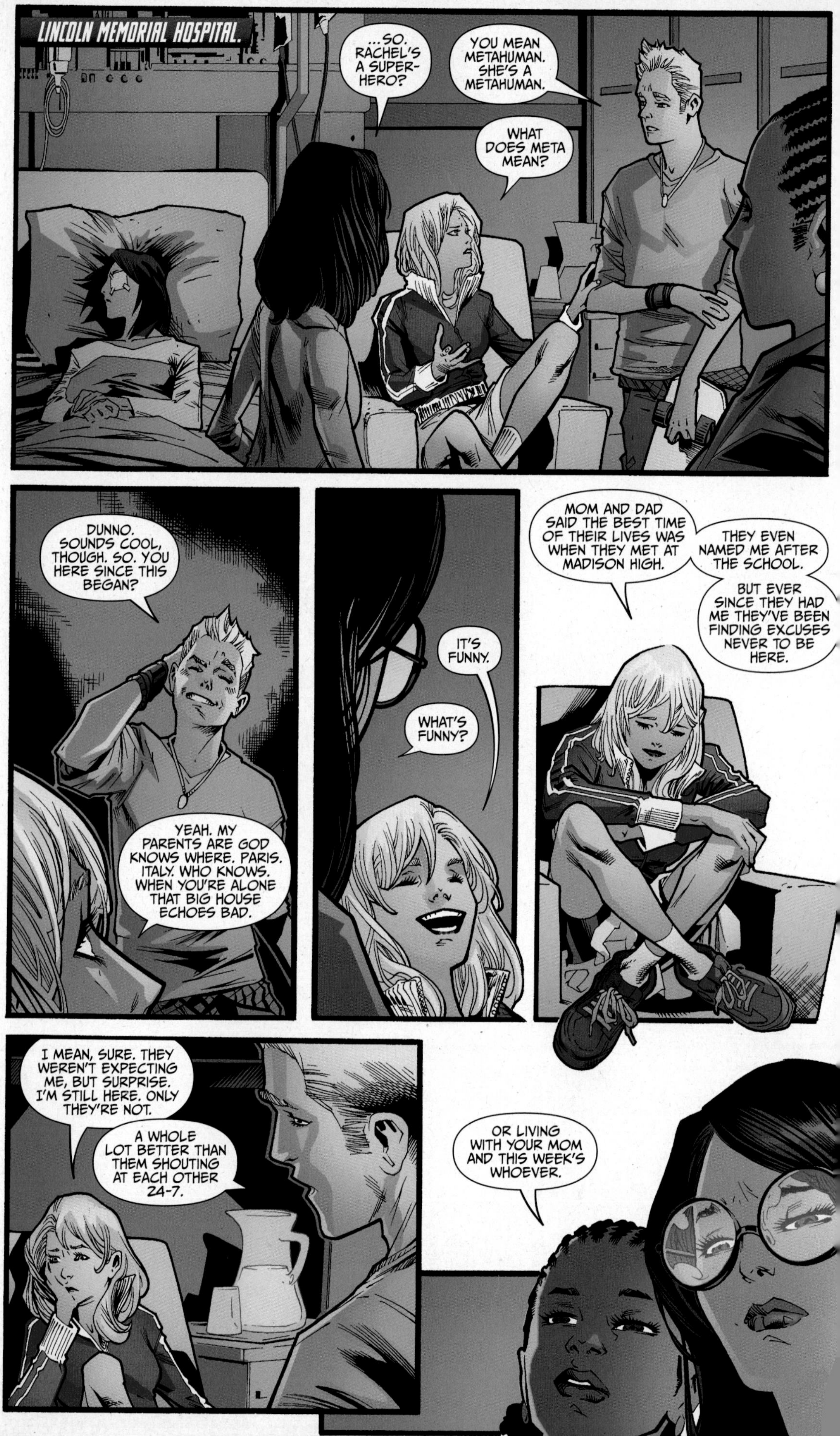
LINCOLN MEMORIAL HOSPITAL.
...SO. RACHEL'S A SUPER-HERO?
YOU MEAN METAHUMAN. SHE'S A METAHUMAN.
WHAT DOES META MEAN?
DUNNO. SOUNDS COOL, THOUGH. SO. YOU HERE SINCE THIS BEGAN?
YEAH. MY PARENTS ARE GOD KNOWS WHERE. PARIS. ITALY. WHO KNOWS. WHEN YOU'RE ALONE THAT BIG HOUSE ECHOES BAD.
IT'S FUNNY.
WHAT'S FUNNY?
MOM AND DAD SAID THE BEST TIME OF THEIR LIVES WAS WHEN THEY MET AT MADISON HIGH.
THEY EVEN NAMED ME AFTER THE SCHOOL.
BUT EVER SINCE THEY HAD ME THEY'VE BEEN FINDING EXCUSES NEVER TO BE HERE.
I MEAN, SURE. THEY WEREN'T EXPECTING ME, BUT SURPRISE. I'M STILL HERE. ONLY THEY'RE NOT.
A WHOLE LOT BETTER THAN THEM SHOUTING AT EACH OTHER 24-7.
OR LIVING WITH YOUR MOM AND THIS WEEK'S WHOEVER.

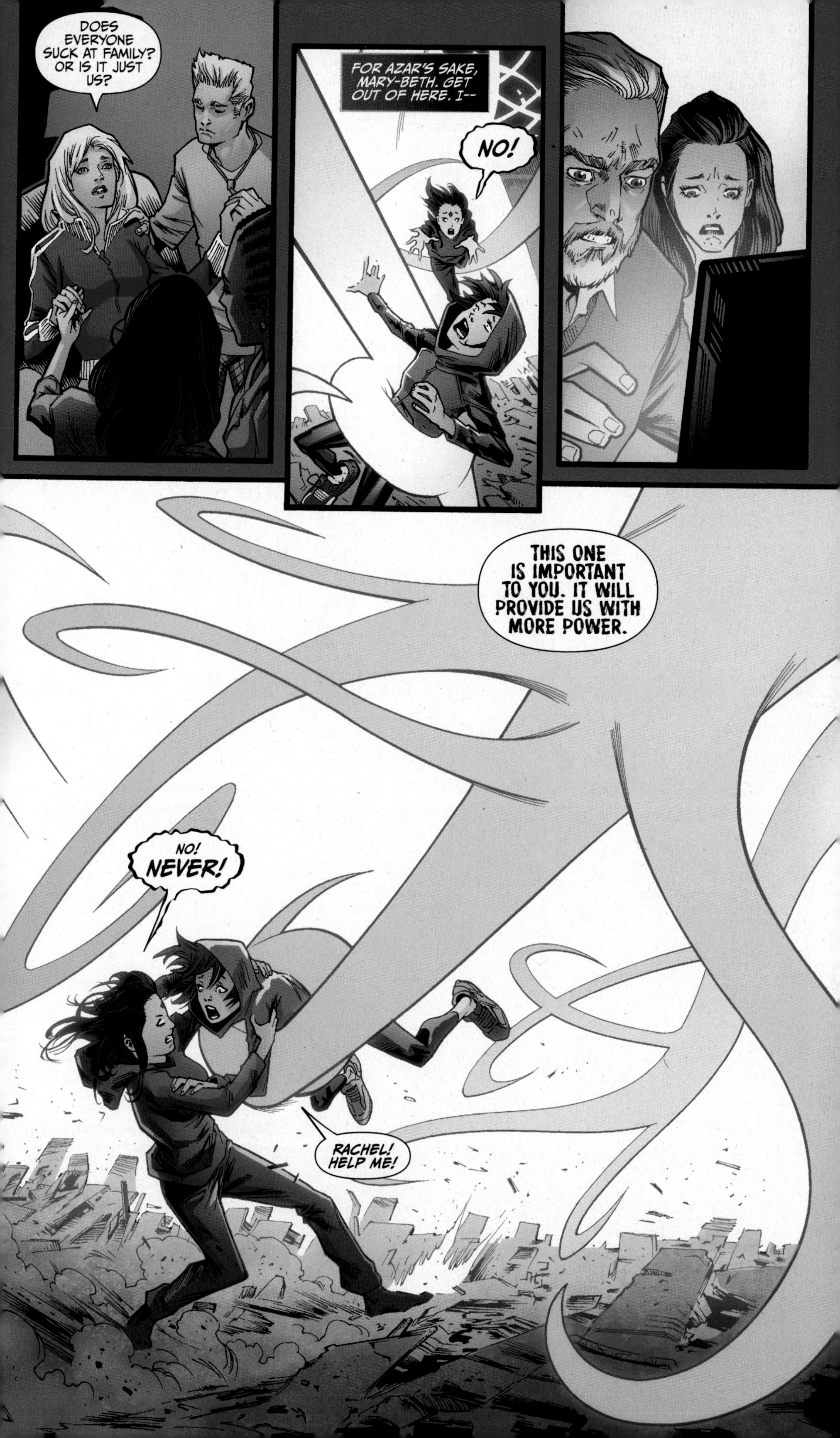
DOES EVERYONE SUCK AT FAMILY? OR IS IT JUST US?
FOR AZAR'S SAKE, MARY-BETH. GET OUT OF HERE. I--
NO!
THIS ONE IS IMPORTANT TO YOU. IT WILL PROVIDE US WITH MORE POWER.
NO! NEVER!
RACHEL! HELP ME!

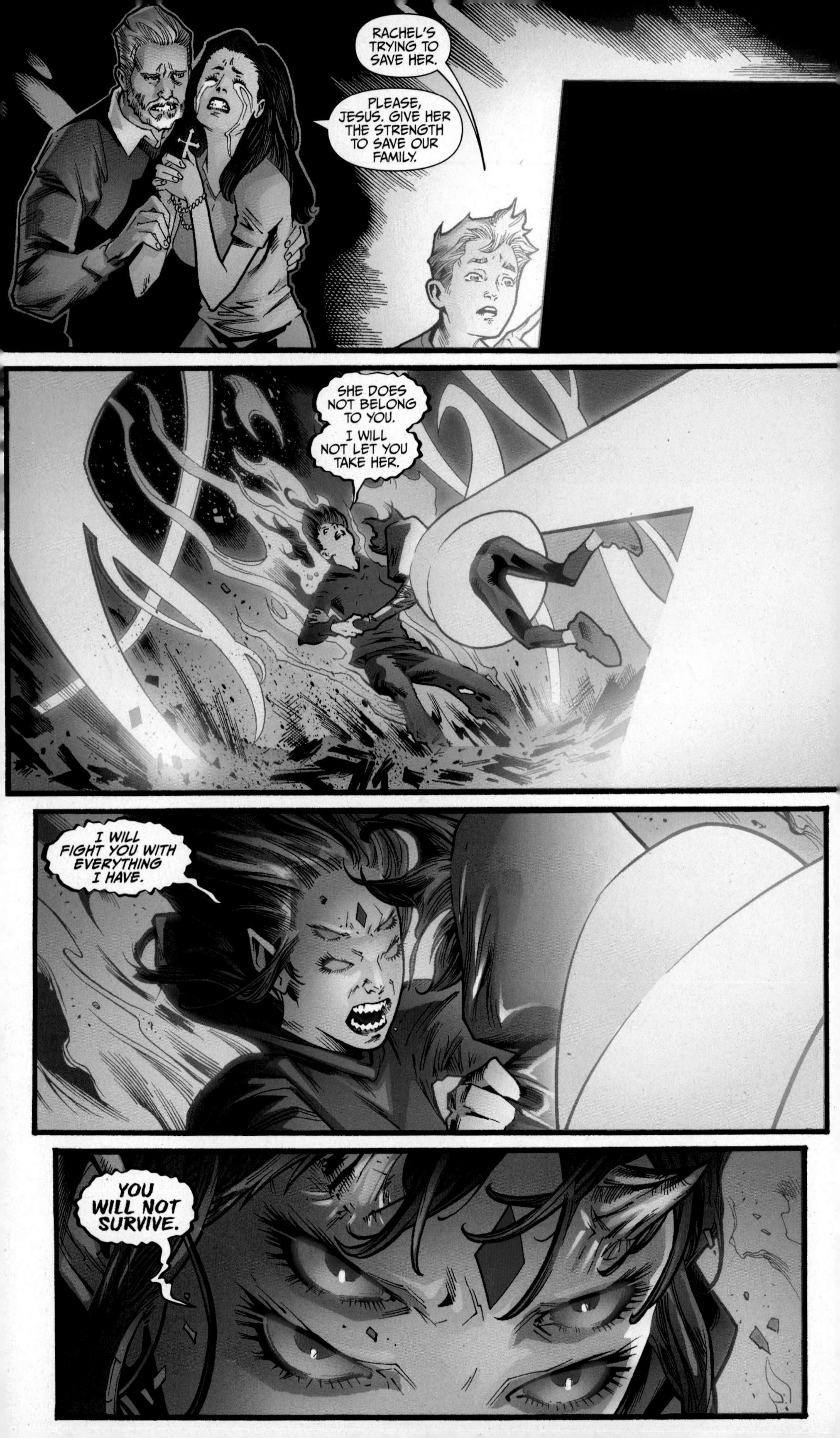
RACHEL'S TRYING TO SAVE HER.
PLEASE, JESUS. GIVE HER THE STRENGTH TO SAVE OUR FAMILY.
SHE DOES NOT BELONG TO YOU.
I WILL NOT LET YOU TAKE HER.
I WILL FIGHT YOU WITH EVERYTHING I HAVE.
YOU WILL NOT SURVIVE.

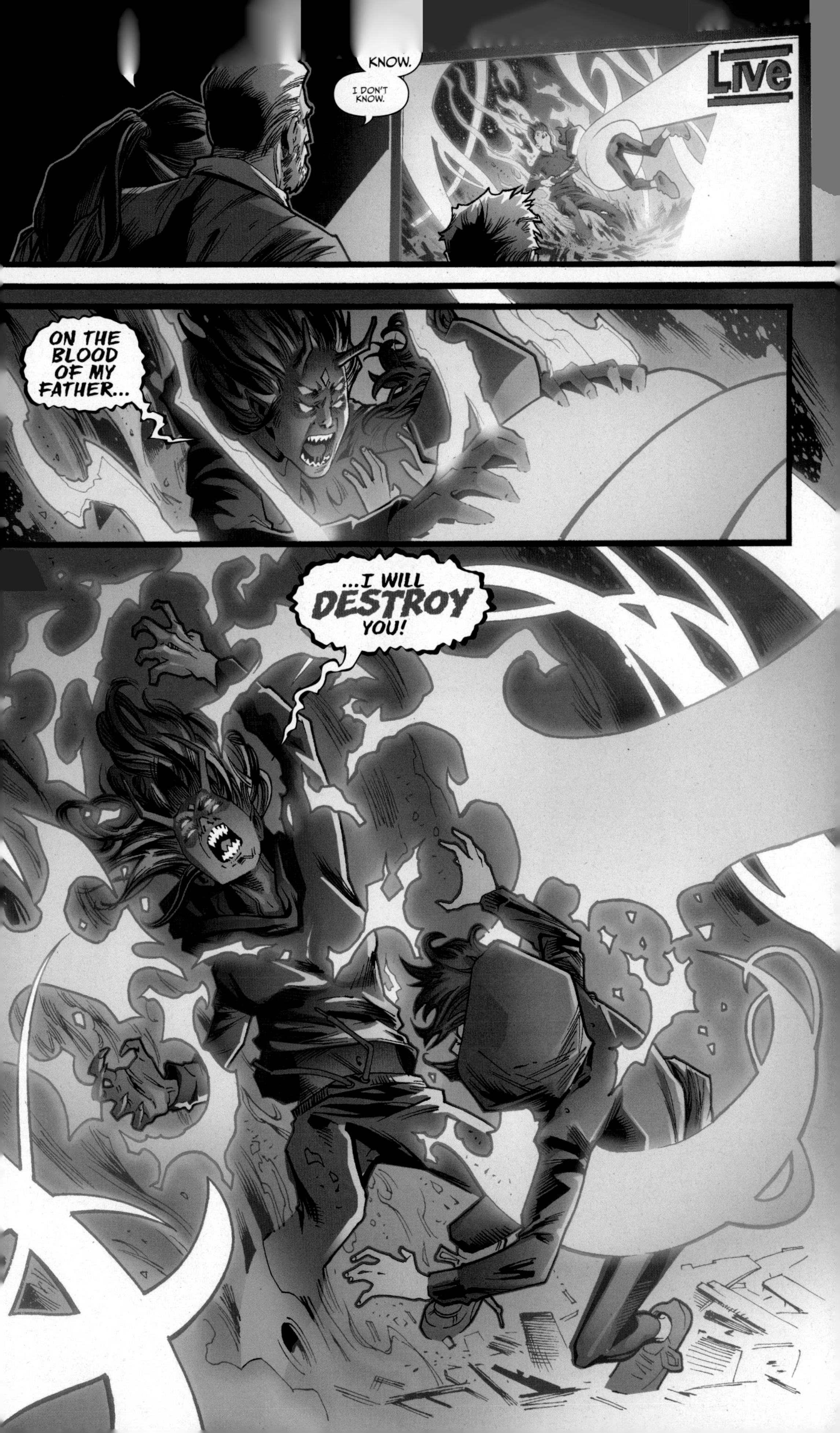
KNOW.
I DON'T KNOW.
LIVE
ON THE BLOOD OF MY FATHER...
...I WILL DESTROY YOU!

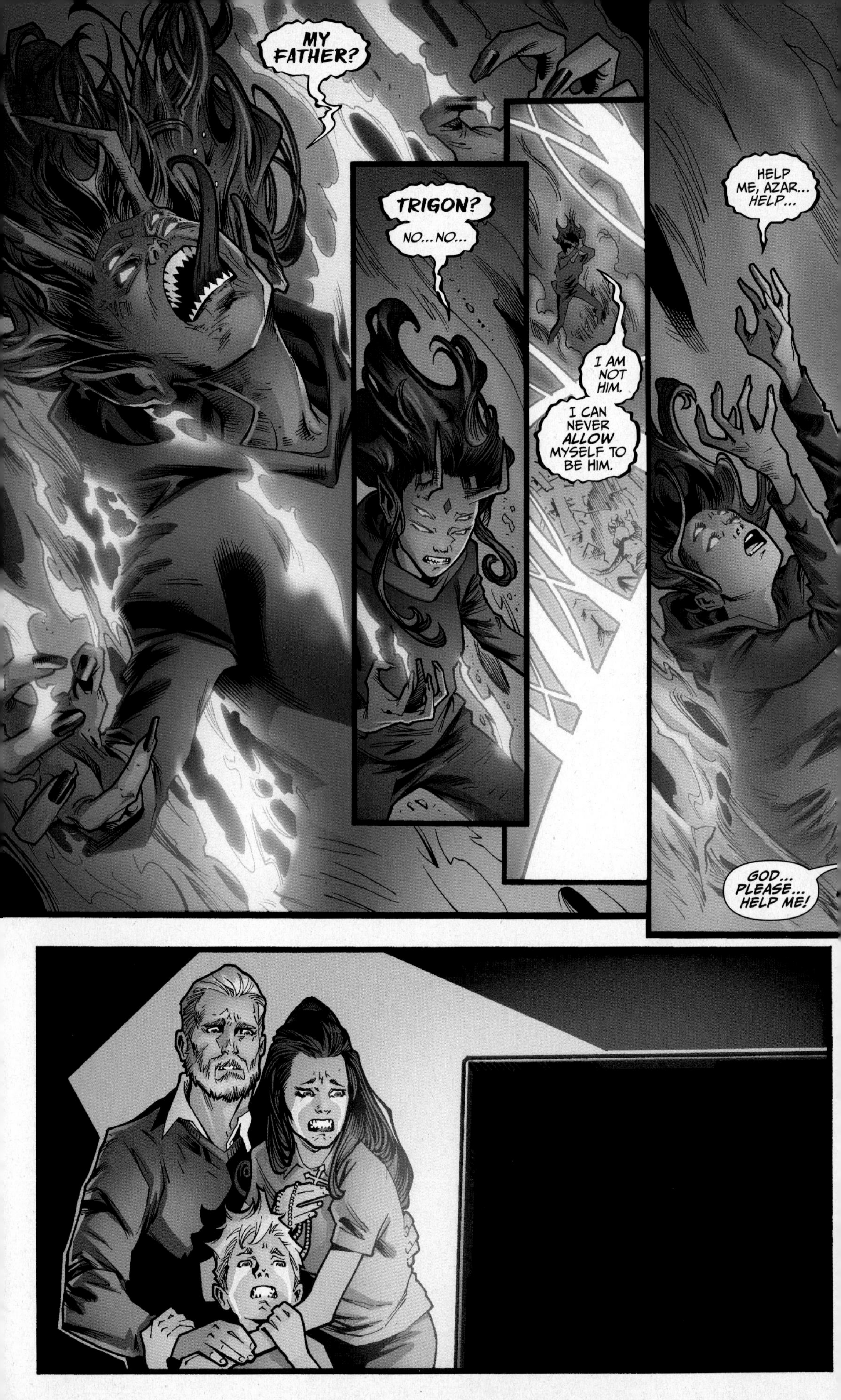
MY FATHER?
TRIGON?
NO... NO...
I AM NOT HIM.
I CAN NEVER ALLOW MYSELF TO BE HIM.
HELP ME, AZAR... HELP...
GOD... PLEASE... HELP ME!

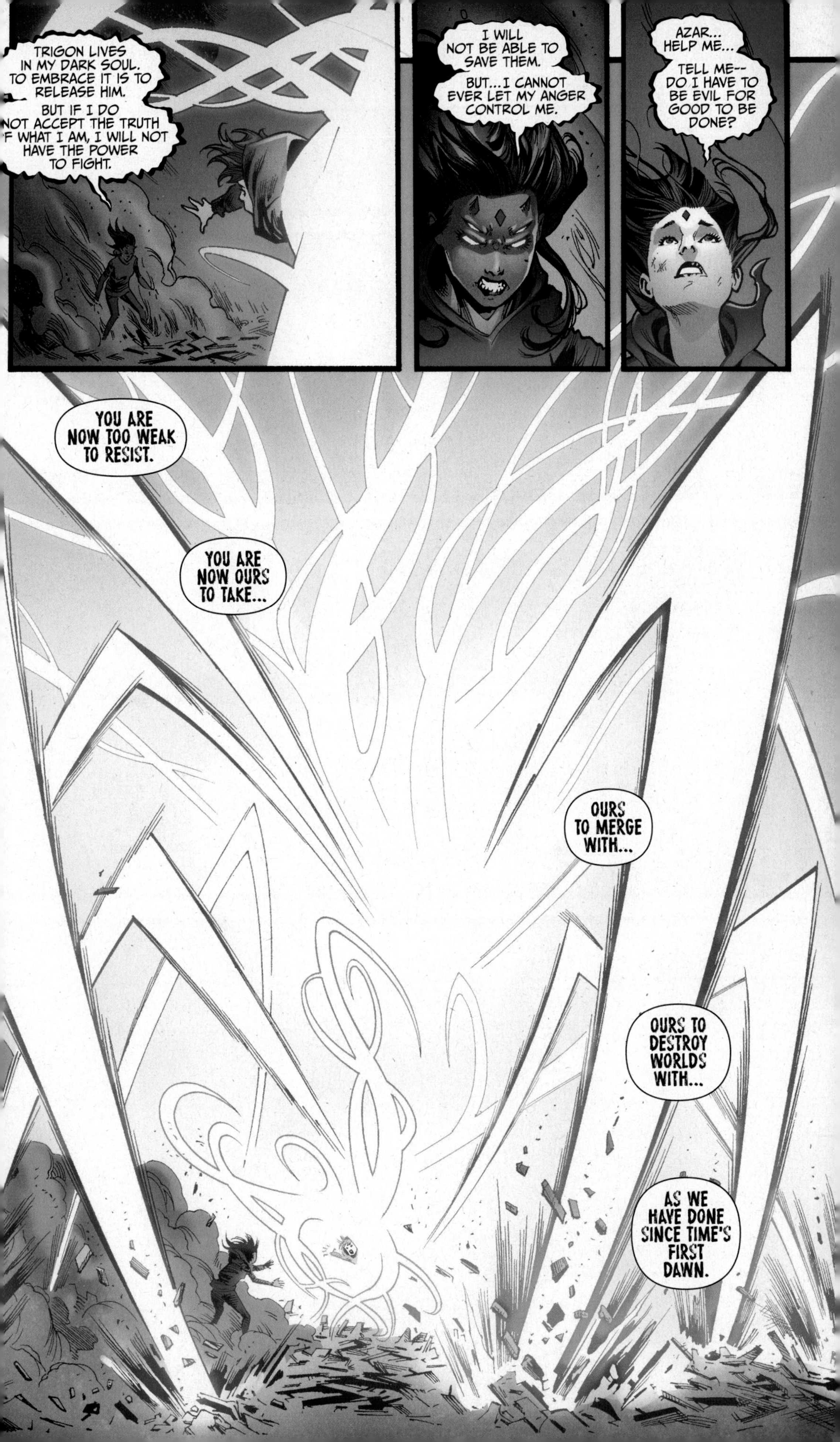
TRIGON LIVES IN MY DARK SOUL. TO EMBRACE IT IS TO RELEASE HIM.
BUT IF I DO NOT ACCEPT THE TRUTH OF WHAT I AM, I WILL NOT HAVE THE POWER TO FIGHT.
I WILL NOT BE ABLE TO SAVE THEM.
BUT...I CANNOT EVER LET MY ANGER CONTROL ME.
AZAR... HELP ME...
TELL ME-- DO I HAVE TO BE EVIL FOR GOOD TO BE DONE?
YOU ARE NOW TOO WEAK TO RESIST.
YOU ARE NOW OURS TO TAKE...
OURS TO MERGE WITH...
OURS TO DESTROY WORLDS WITH...
AS WE HAVE DONE SINCE TIME'S FIRST DAWN.

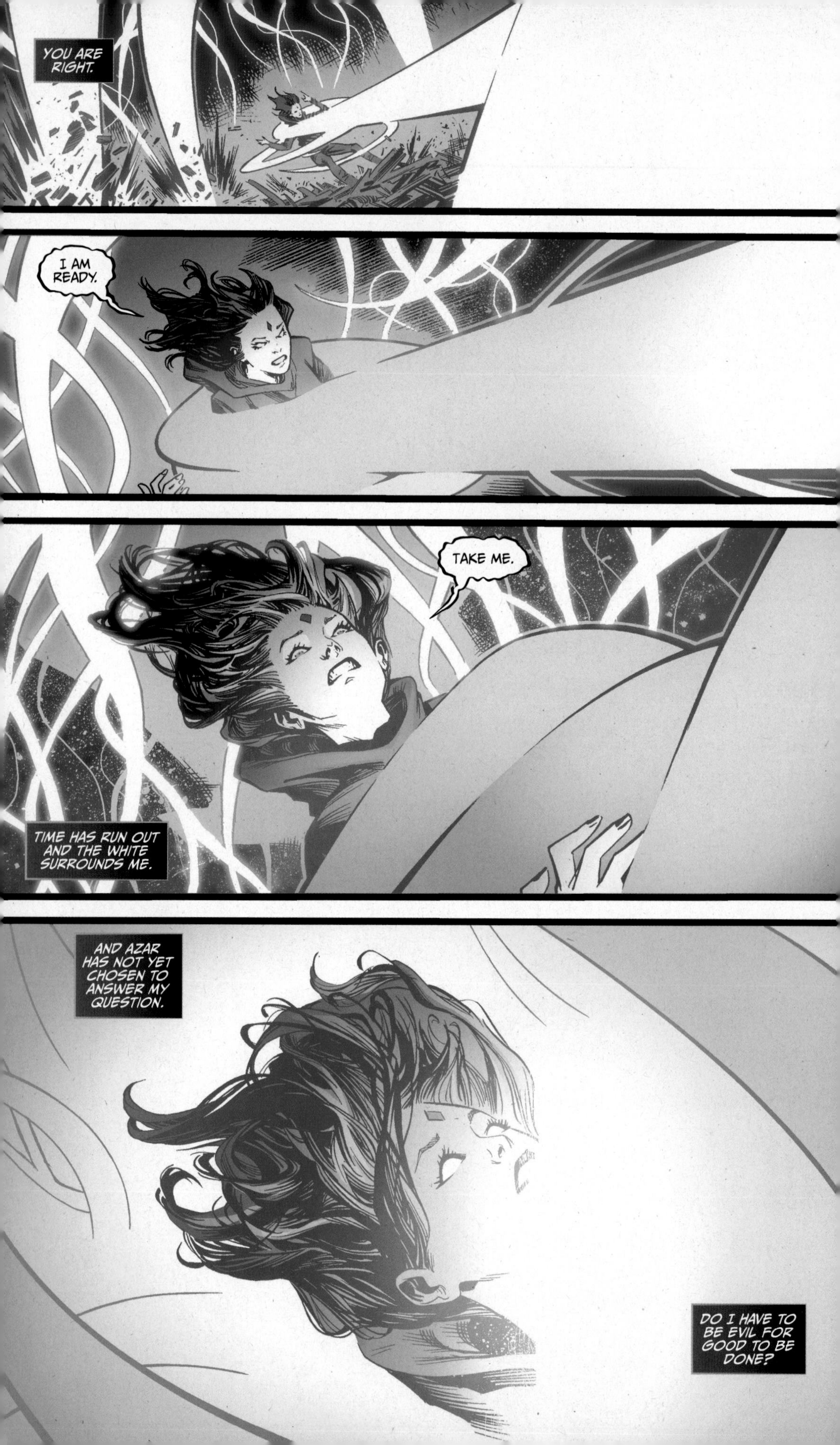
YOU ARE RIGHT.
I AM READY.
TAKE ME.
TIME HAS RUN OUT AND THE WHITE SURROUNDS ME.
AND AZAR HAS NOT YET CHOSEN TO ANSWER MY QUESTION.
DO I HAVE TO BE EVIL FOR GOOD TO BE DONE?

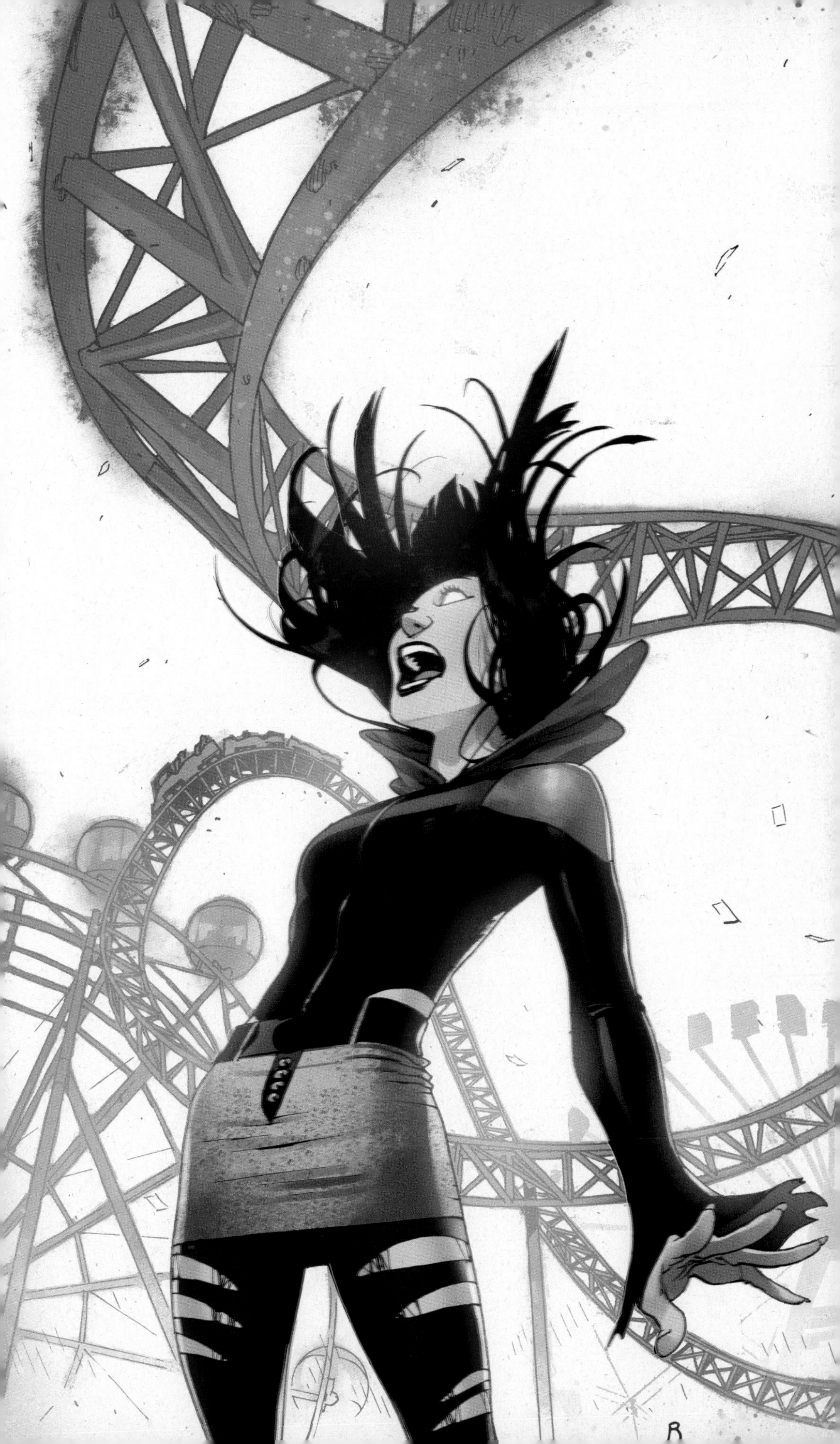

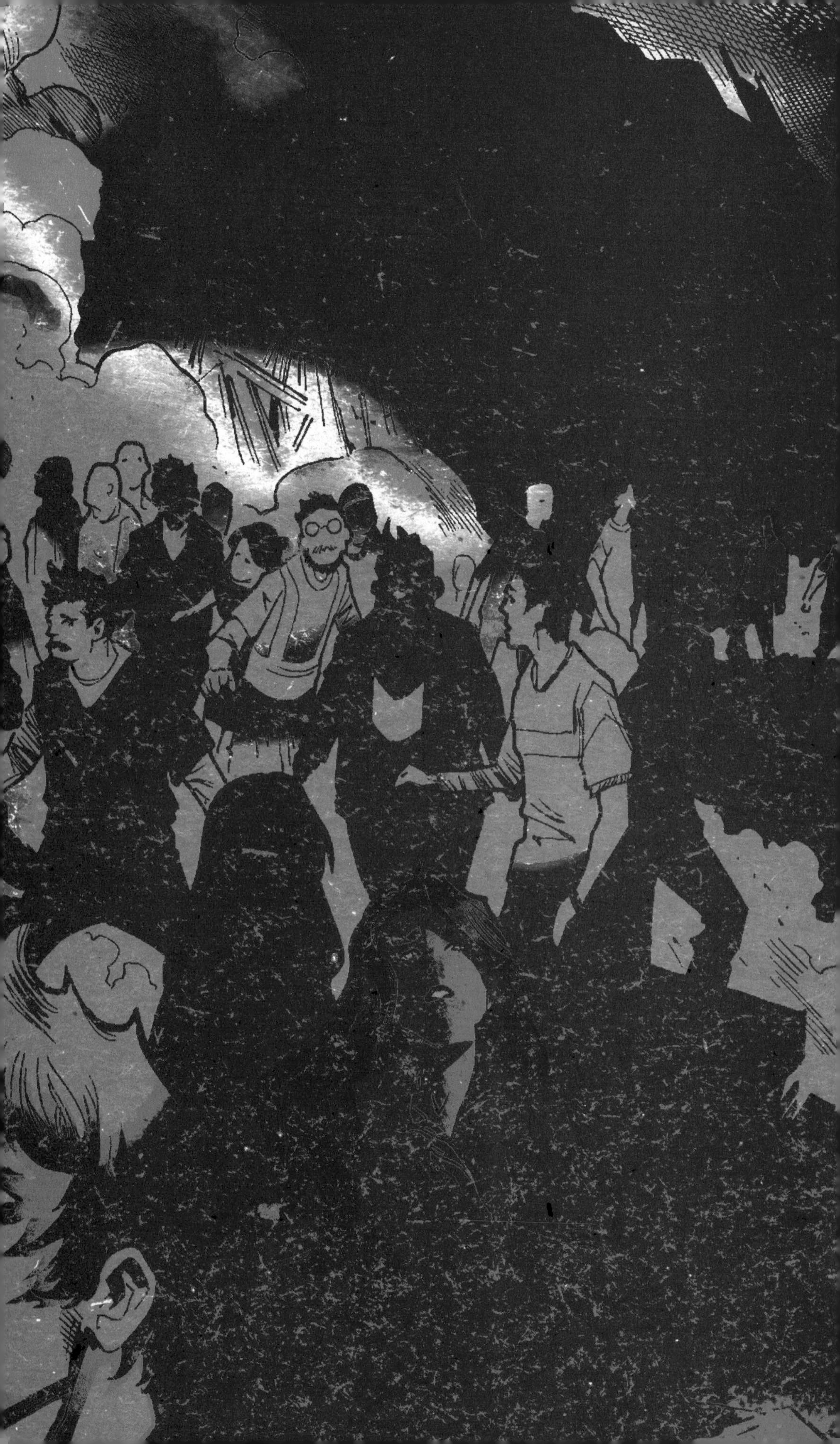

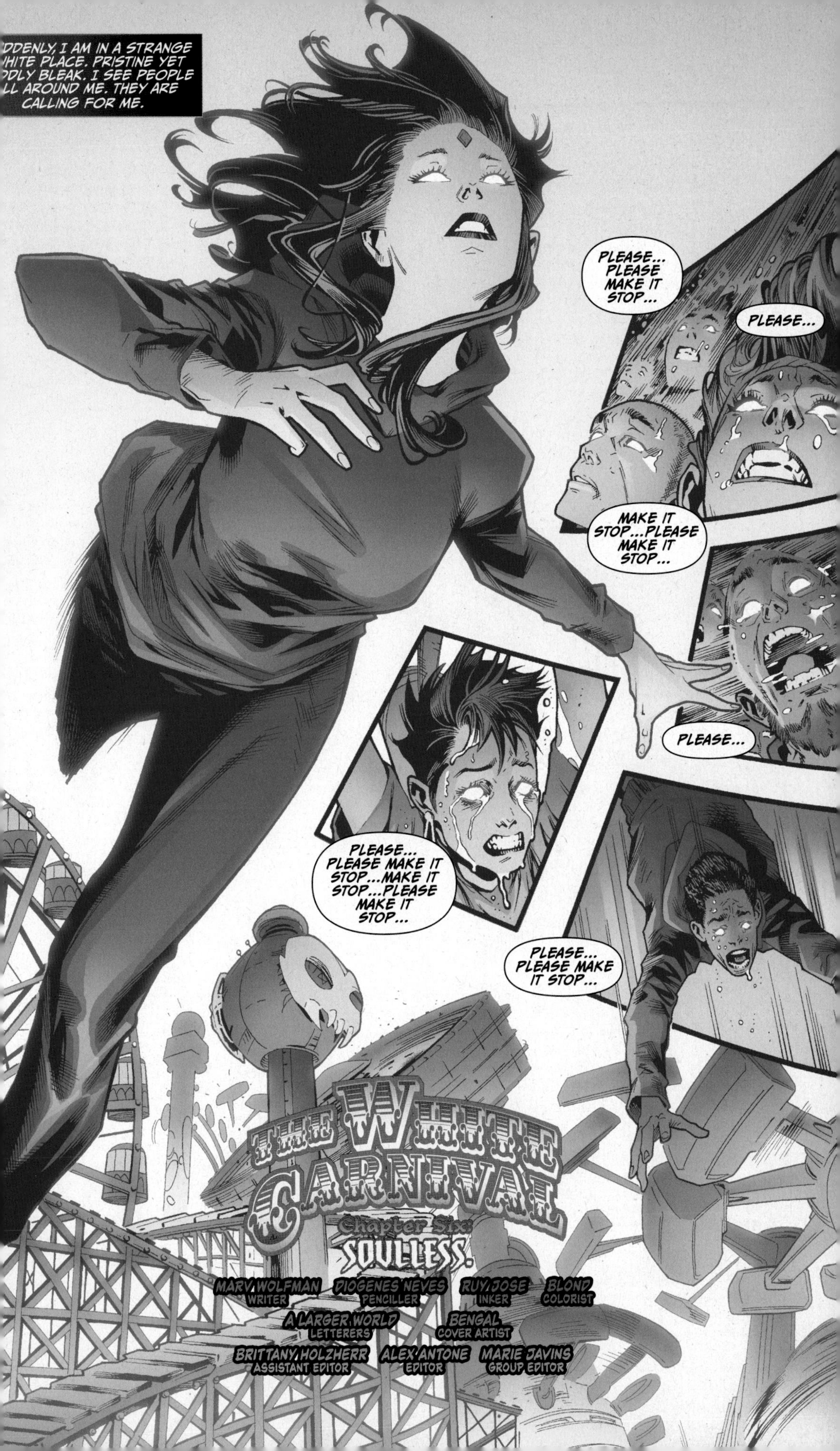

DDENLY, I AM IN A STRANGE
WHITE PLACE. PRISTINE YET
DDLY BLEAK. I SEE PEOPLE
LL AROUND ME. THEY ARE
CALLING FOR ME.
PLEASE... PLEASE MAKE IT STOP...
PLEASE...
MAKE IT STOP...PLEASE MAKE IT STOP...
PLEASE...
PLEASE... PLEASE MAKE IT STOP...MAKE IT STOP...PLEASE MAKE IT STOP...
PLEASE... PLEASE MAKE IT STOP...
THE WHITE CARNIVAL
Chapter Six: SOULLESS.
MARV WOLFMAN WRITER
DIOGENES NEVES PENCILLER
RUY JOSE INKER
BLOND COLORIST
A LARGER WORLD LETTERERS
BENGAL COVER ARTIST
BRITTANY HOLZHERR ASSISTANT EDITOR
ALEX ANTONE EDITOR
MARIE JAVINS GROUP EDITOR

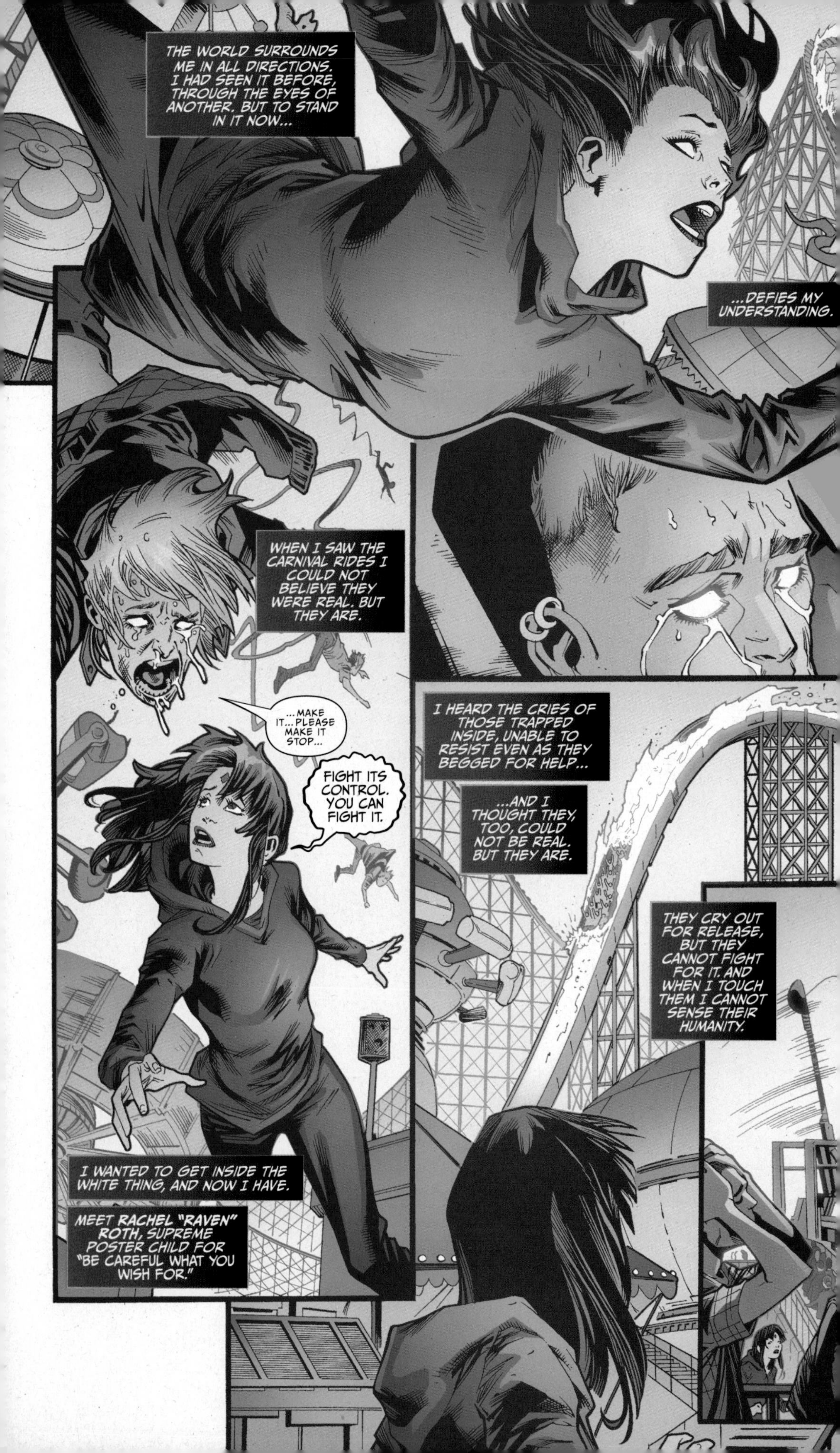
THE WORLD SURROUNDS ME IN ALL DIRECTIONS. I HAD SEEN IT BEFORE, THROUGH THE EYES OF ANOTHER. BUT TO STAND IN IT NOW...
...DEFIES MY UNDERSTANDING.
WHEN I SAW THE CARNIVAL RIDES I COULD NOT BELIEVE THEY WERE REAL. BUT THEY ARE.
...MAKE IT... PLEASE MAKE IT STOP...
FIGHT ITS CONTROL. YOU CAN FIGHT IT.
I WANTED TO GET INSIDE THE WHITE THING, AND NOW I HAVE.
MEET RACHEL "RAVEN" ROTH, SUPREME POSTER CHILD FOR "BE CAREFUL WHAT YOU WISH FOR."
I HEARD THE CRIES OF THOSE TRAPPED INSIDE, UNABLE TO RESIST EVEN AS THEY BEGGED FOR HELP...
...AND I THOUGHT THEY, TOO, COULD NOT BE REAL. BUT THEY ARE.
THEY CRY OUT FOR RELEASE, BUT THEY CANNOT FIGHT FOR IT. AND WHEN I TOUCH THEM I CANNOT SENSE THEIR HUMANITY.

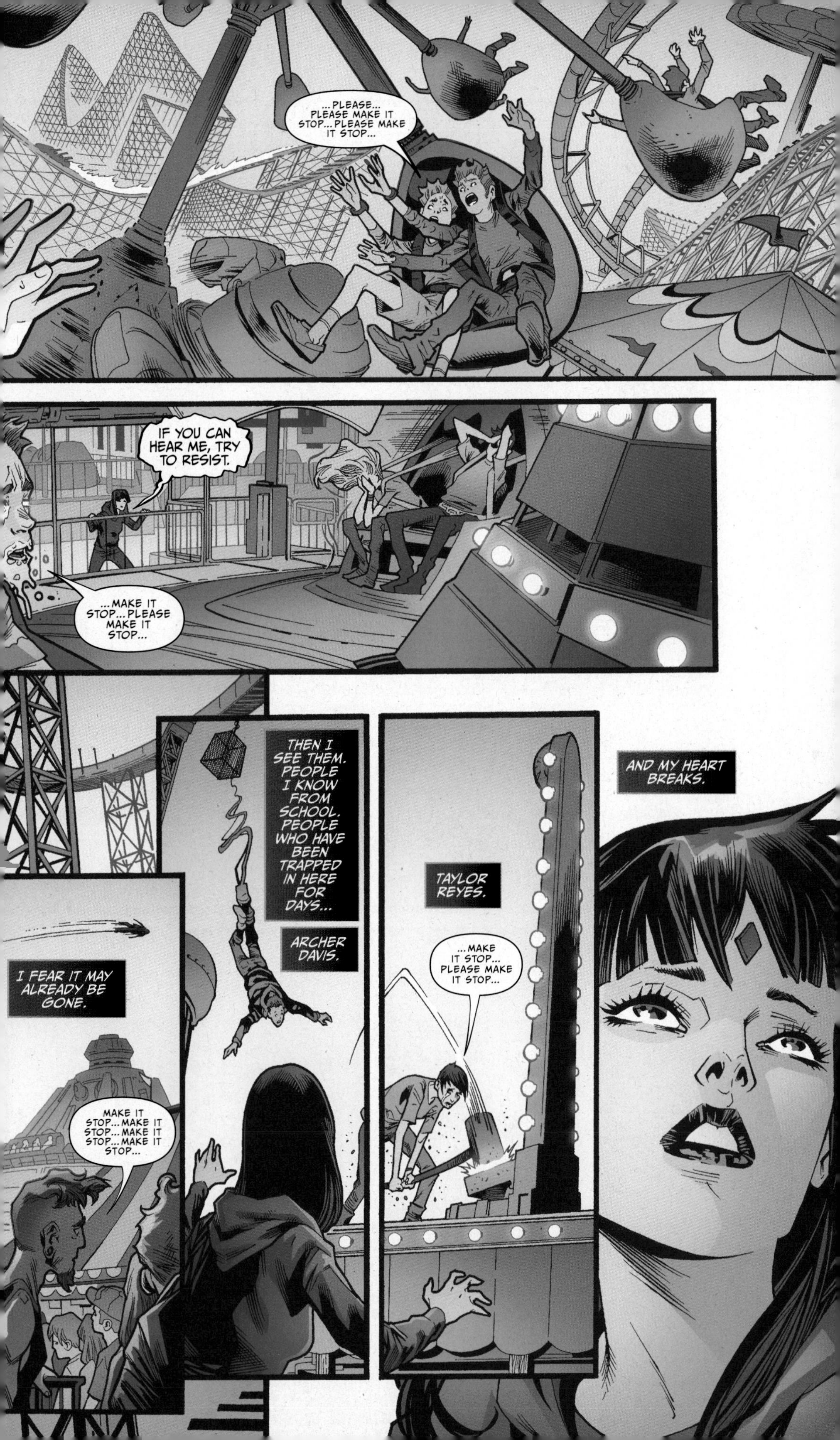
...PLEASE... PLEASE MAKE IT STOP...PLEASE MAKE IT STOP...
IF YOU CAN HEAR ME, TRY TO RESIST.
...MAKE IT STOP...PLEASE MAKE IT STOP...
THEN I SEE THEM. PEOPLE I KNOW FROM SCHOOL. PEOPLE WHO HAVE BEEN TRAPPED IN HERE FOR DAYS...
ARCHER DAVIS.
TAYLOR REYES.
...MAKE IT STOP... PLEASE MAKE IT STOP...
AND MY HEART BREAKS.
I FEAR IT MAY ALREADY BE GONE.
MAKE IT STOP...MAKE IT STOP...MAKE IT STOP...MAKE IT STOP...

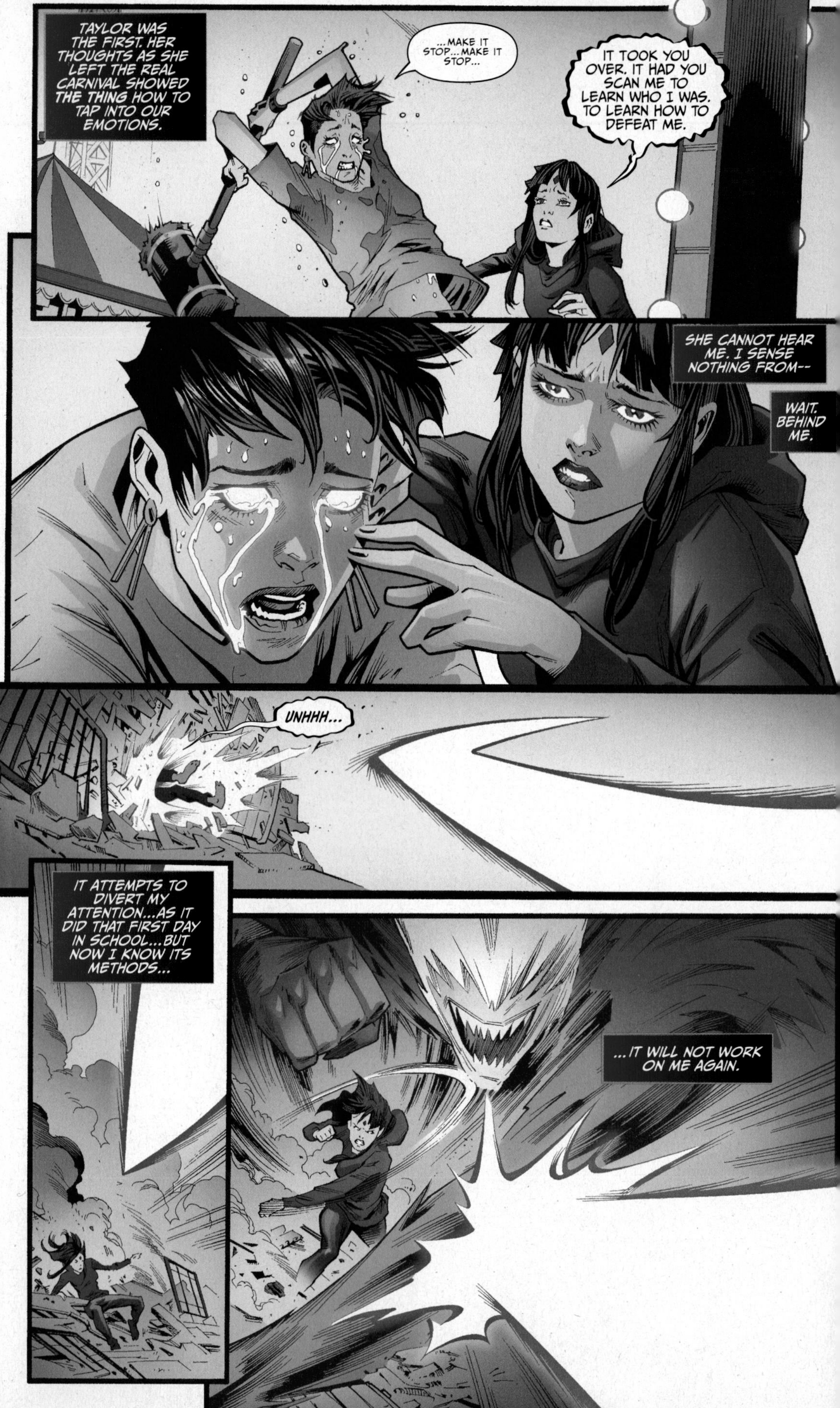
TAYLOR WAS THE FIRST. HER THOUGHTS AS SHE LEFT THE REAL CARNIVAL SHOWED THE THING HOW TO TAP INTO OUR EMOTIONS.
...MAKE IT STOP...MAKE IT STOP...
IT TOOK YOU OVER. IT HAD YOU SCAN ME TO LEARN WHO I WAS. TO LEARN HOW TO DEFEAT ME.
SHE CANNOT HEAR ME. I SENSE NOTHING FROM--
WAIT. BEHIND ME.
UNHHH...
IT ATTEMPTS TO DIVERT MY ATTENTION...AS IT DID THAT FIRST DAY IN SCHOOL...BUT NOW I KNOW ITS METHODS...
...IT WILL NOT WORK ON ME AGAIN.

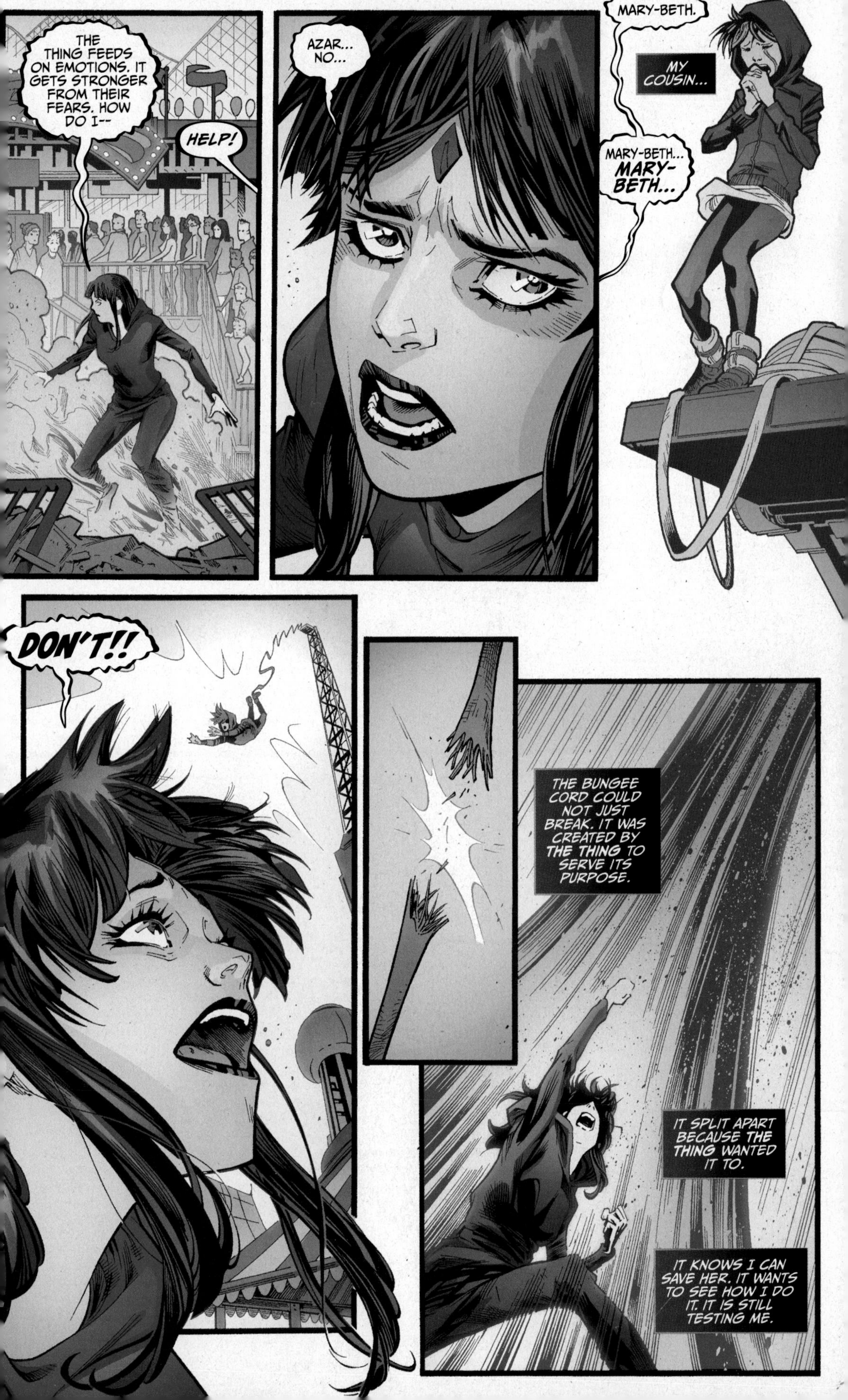
THE THING FEEDS ON EMOTIONS. IT GETS STRONGER FROM THEIR FEARS. HOW DO I--
HELP!
AZAR... NO...
MARY-BETH.
MY COUSIN...
MARY-BETH... MARY-BETH...
DON'T!!
THE BUNGEE CORD COULD NOT JUST BREAK. IT WAS CREATED BY THE THING TO SERVE ITS PURPOSE.
IT SPLIT APART BECAUSE THE THING WANTED IT TO.
IT KNOWS I CAN SAVE HER. IT WANTS TO SEE HOW I DO IT. IT IS STILL TESTING ME.

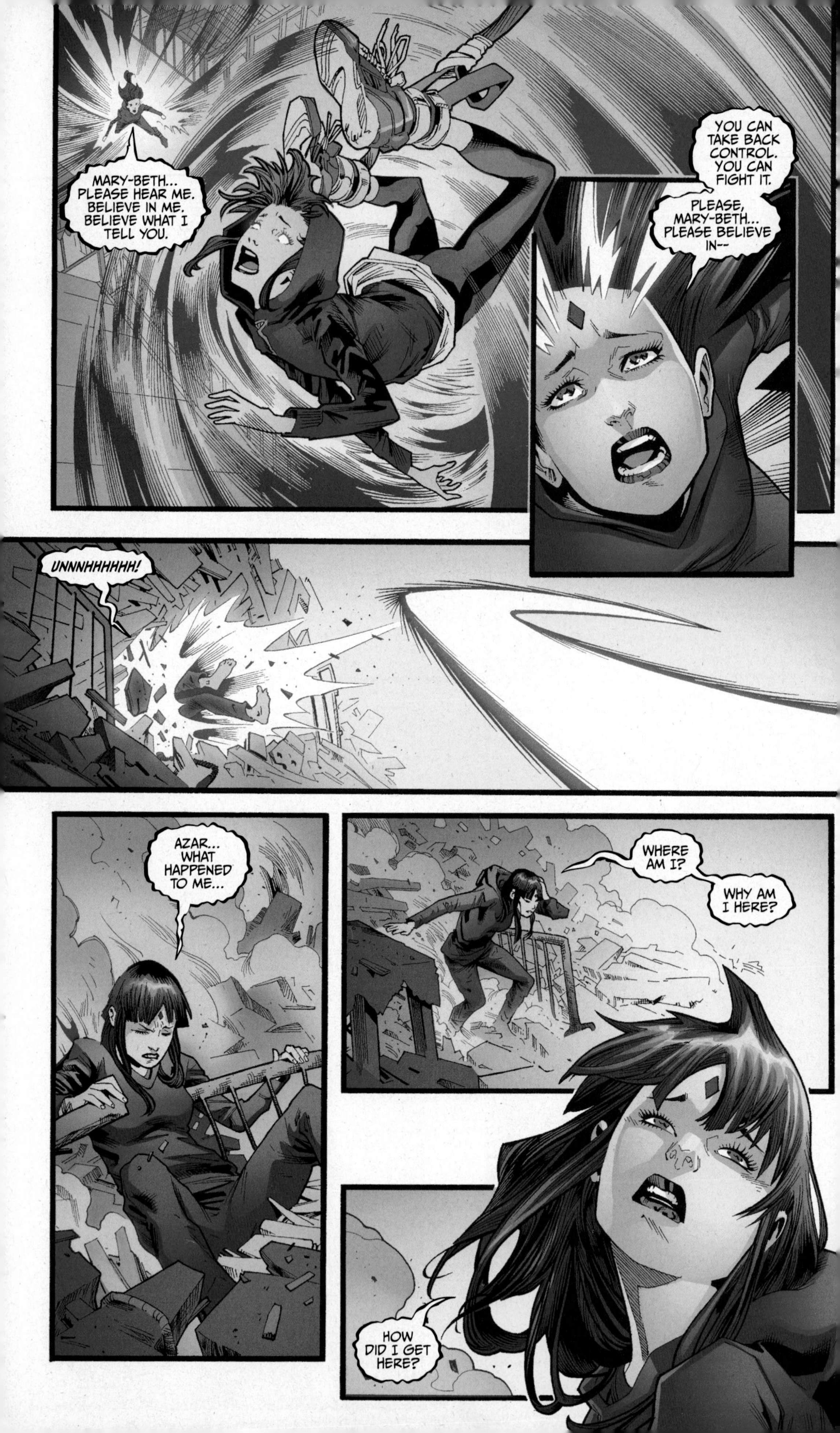
MARY-BETH... PLEASE HEAR ME. BELIEVE IN ME. BELIEVE WHAT I TELL YOU.
YOU CAN TAKE BACK CONTROL. YOU CAN FIGHT IT.
PLEASE, MARY-BETH... PLEASE BELIEVE IN--
UNNNHHHHHH!
AZAR... WHAT HAPPENED TO ME...
WHERE AM I?
WHY AM I HERE?
HOW DID I GET HERE?

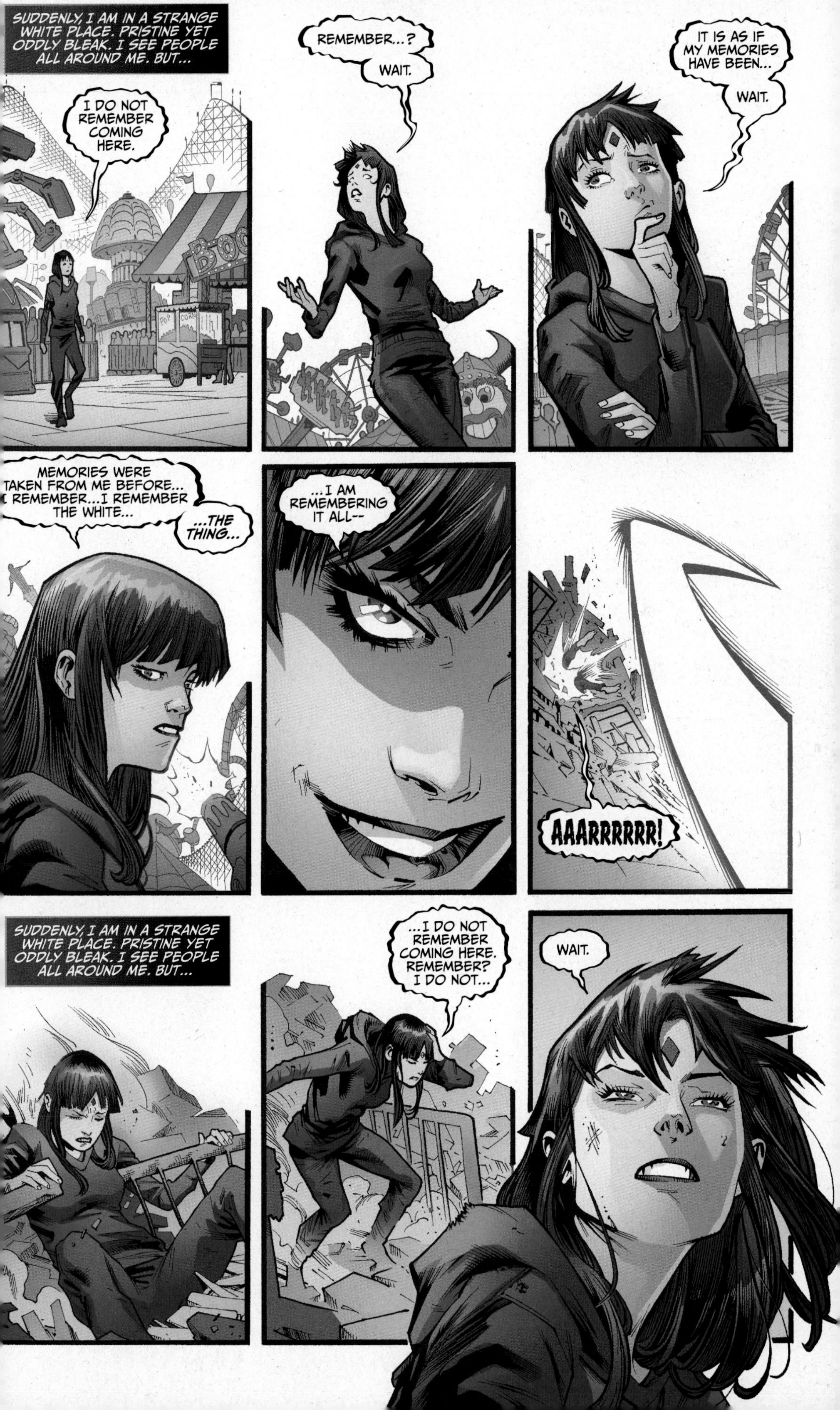

SUDDENLY, I AM IN A STRANGE WHITE PLACE. PRISTINE YET ODDLY BLEAK. I SEE PEOPLE ALL AROUND ME. BUT...
I DO NOT REMEMBER COMING HERE.
REMEMBER...?
WAIT.
IT IS AS IF MY MEMORIES HAVE BEEN...
WAIT.
MEMORIES WERE TAKEN FROM ME BEFORE... I REMEMBER...I REMEMBER THE WHITE...
...THE THING...
...I AM REMEMBERING IT ALL--
AAARRRRRR!
SUDDENLY, I AM IN A STRANGE WHITE PLACE. PRISTINE YET ODDLY BLEAK. I SEE PEOPLE ALL AROUND ME. BUT...
...I DO NOT REMEMBER COMING HERE. REMEMBER? I DO NOT...
WAIT.

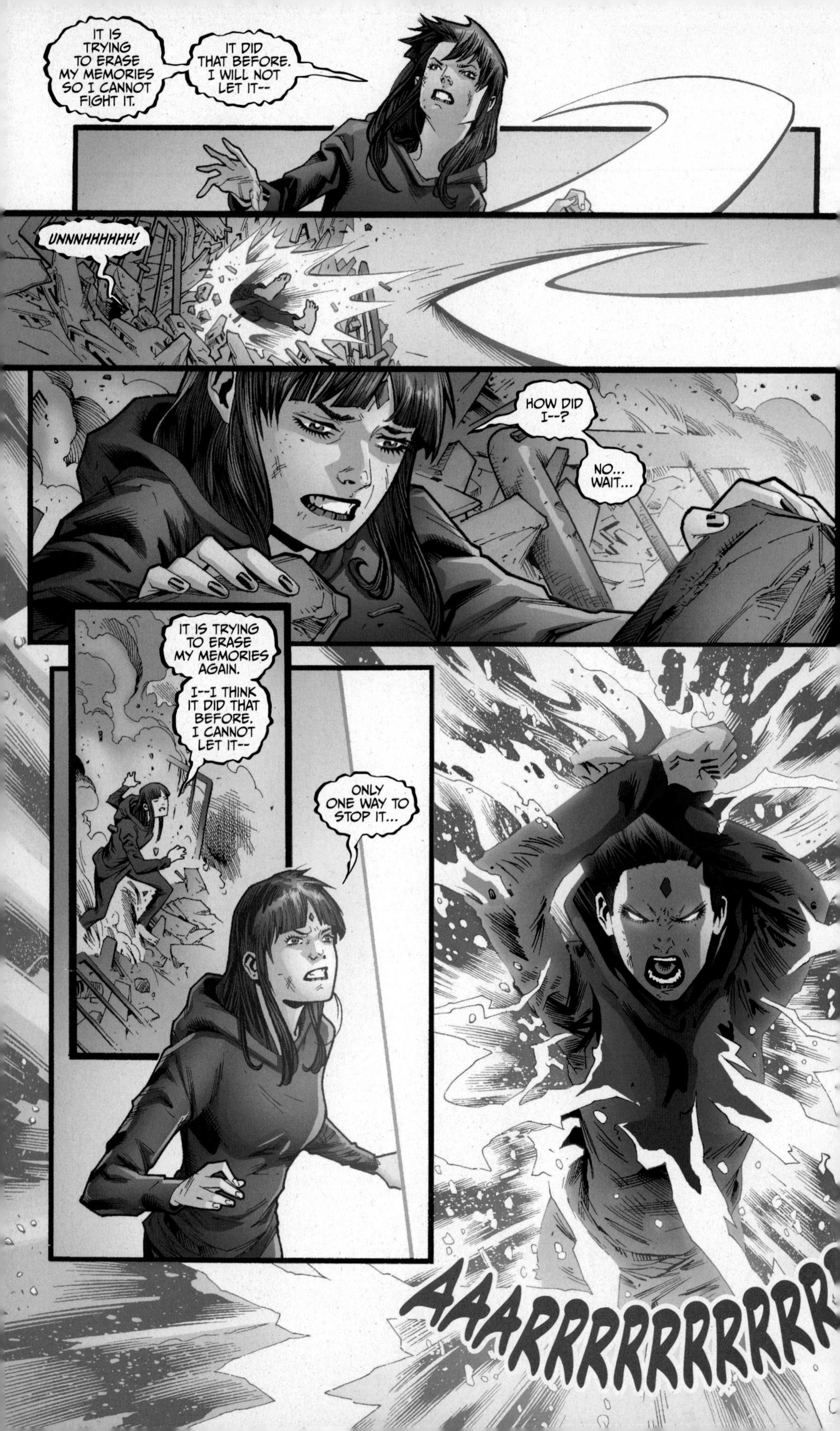
IT IS TRYING TO ERASE MY MEMORIES SO I CANNOT FIGHT IT.
IT DID THAT BEFORE. I WILL NOT LET IT--
UNNNHHHHHH!
HOW DID I--?
NO... WAIT...
IT IS TRYING TO ERASE MY MEMORIES AGAIN.
I--I THINK IT DID THAT BEFORE. I CANNOT LET IT--
ONLY ONE WAY TO STOP IT...
AAARRRRRRRRRR

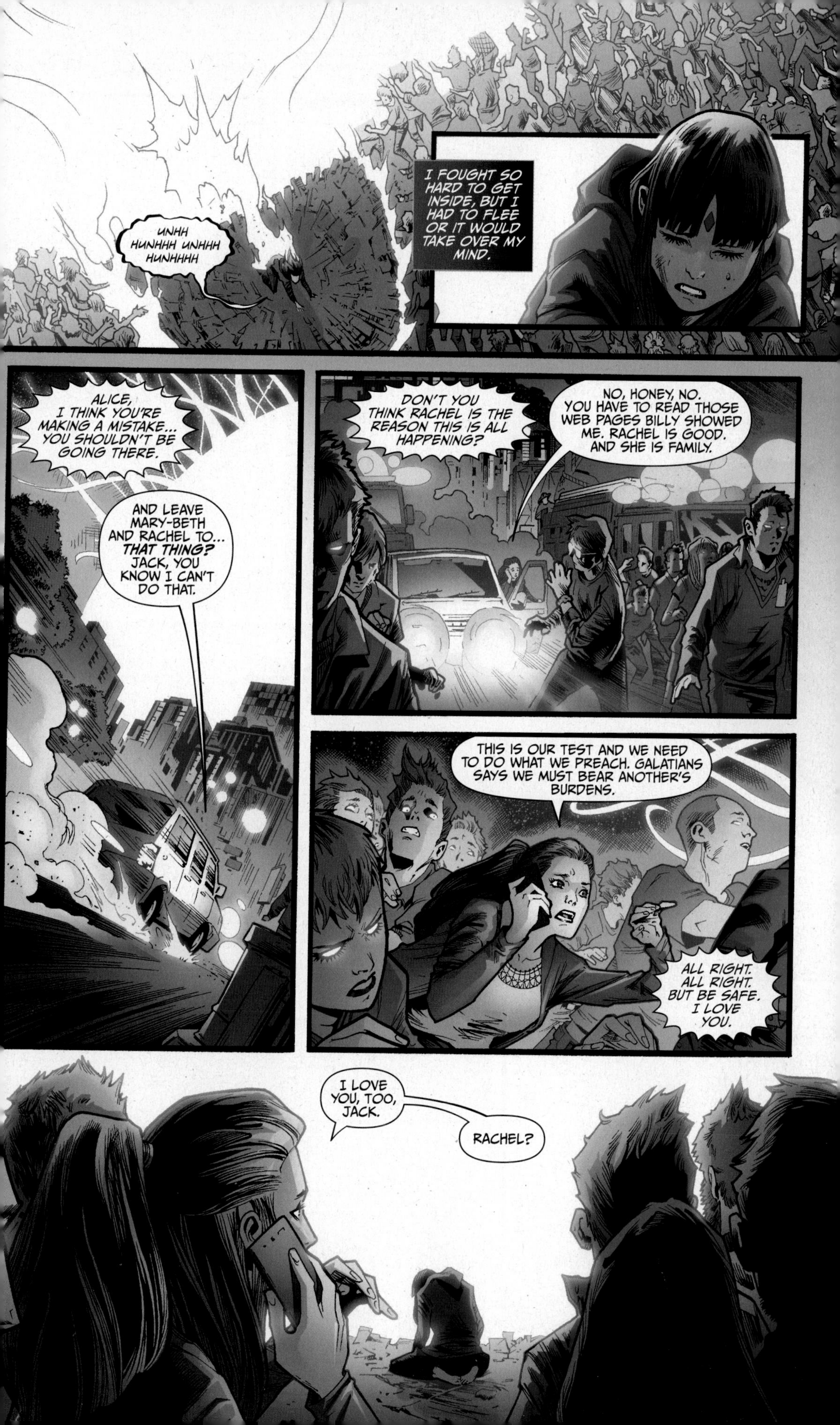

UNHH HUNHHH UNHHH HUNHHHH
I FOUGHT SO HARD TO GET INSIDE, BUT I HAD TO FLEE OR IT WOULD TAKE OVER MY MIND.
ALICE, I THINK YOU'RE MAKING A MISTAKE... YOU SHOULDN'T BE GOING THERE.
AND LEAVE MARY-BETH AND RACHEL TO... THAT THING? JACK, YOU KNOW I CAN'T DO THAT.
DON'T YOU THINK RACHEL IS THE REASON THIS IS ALL HAPPENING?
NO, HONEY, NO. YOU HAVE TO READ THOSE WEB PAGES BILLY SHOWED ME. RACHEL IS GOOD. AND SHE IS FAMILY.
THIS IS OUR TEST AND WE NEED TO DO WHAT WE PREACH. GALATIANS SAYS WE MUST BEAR ANOTHER'S BURDENS.
ALL RIGHT. ALL RIGHT. BUT BE SAFE. I LOVE YOU.
I LOVE YOU, TOO, JACK.
RACHEL?

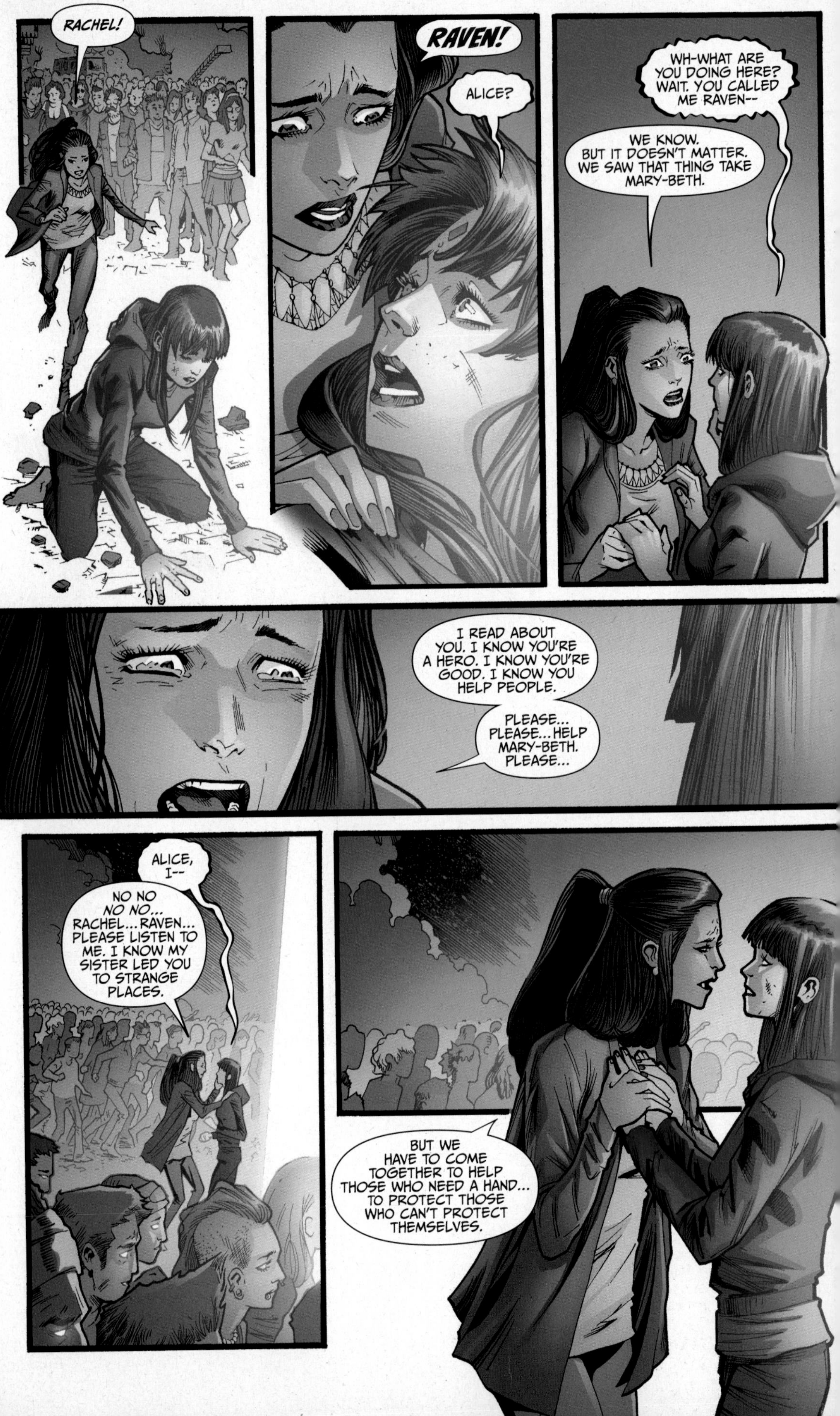
RACHEL!
RAVEN!
ALICE?
WH-WHAT ARE YOU DOING HERE? WAIT. YOU CALLED ME RAVEN--
WE KNOW. BUT IT DOESN'T MATTER. WE SAW THAT THING TAKE MARY-BETH.
I READ ABOUT YOU. I KNOW YOU'RE A HERO. I KNOW YOU'RE GOOD. I KNOW YOU HELP PEOPLE.
PLEASE... PLEASE...HELP MARY-BETH. PLEASE...
ALICE, I--
NO NO NO NO... RACHEL...RAVEN... PLEASE LISTEN TO ME. I KNOW MY SISTER LED YOU TO STRANGE PLACES.
BUT WE HAVE TO COME TOGETHER TO HELP THOSE WHO NEED A HAND... TO PROTECT THOSE WHO CAN'T PROTECT THEMSELVES.

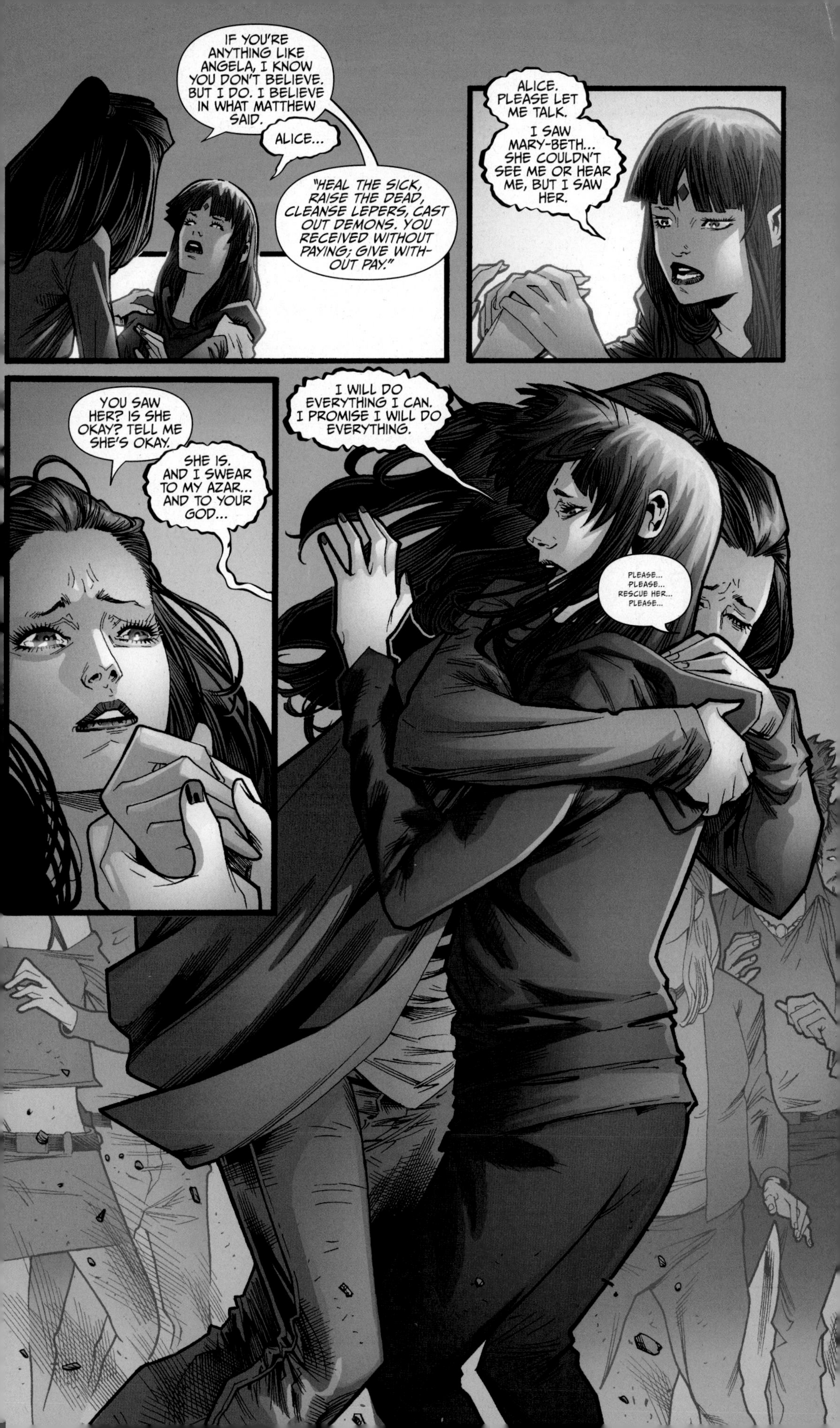
IF YOU'RE ANYTHING LIKE ANGELA, I KNOW YOU DON'T BELIEVE. BUT I DO. I BELIEVE IN WHAT MATTHEW SAID.
ALICE...
"HEAL THE SICK, RAISE THE DEAD, CLEANSE LEPERS, CAST OUT DEMONS. YOU RECEIVED WITHOUT PAYING; GIVE WITH-OUT PAY."
ALICE. PLEASE LET ME TALK.
I SAW MARY-BETH... SHE COULDN'T SEE ME OR HEAR ME, BUT I SAW HER.
YOU SAW HER? IS SHE OKAY? TELL ME SHE'S OKAY.
SHE IS. AND I SWEAR TO MY AZAR... AND TO YOUR GOD...
I WILL DO EVERYTHING I CAN. I PROMISE I WILL DO EVERYTHING.
PLEASE... PLEASE... RESCUE HER... PLEASE...

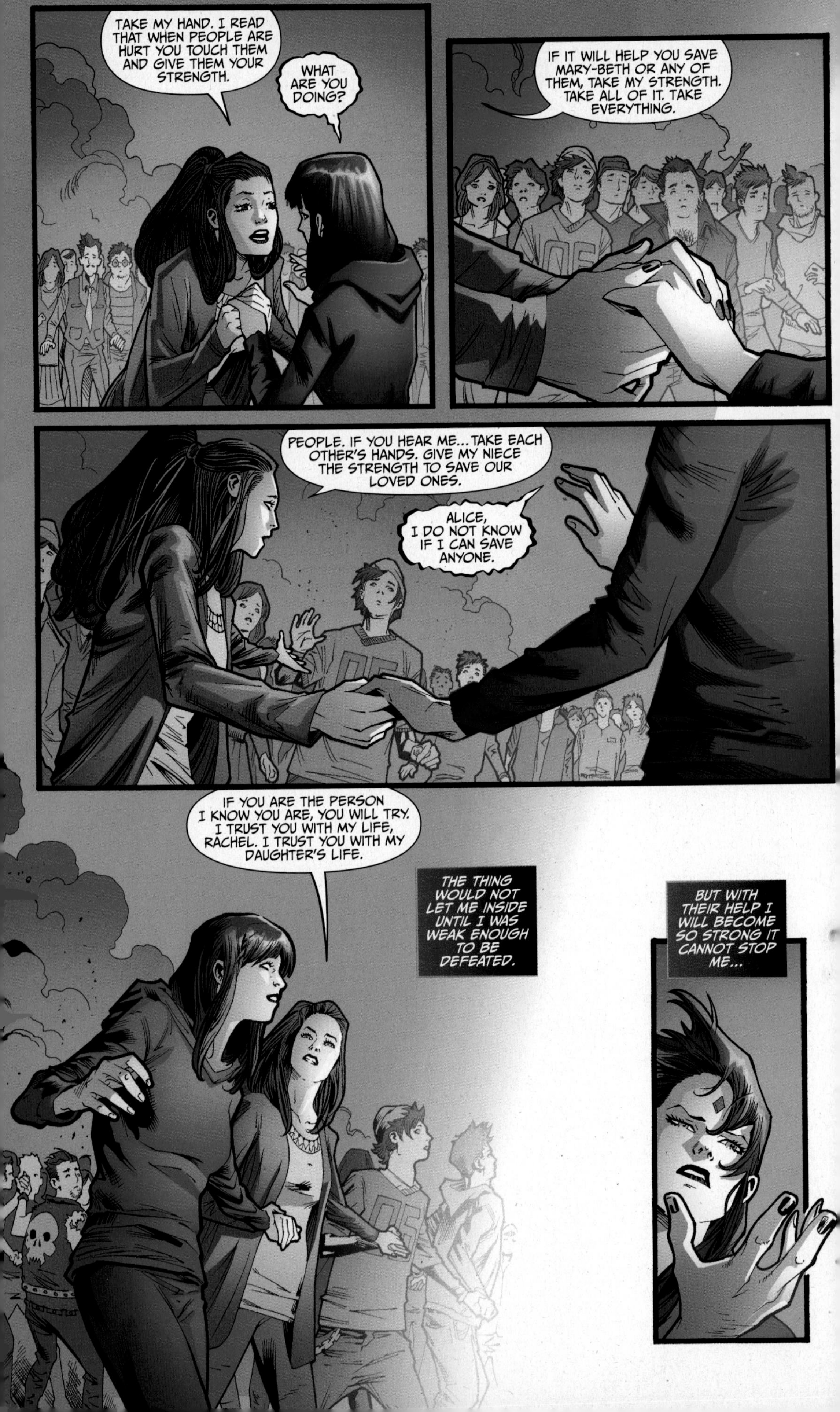
TAKE MY HAND. I READ THAT WHEN PEOPLE ARE HURT YOU TOUCH THEM AND GIVE THEM YOUR STRENGTH.
WHAT ARE YOU DOING?
IF IT WILL HELP YOU SAVE MARY-BETH OR ANY OF THEM, TAKE MY STRENGTH. TAKE ALL OF IT. TAKE EVERYTHING.
PEOPLE. IF YOU HEAR ME... TAKE EACH OTHER'S HANDS. GIVE MY NIECE THE STRENGTH TO SAVE OUR LOVED ONES.
ALICE, I DO NOT KNOW IF I CAN SAVE ANYONE.
IF YOU ARE THE PERSON I KNOW YOU ARE, YOU WILL TRY. I TRUST YOU WITH MY LIFE, RACHEL. I TRUST YOU WITH MY DAUGHTER'S LIFE.
THE THING WOULD NOT LET ME INSIDE UNTIL I WAS WEAK ENOUGH TO BE DEFEATED.
BUT WITH THEIR HELP I WILL BECOME SO STRONG IT CANNOT STOP ME...

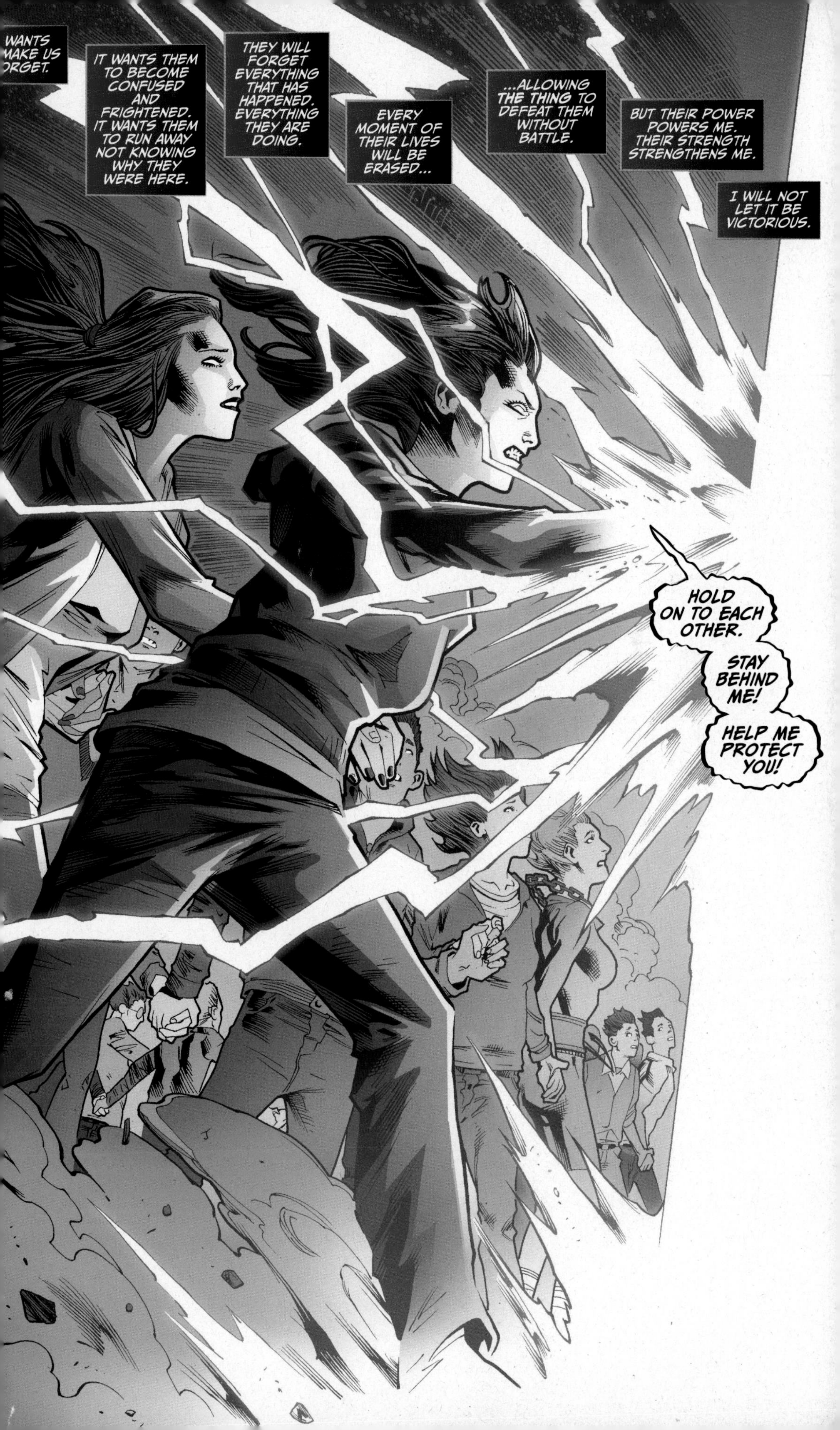
WANTS
MAKE US
ORGET.
IT WANTS THEM TO BECOME CONFUSED AND FRIGHTENED. IT WANTS THEM TO RUN AWAY NOT KNOWING WHY THEY WERE HERE.
THEY WILL FORGET EVERYTHING THAT HAS HAPPENED. EVERYTHING THEY ARE DOING.
EVERY MOMENT OF THEIR LIVES WILL BE ERASED...
...ALLOWING THE THING TO DEFEAT THEM WITHOUT BATTLE.
BUT THEIR POWER POWERS ME. THEIR STRENGTH STRENGTHENS ME.
I WILL NOT LET IT BE VICTORIOUS.
HOLD ON TO EACH OTHER.
STAY BEHIND ME!
HELP ME PROTECT YOU!

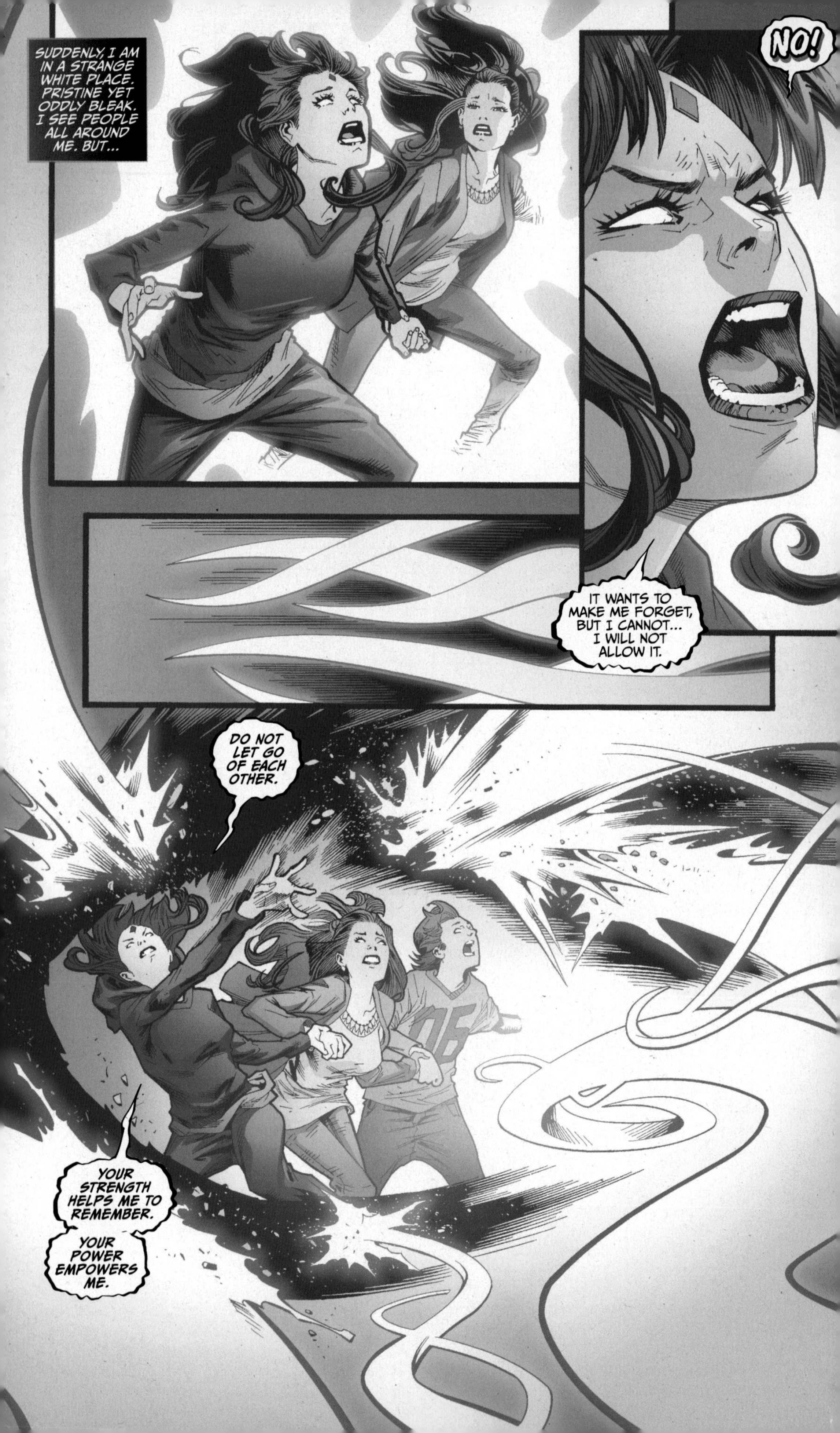
SUDDENLY, I AM IN A STRANGE WHITE PLACE. PRISTINE YET ODDLY BLEAK. I SEE PEOPLE ALL AROUND ME. BUT...
NO!
IT WANTS TO MAKE ME FORGET, BUT I CANNOT... I WILL NOT ALLOW IT.
DO NOT LET GO OF EACH OTHER.
YOUR STRENGTH HELPS ME TO REMEMBER.
YOUR POWER EMPOWERS ME.

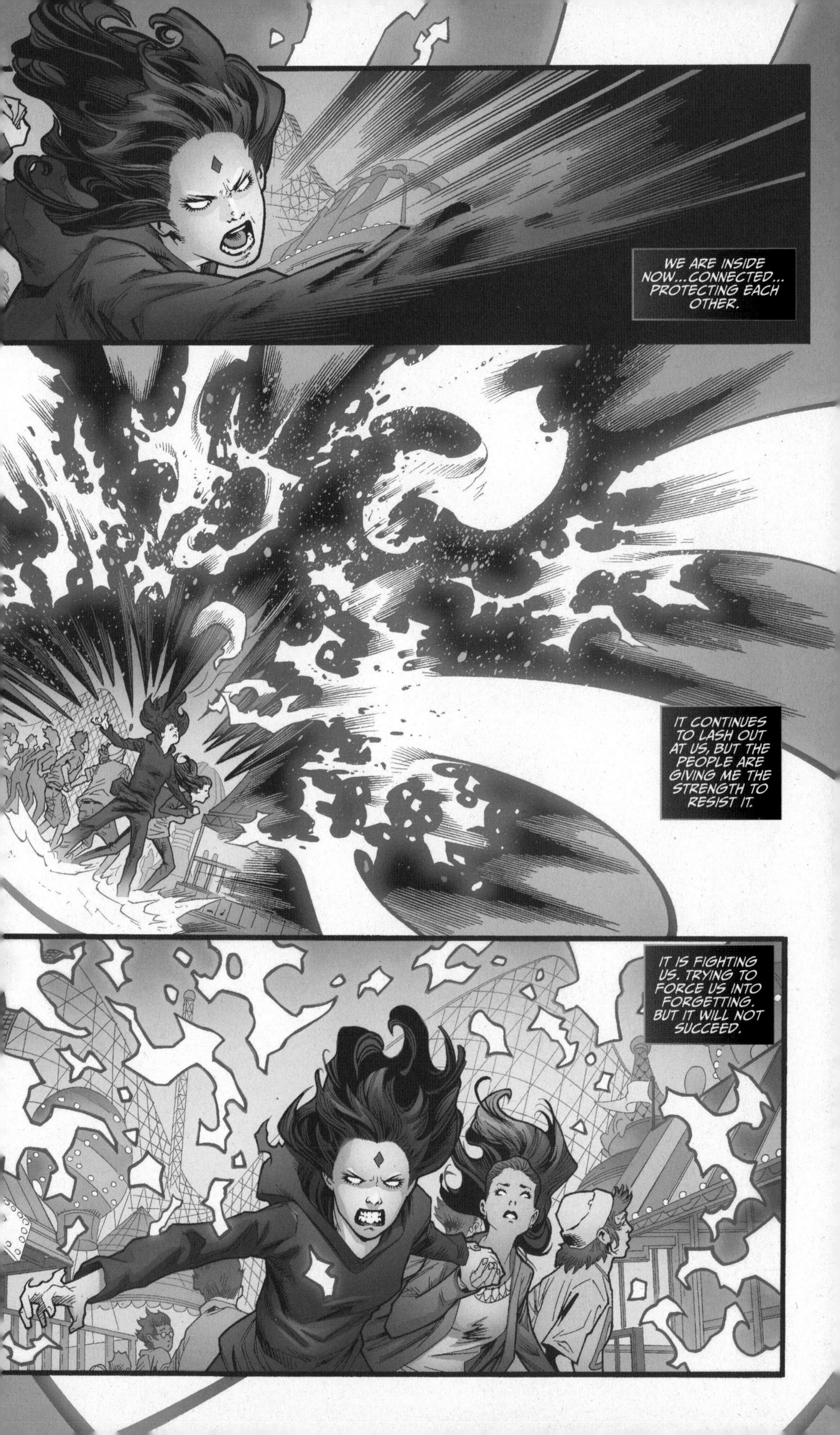

WE ARE INSIDE NOW...CONNECTED... PROTECTING EACH OTHER.
IT CONTINUES TO LASH OUT AT US, BUT THE PEOPLE ARE GIVING ME THE STRENGTH TO RESIST IT.
IT IS FIGHTING US, TRYING TO FORCE US INTO FORGETTING. BUT IT WILL NOT SUCCEED.

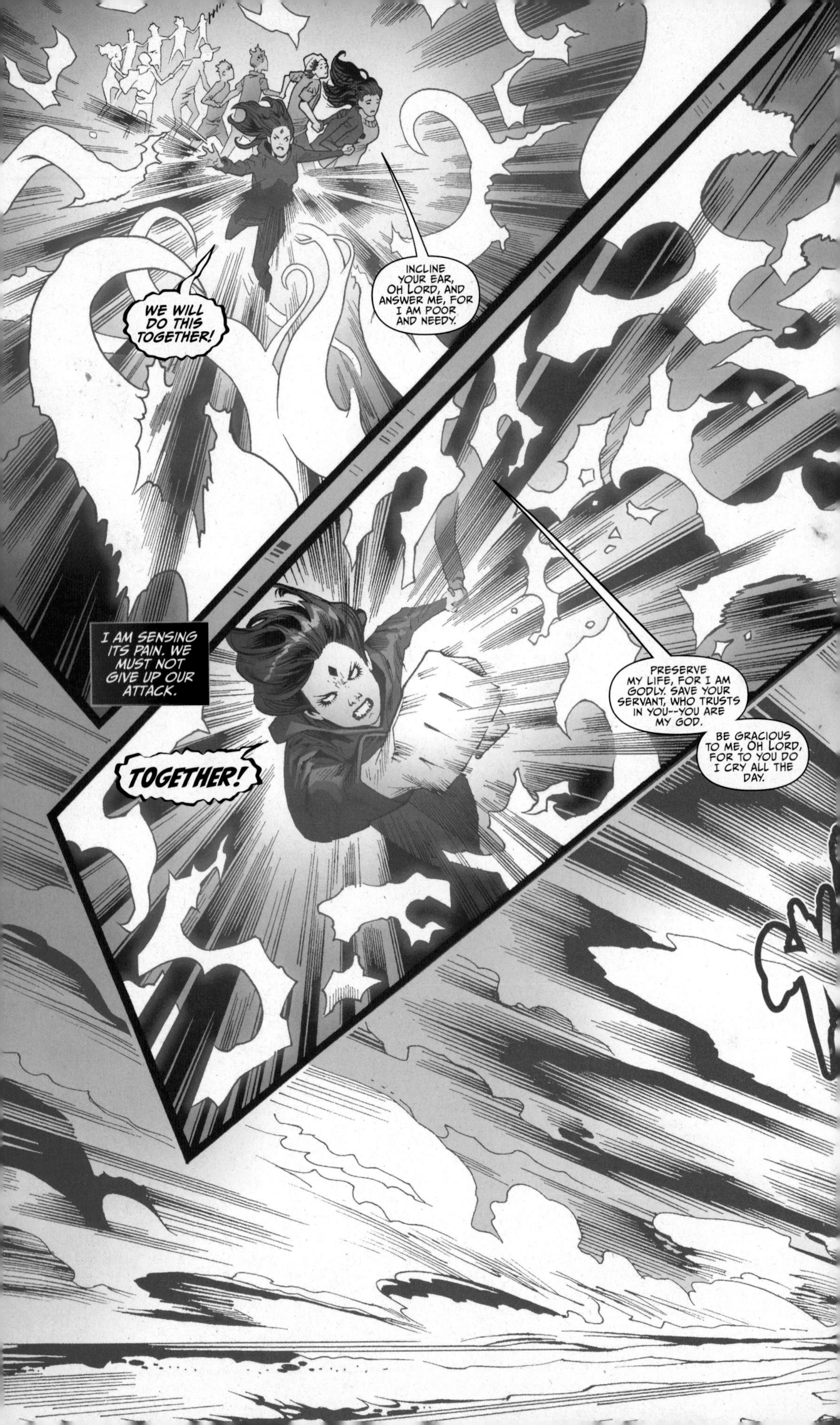
WE WILL DO THIS TOGETHER!
INCLINE YOUR EAR, OH LORD, AND ANSWER ME, FOR I AM POOR AND NEEDY.
I AM SENSING ITS PAIN. WE MUST NOT GIVE UP OUR ATTACK.
TOGETHER!
PRESERVE MY LIFE, FOR I AM GODLY. SAVE YOUR SERVANT, WHO TRUSTS IN YOU--YOU ARE MY GOD.
BE GRACIOUS TO ME, OH LORD, FOR TO YOU DO I CRY ALL THE DAY.

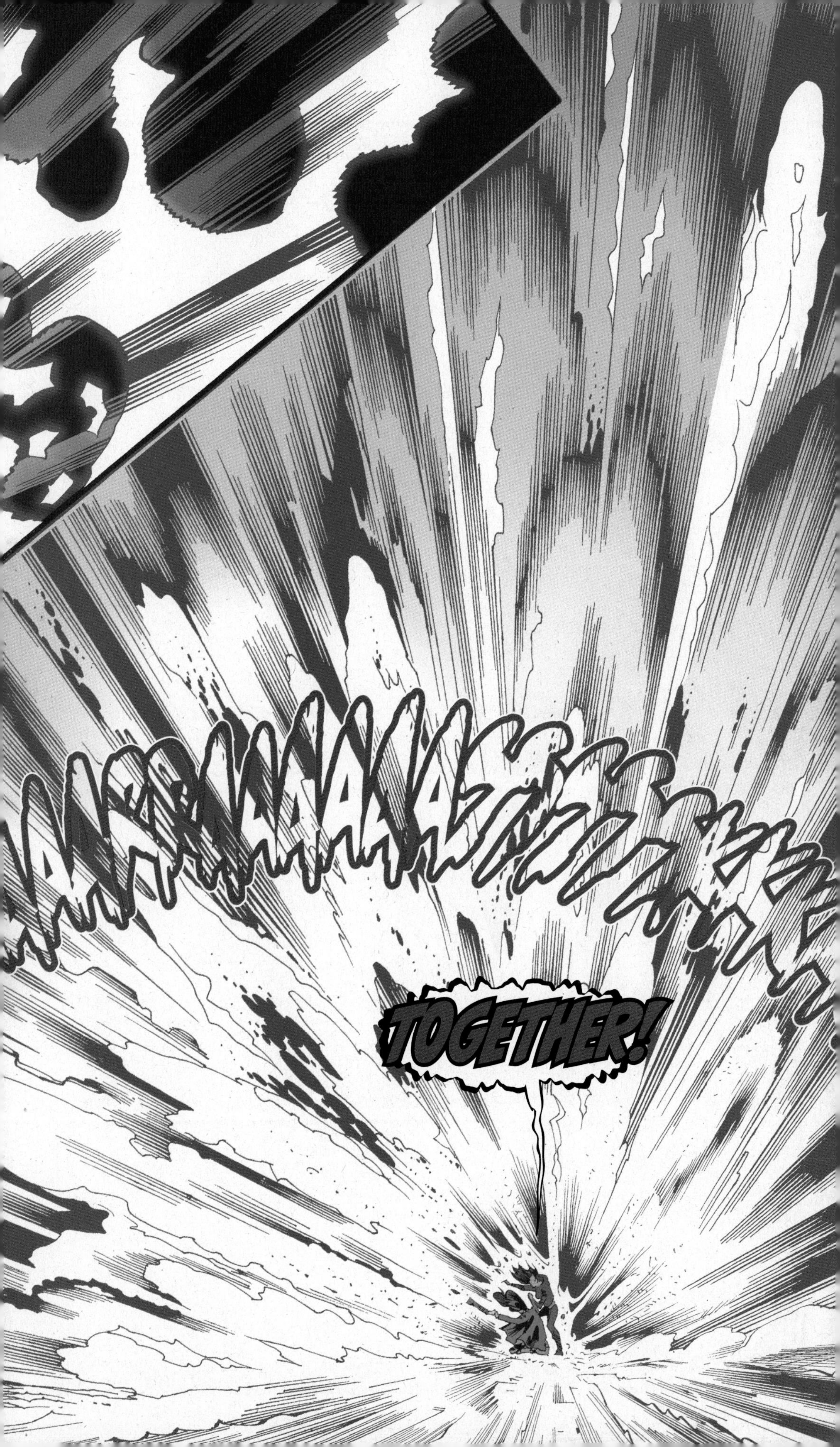
TOGETHER!

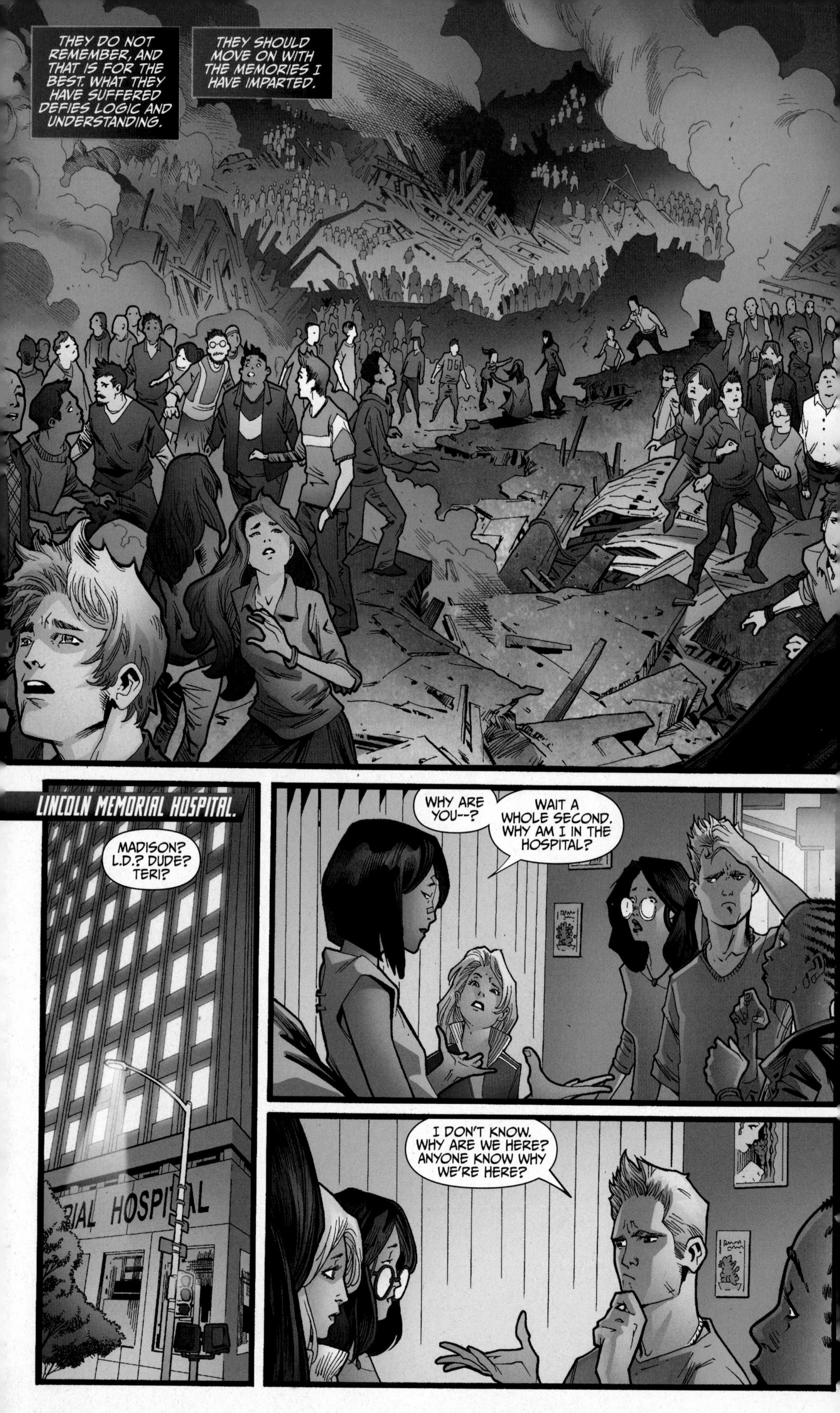
THEY DO NOT REMEMBER, AND THAT IS FOR THE BEST. WHAT THEY HAVE SUFFERED DEFIES LOGIC AND UNDERSTANDING.
THEY SHOULD MOVE ON WITH THE MEMORIES I HAVE IMPARTED.
LINCOLN MEMORIAL HOSPITAL.
MADISON? L.D.? DUDE? TERI?
RIAL HOSPITAL
WHY ARE YOU--?
WAIT A WHOLE SECOND. WHY AM I IN THE HOSPITAL?
I DON'T KNOW. WHY ARE WE HERE? ANYONE KNOW WHY WE'RE HERE?

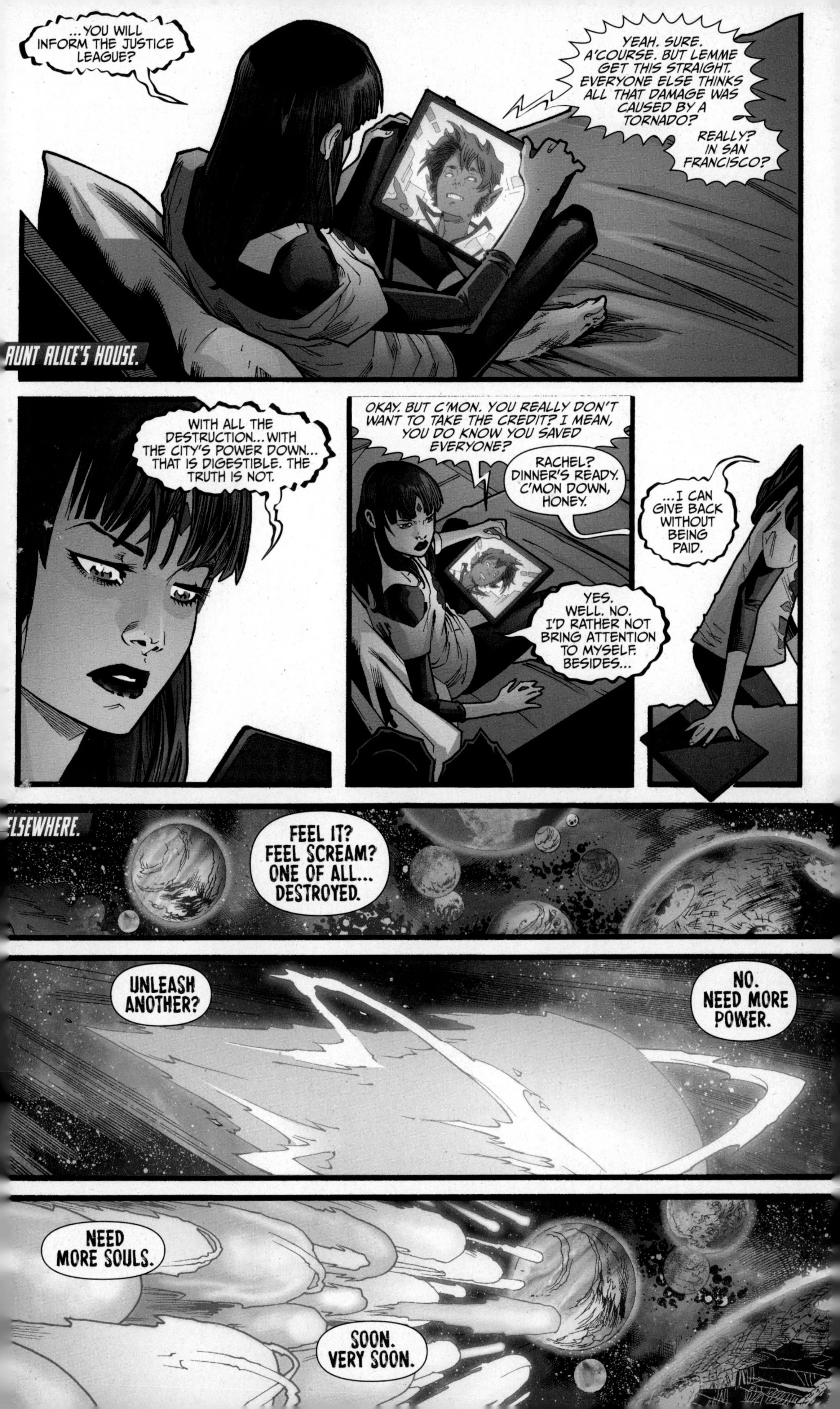
...YOU WILL INFORM THE JUSTICE LEAGUE?
YEAH. SURE. A'COURSE. BUT LEMME GET THIS STRAIGHT. EVERYONE ELSE THINKS ALL THAT DAMAGE WAS CAUSED BY A TORNADO?
REALLY? IN SAN FRANCISCO?
AUNT ALICE'S HOUSE.
WITH ALL THE DESTRUCTION... WITH THE CITY'S POWER DOWN... THAT IS DIGESTIBLE. THE TRUTH IS NOT.
OKAY. BUT C'MON. YOU REALLY DON'T WANT TO TAKE THE CREDIT? I MEAN, YOU DO KNOW YOU SAVED EVERYONE?
YES. WELL. NO. I'D RATHER NOT BRING ATTENTION TO MYSELF. BESIDES...
RACHEL? DINNER'S READY. C'MON DOWN, HONEY.
...I CAN GIVE BACK WITHOUT BEING PAID.
ELSEWHERE.
FEEL IT? FEEL SCREAM? ONE OF ALL... DESTROYED.
UNLEASH ANOTHER?
NO. NEED MORE POWER.
NEED MORE SOULS.
SOON. VERY SOON.

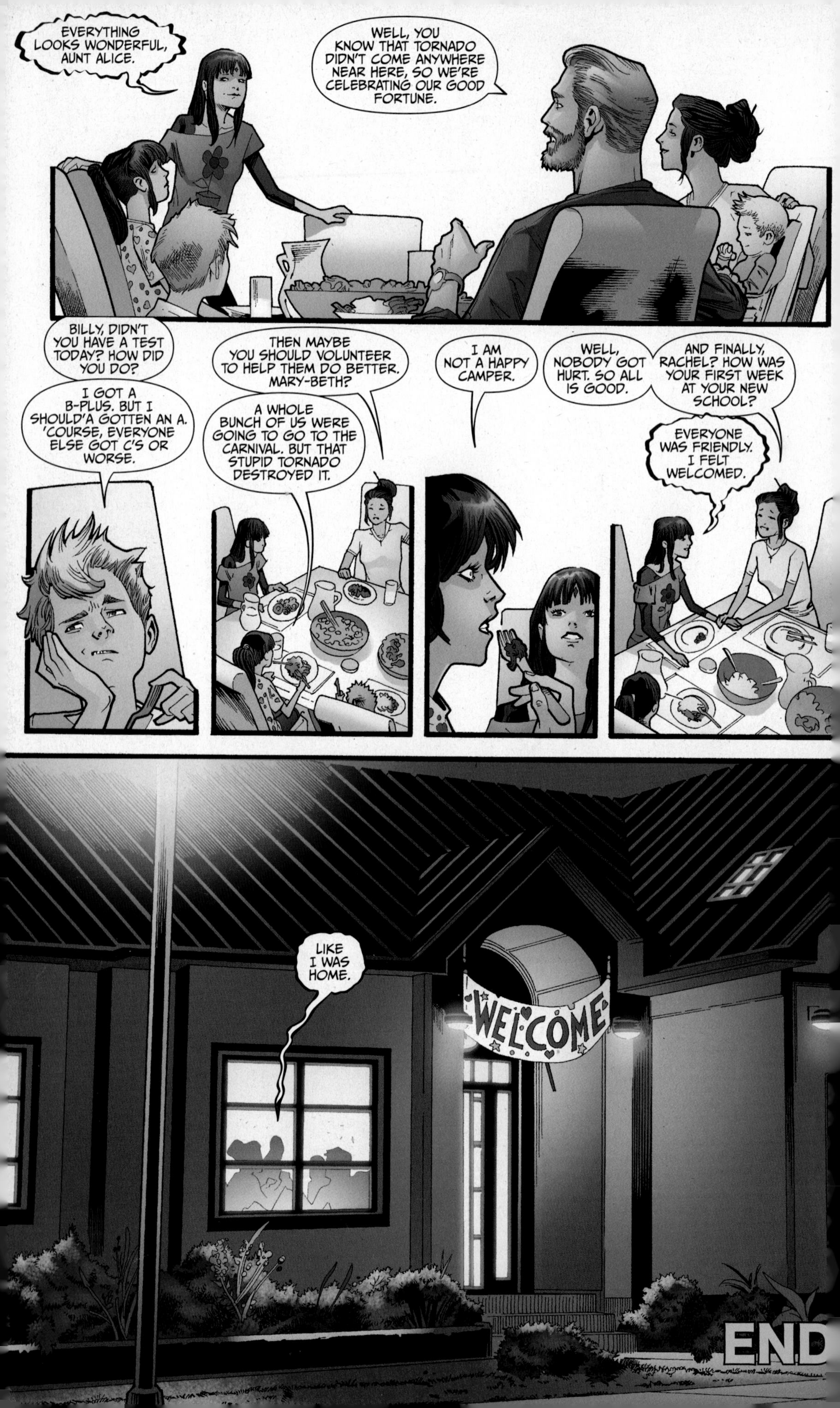
EVERYTHING LOOKS WONDERFUL, AUNT ALICE.
WELL, YOU KNOW THAT TORNADO DIDN'T COME ANYWHERE NEAR HERE, SO WE'RE CELEBRATING OUR GOOD FORTUNE.
BILLY, DIDN'T YOU HAVE A TEST TODAY? HOW DID YOU DO?
I GOT A B-PLUS. BUT I SHOULD'A GOTTEN AN A. 'COURSE, EVERYONE ELSE GOT C'S OR WORSE.
THEN MAYBE YOU SHOULD VOLUNTEER TO HELP THEM DO BETTER. MARY-BETH?
A WHOLE BUNCH OF US WERE GOING TO GO TO THE CARNIVAL. BUT THAT STUPID TORNADO DESTROYED IT.
I AM NOT A HAPPY CAMPER.
WELL, NOBODY GOT HURT. SO ALL IS GOOD.
AND FINALLY, RACHEL? HOW WAS YOUR FIRST WEEK AT YOUR NEW SCHOOL?
EVERYONE WAS FRIENDLY. I FELT WELCOMED.
LIKE I WAS HOME.
WELCOME
END

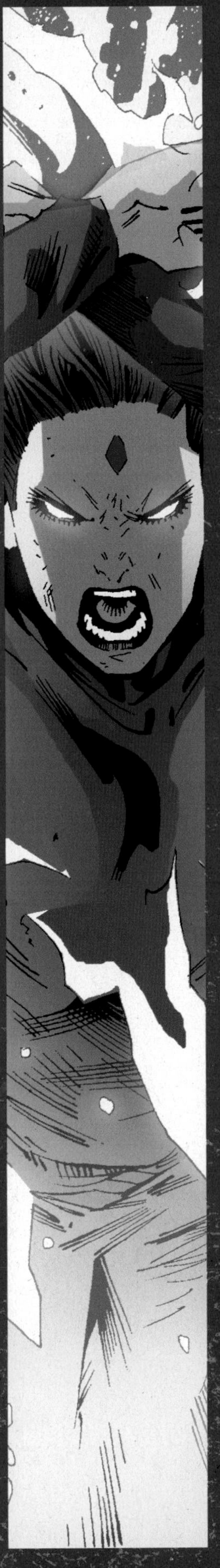

ORIGINAL PITCH By Marv Wolfman

"MY NAME IS RAVEN... I LIVE IN A DARK, DARK WORLD. MAYBE THAT'S WHY I AM ALWAYS SEEKING THE LIGHT."

"Here's the scoop. I'm a few months shy of 17, but I have learned more than a lot in those few, brief years. For example, when it turns out you are the only surviving daughter of an interdimensional-doom-demon who gets off destroying entire galaxies, and that you are then raised by a bizarre other-worldly cult that is trying to protect you from said poppa monster, well, you are probably not going to have a whole lot in common with the other students in your high school.

"I mean, they won't ever have to worry about finding something so funny they cannot stop laughing, or so sad they want to cry. But if I do any of those things, or actually show any kind of feelings at all—which, by the way, includes liking someone a whole lot—I am in real danger of freeing daddy dreadful from his other-dimensional Guantanamo and releasing him on an unsuspecting Earth.

"Trust me, that is as far from a good thing as you can get.

"Then, if you throw in also trying to stop the evil machinations of BELIAL, RUSKOFF & SUGE, my three artificially hatched demon-brothers, well, you've pretty much summed up my so-called life: Go to school. Try to co-exist with other students. Figure out what the Family Bad is planning, and then save the Universe from them.

"And somehow I still have to find time to do my homework.

"Yay, me."

IF I ALLOW MYSELF TO FEEL, TO CARE, TO HATE OR EVEN TO LOVE, THE UNIVERSE WILL DIE!

RAVEN

SOMEONE NEEDS TO SHINE LIGHT INTO THE DARK

DESIGNS BY EDUARDO PANSICA

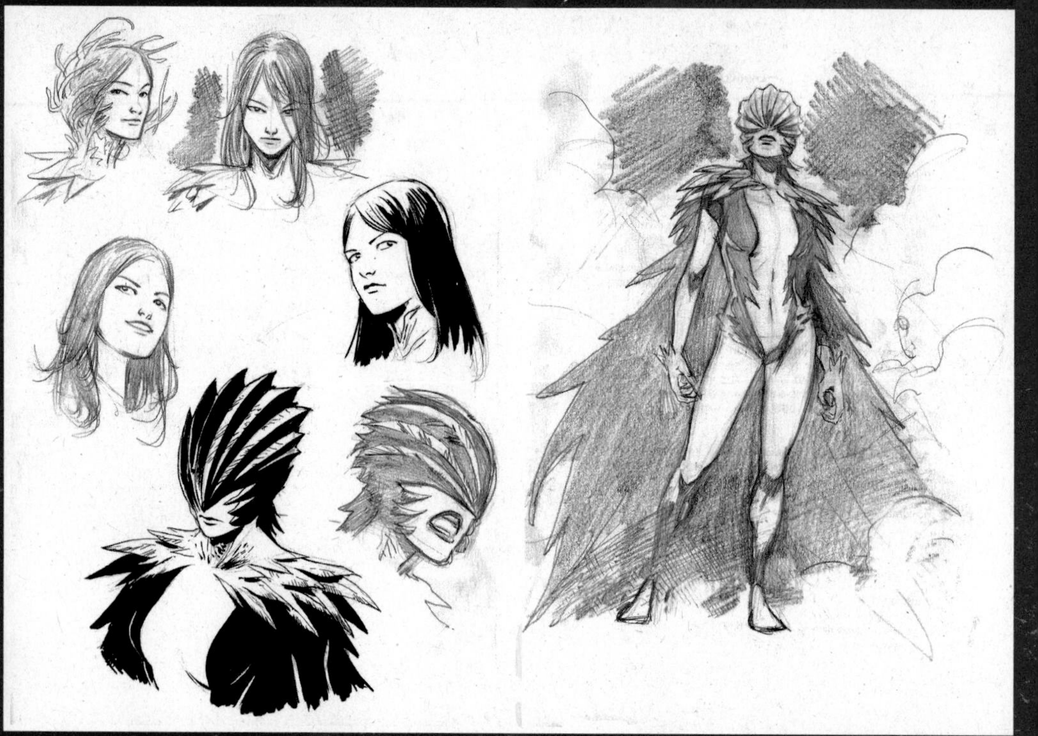

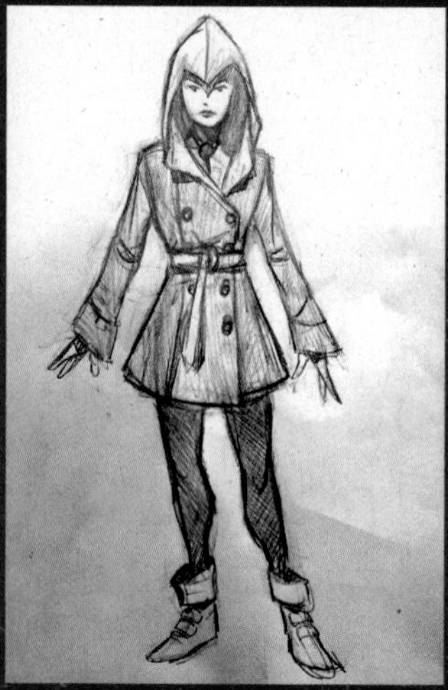

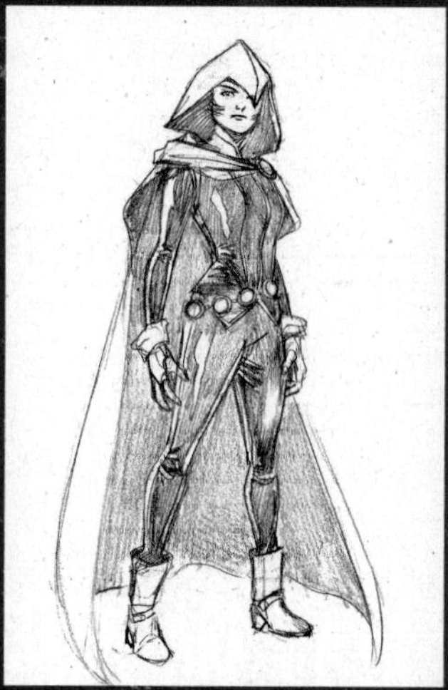

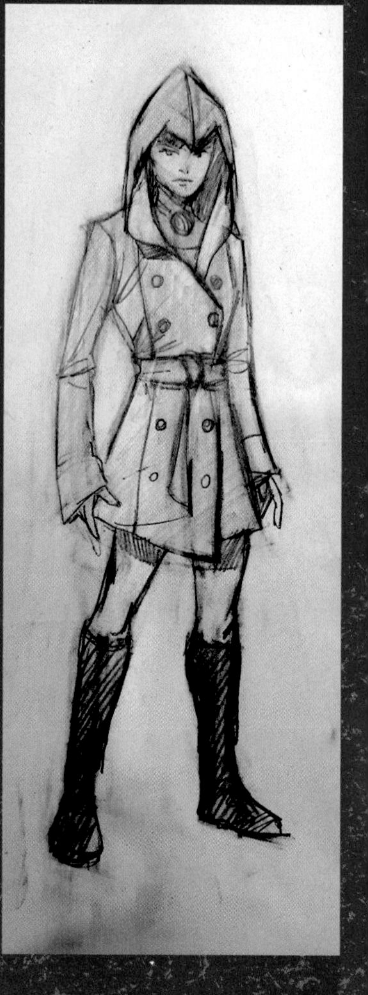

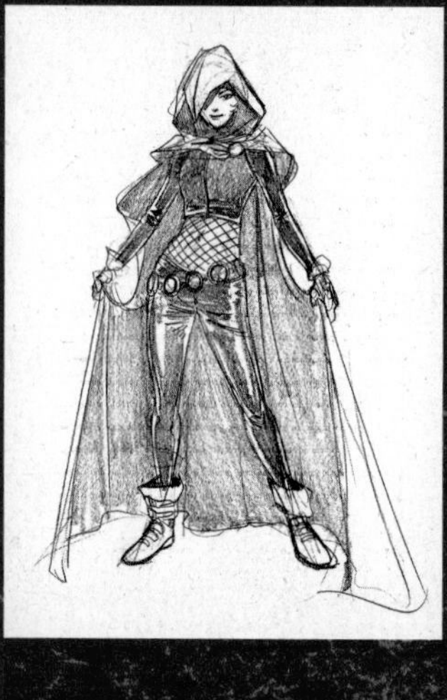

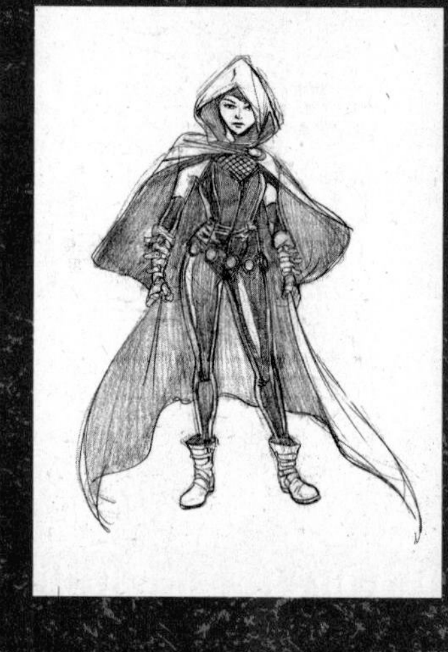

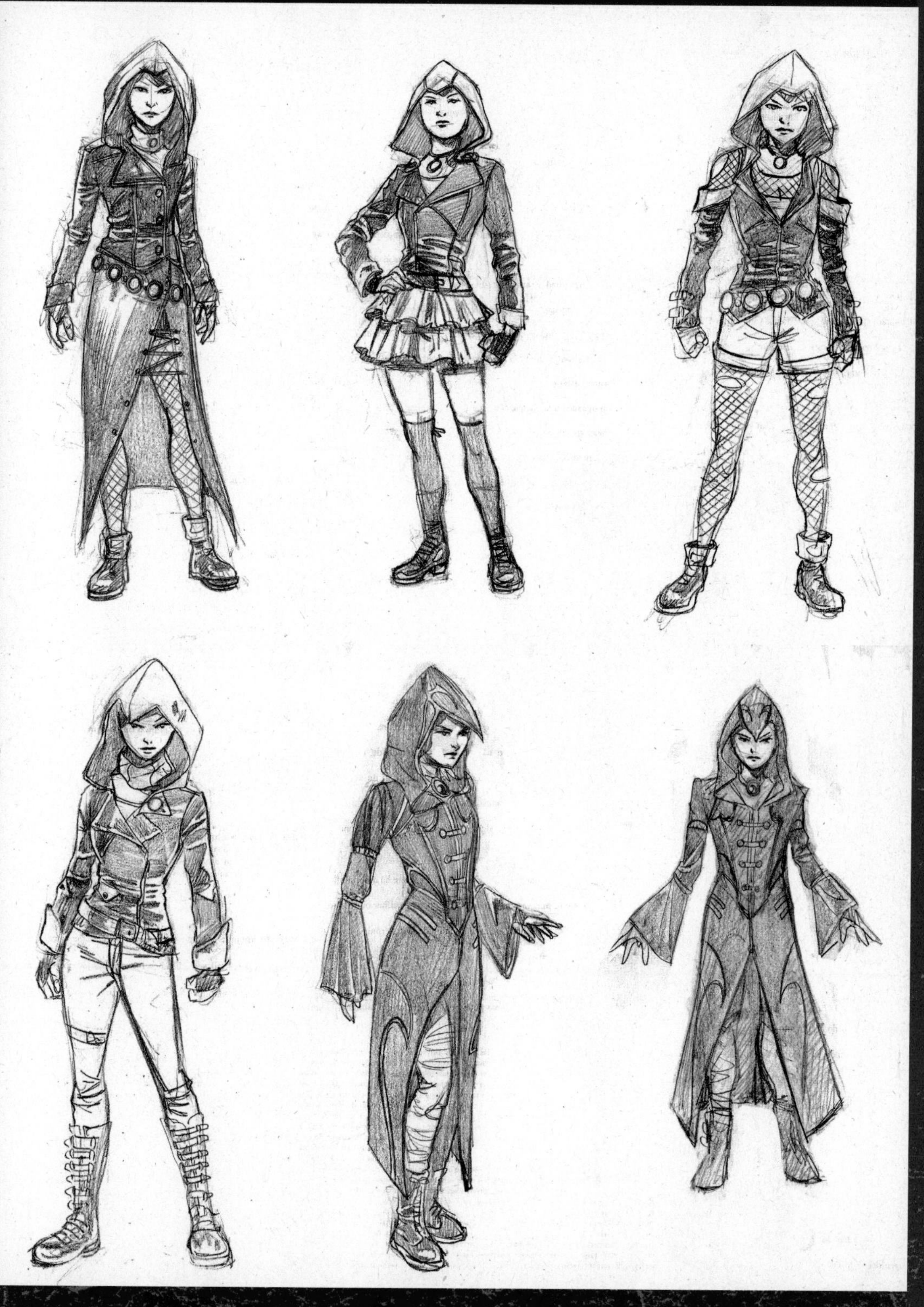

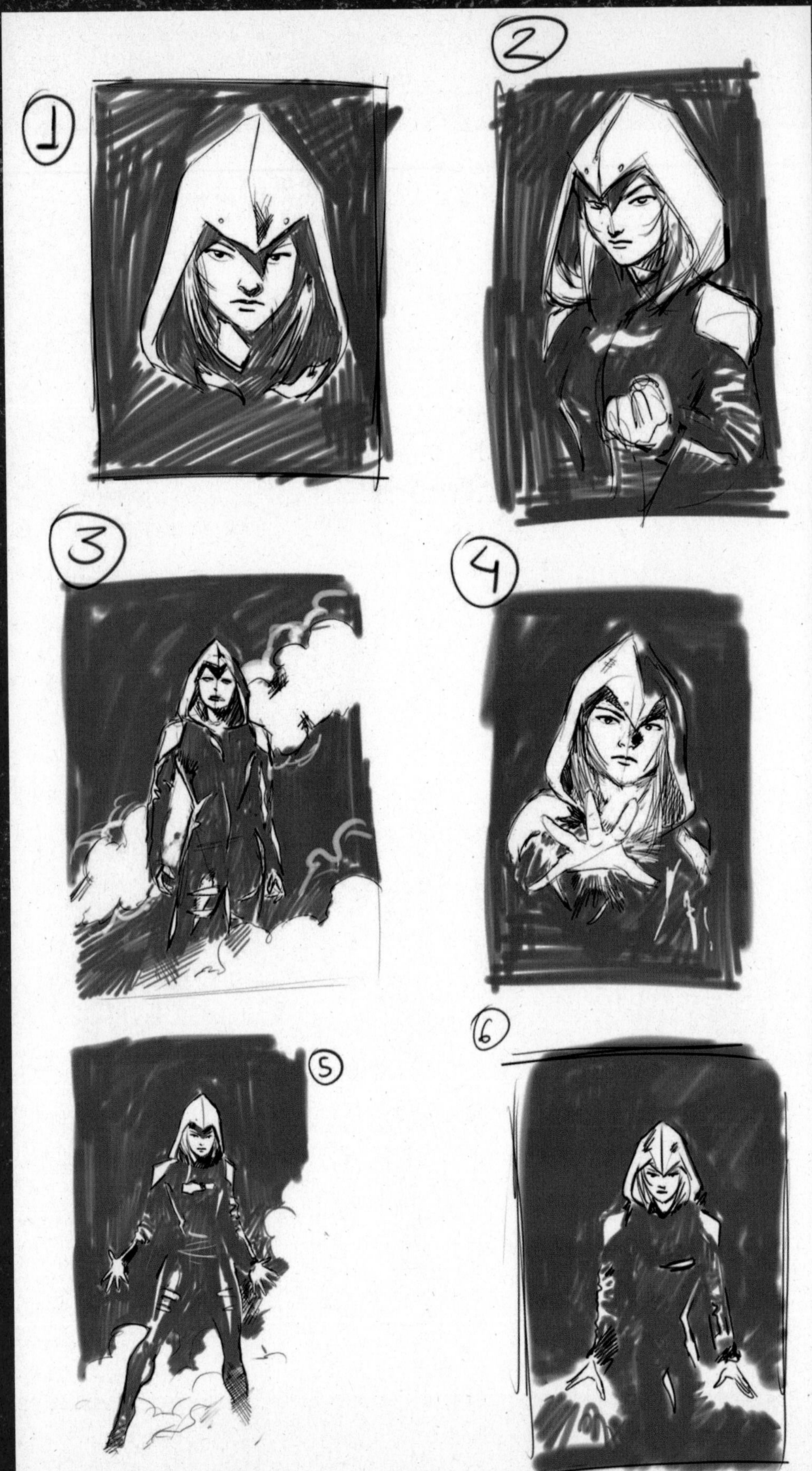

1
2
3
4
5
6

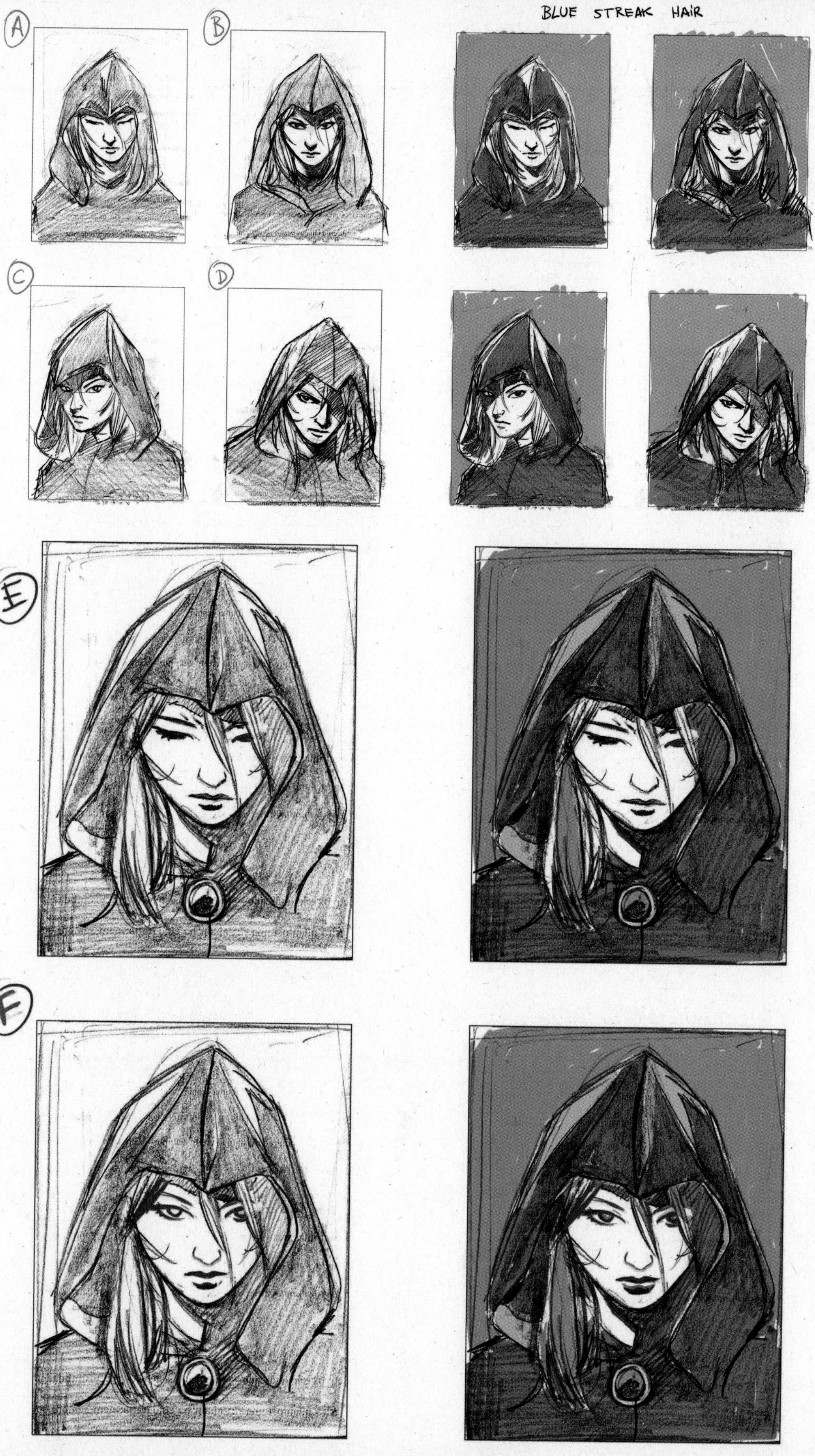
A
B
BLUE STREAK HAIR
C
D
E
F

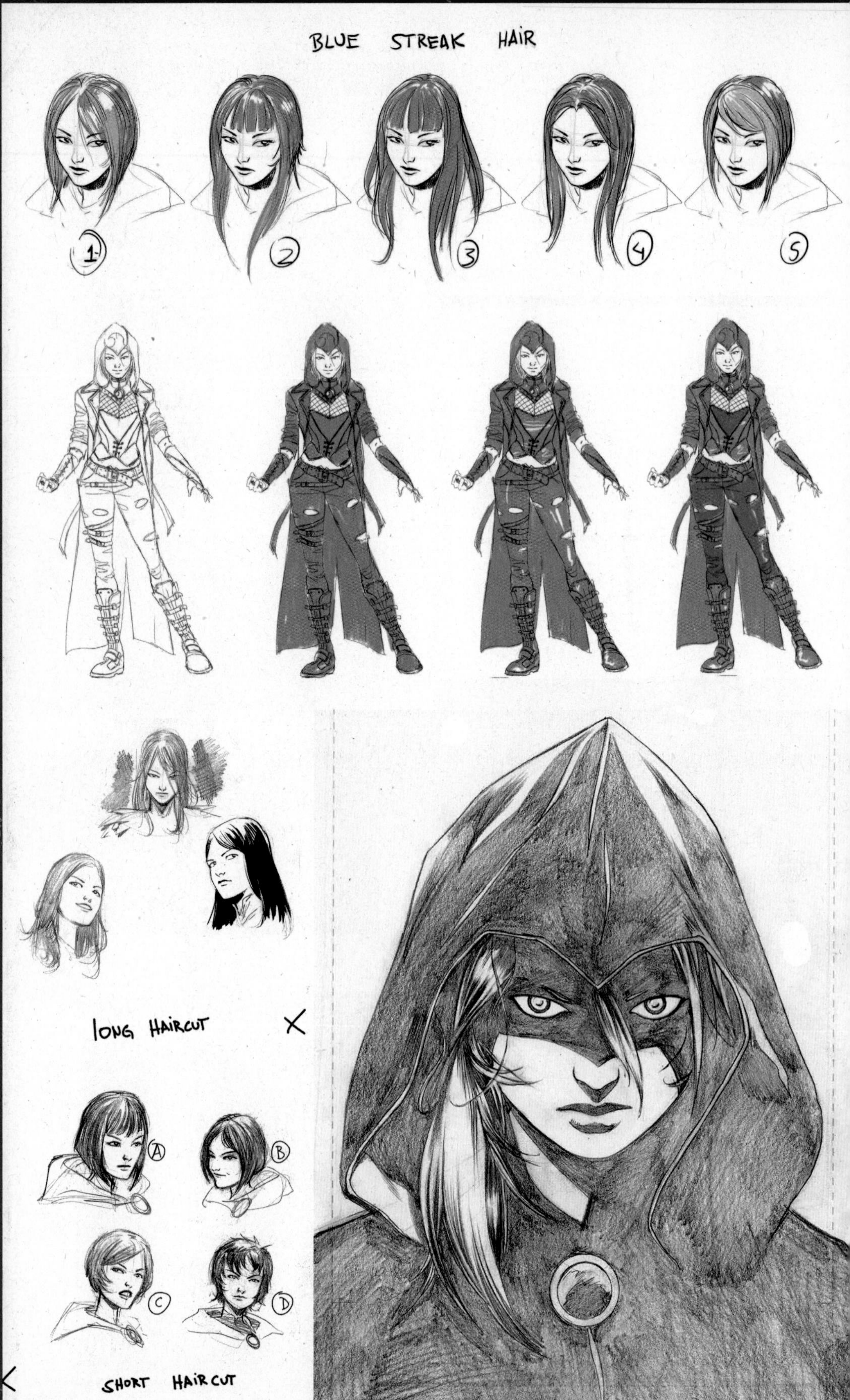
BLUE STREAK HAIR
1
2
3
4
5
LONG HAIRCUT
A
B
C
D
SHORT HAIRCUT

DESIGNS BY JORGE JIMÉNEZ

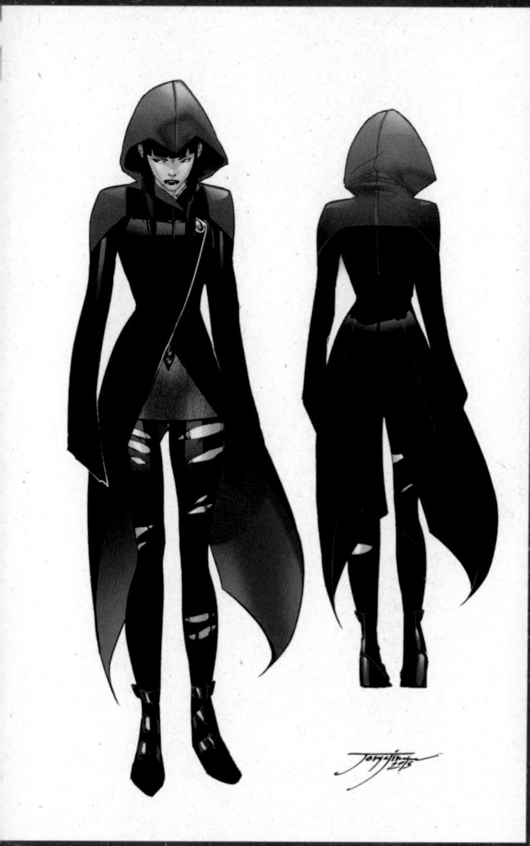

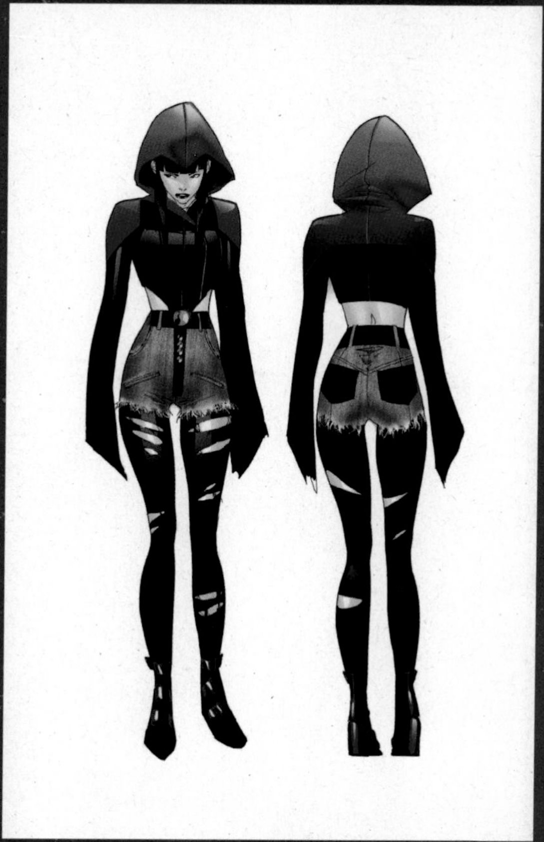

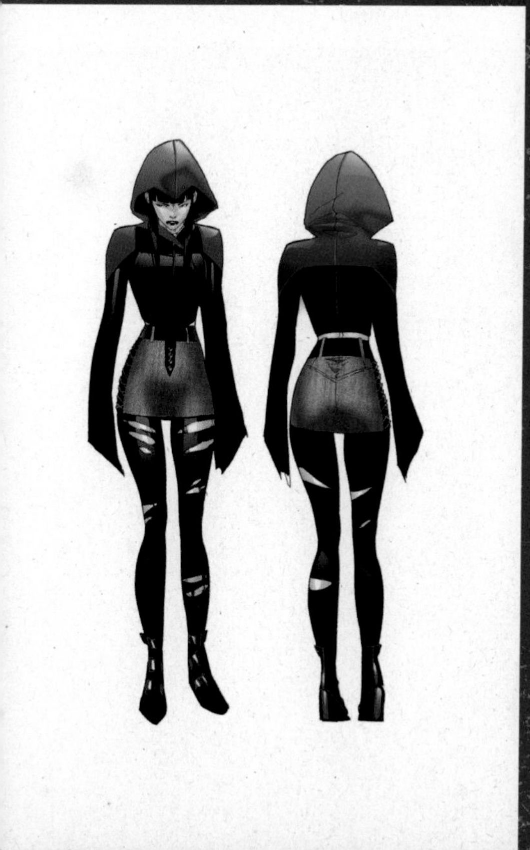

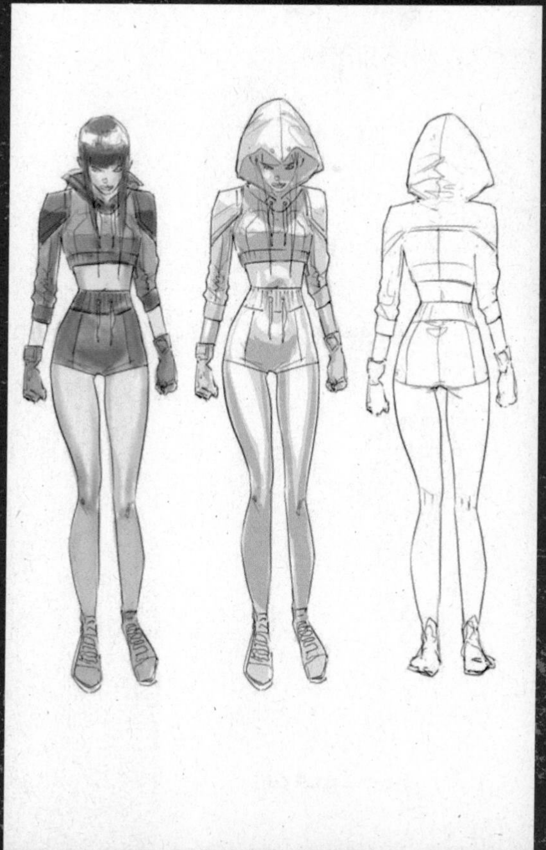

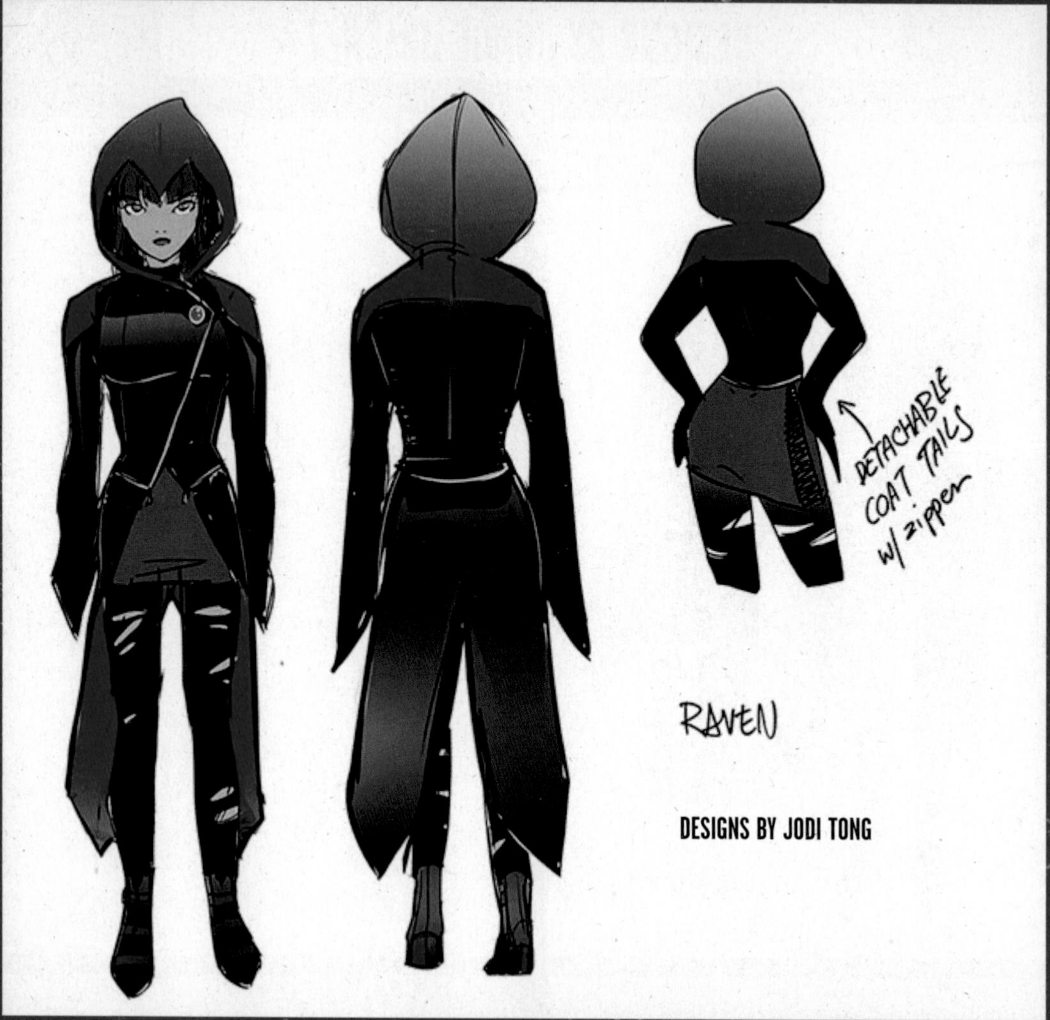
DETACHABLE COAT TAILS w/ zipper
RAVEN
DESIGNS BY JODI TONG

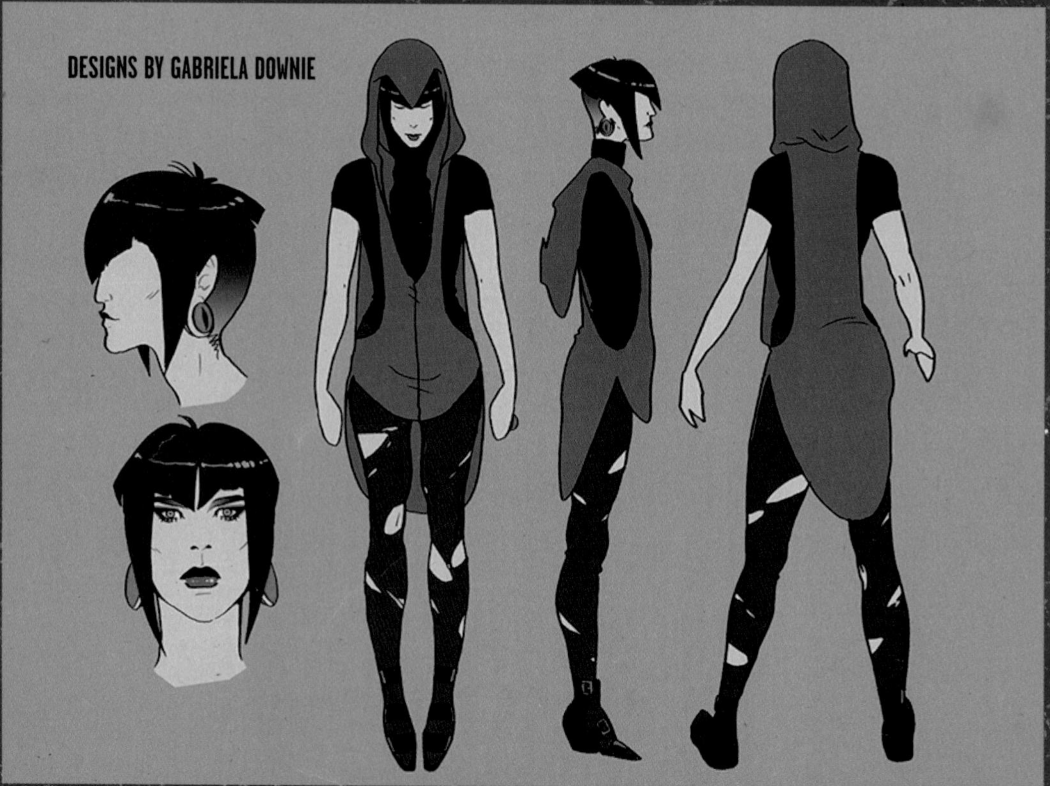
DESIGNS BY GABRIELA DOWNIE